From Can See to Can't

From Can See *to* Can't

Texas Cotton Farmers
on the Southern Prairies

By Thad Sitton and Dan K. Utley

University of Texas Press Austin

Requests for permission to reproduce material from this work should be sent to Permissions, University of Texas Press, P.O. Box 7819, Austin, TX 78713-7819.

∞ The paper used in this publication meets the minimum requirements of American National Standard for Information Sciences—Permanence of Paper for Printed Library Materials, ANSI Z39.48-1984.

Library of Congress Cataloging-in-Publication Data

Sitton, Thad, 1941–
   From can see to can't : Texas cotton farmers on the southern prairies / by Thad Sitton and Dan K. Utley. — 1st ed.
      p.   cm.
   Includes bibliographical references and index.
   ISBN 0-292-77720-5 (cloth : alk. paper). — ISBN 0-292-77721-3 (pbk. : alk. paper)
      1. Farm life—Texas—Fayette County.   2. Farm life—Texas—Washington County.   3. Cotton farmers—Texas—Fayette County.   4. Cotton farmers—Texas—Washington County.   5. Ethnology—Texas—Fayette County.   6. Ethnology—Texas—Washington County.   7. Fayette County (Tex.)—Social life and customs.   8. Washington County (Tex.)—Social life and customs.   9. Oral history.
      I. Utley, Dan K.   II. Title.
   F392.F2S58   1997
   976.4'251062—dc21   96-37625

Contents

Acknowledgments

First and foremost, the authors are indebted to archivist James H. Conrad of East Texas State University, whose generous contributions to the research and writing of this book approached that of a coauthor. We enthusiastically second the comment of historian Kyle Wilkison, who once remarked, "Having Jim Conrad as a friend is better than having a grant."

However, many other people also deserve our thanks. Rebecca Sharpless and the staff of the Baylor University Institute for Oral History allowed us access to their oral history archives. John Wheat of the Center for American History, the University of Texas at Austin, assisted us with the Lipscomb-Myers Collection and the early tape recordings of John Henry Faulk. Members of Operation Restoration, Burton, provided leads on people to interview and opened their archival materials for our use. T. Lindsay Baker of the Baylor University Department of Museum Studies and Larry N. Jones of the Smithsonian Institution offered technical assistance. Gloria Jaster and Delores Gummelt of the Winedale Historical Center of the University of Texas at Austin gave access to oral history tapes and advice about additional persons to interview. Staffs of the Fayette Heritage Museum and Archives, the Winedale Historical Center, the Special Collections of the Sterling Evans Library at Texas A&M University, the Smithsonian Institution, and the Institute of Texan Cultures in San

Antonio, as well as Wanda Whitener, Louis J. ("Buddy") Polansky, Howard Matthies, Dr. Kermit Fox, and Robert Wilhelmsen, assisted us in locating historic photographs for the book.

Finally, we offer emphatic thanks to our many interviewees, whose rich recollections of life on the cotton farms of south-central Texas made this account possible.

From Can See to Can't

Those who labor in the earth are the chosen people of God, if ever He had a chosen people, whose breasts he has made his peculiar deposit for substantial and germane virtue. It is the focus in which He keeps alive that sacred fire, which otherwise might escape from the face of the earth.

— THOMAS JEFFERSON

CHAPTER I

Introduction

In late nineteenth and early twentieth century Texas, farmers were not just one economic interest group among many. Their story—in many ways—is the story of the people.

—KYLE WILKISON

On October 10, 1907, farm families living near the little Henninger community of Fayette County, Texas, held a harvest parade as preliminary to the barbecue and dance that evening. First came Herman Bunger carrying the United States flag, then a wagon with the small Henninger Band, then a float representing the local blacksmith. Then, one by one, came the farmers, proudly parading the decorated tools of their craft before an audience that must have had tools just like theirs back at their own farms. Driven by individual farmers and pulled by mules and horses, turning plow, middle-buster plow, sweep plow, harrow, planter, root cutter, cultivator, mowing machine, and hay rake each passed in its turn, followed by wagonloads of cotton choppers holding hoes, cotton pickers wearing pick sacks, and finally a bale of cotton.[1] Thomas Jefferson's proud yeoman farmers were on the march, and when they paraded they chose to celebrate themselves.

Many people still live in the Fayette County countryside, but the world the Henninger farmers celebrated has passed away in a generation, so swiftly that, as one historian observed, "the rural traveler sees constant reminders of the agricultural system that once characterized the South": decaying barns and country schools, falling-down gins, empty mule lots, and rusty farming equipment in front of rural antique stores. These museum pieces stand juxtaposed with a New South of brick houses, mobile homes, tractors, and cattle pastures.[2]

Understandably, historians have been so impressed with the enormity of the transformation of the Southern cotton-farming life—what Jack Temple Kirby called "the Southern exodus"—that they have focused primarily upon the change itself: the impacts upon the farmers' world of a growing rural population, rising tenancy rates, the Great Depression, New Deal programs, World War II, and the mechanization and commercialization of agriculture that took place in the two decades after the war. The titles of major histories interpreting Southern rural life during the twentieth century clearly demonstrate this preoccupation with transformation and change: Gilbert Fite's *Cotton Fields No More: Cotton Agriculture, 1865-1980* (1984), Pete Daniel's *Breaking the Land: The Transformation of Cotton, Tobacco, and Rice Cultures Since 1880* (1986), and Jack Temple Kirby's *Rural Worlds Lost: The American South, 1920–1960* (1987). In Texas, dissertation scholars also have been in the field, and some of the same focus on change permeates their work. The long lapse in historiography since Samuel Lee Evans's pioneering study, "Texas Agriculture, 1880–1930" (1960), ended in the 1990s with important dissertations by Neil Foley, Mary Rebecca Sharpless, and Kyle Wilkison.[3]

While agreeing about most of the factors making for change, including the disastrous, and probably intentional, effects of New Deal programs on renters and small landowners, these historians disagree profoundly about whether the displacement of millions of American farm families from the land was inevitable or for the best. Demographic change was massive, all admit. As summarized by Pete Daniel: "In the eleven southern states, farms declined from 2.4 million in 1940 to 723,000 in 1974, while the average size grew from 86 to 235 acres." In the end, "Farming as a culture was superseded by large-scale farming as a commercial enterprise."[4]

The interpretations of Gilbert Fite and Pete Daniel stand in sharpest contrast. To economic historian Fite, depopulation of the countryside and commercialization of agriculture were a merciful transformation of a rural world where farmers had been caught in an "agricultural trap" of too small farms, too much cotton, and not enough money. "The answers to the condition of farm poverty could not be found within the agricultural sector," Fite believed.[5] Nor was there much to salvage in the rural world, where Southern farm families lived Hobbsian lives, nasty, brutish, and short. "Life was dull and difficult for the great majority of people on American farms, but nowhere was this more evident than among Southern farmers. Their low incomes were reflected in poor housing, inadequate diets, lack of education and health care, and hopelessness that permeated so much of farm life."[6]

Pete Daniel disagreed, believing that much had been lost with the demise of Southern farming cultures.

> Cotton farmers lived in a fragile balance with nature. They constantly studied such variables as soil, insects, climate, and seasons and cultivated their crops with individual flourishes. There were almost as many nuances in growing a crop as there were cotton farmers. They watched the sky and the earth and moved in harmony with nature and in accordance with the collected wisdom of their forbears. Whether tenant or owner, each cotton farmer had certain tasks that were tied to the pages of an almanac, to experience and the weather.[7]

Nor was the demise of the rural world inevitable, or even for the best; the United States could have preserved Southern rural folk cultures and the small-farming life, as some nations of Western Europe had successfully preserved their traditional farming cultures.

> It is far too easy to see technological change as inevitable, as part of some cosmic predestination. The South contained one of the richest folk cultures in the nation — or, rather, contained some of the richest folk cultures, for the South was as diverse culturally as it was in other ways. Building on the strengths of the old culture and reforming its abuses, there were options that could have kept people farming and preserved the culture and community that gave a deeper

meaning to life in the rural South. Larger farms, mammoth implements, killer chemicals, and government intrusion were not inevitable.[8]

For Daniel, a single, prosperous, horse-powered, Amish farm, flourishing in the Pennsylvania countryside of 1990, rebutted economic historians' arguments of economic inevitability. Having judiciously considered the first generation of tractors available to them, the Amish long ago had decided what they thought about them and never changed their minds: "They don't make manure."[9]

While readers may surmise which scholar the Henninger farmers might have agreed with, virtually all historians participating in the great debate about the transformation of Southern rural society in the twentieth century are open to one criticism; they have written little about how farm families actually farmed and lived their lives—the subject of this informal ethnography of the farming life in Fayette and Washington counties of south-central Texas. Until recently, few oral historians have ventured out to collect the recollections and opinions of the farm families themselves, while there is still time to do so.[10] This was an animal-powered society, but little research has been done about work stock. It was a society of plowmen, but little has been written about techniques of breaking the land. And it was a society where "self-sufficiency had been a way of life as well as an economic practice,"[11] but little data has been collected about the subsistence side of farming: gardening, domestic livestock, food preservation, and all the rest. Is there so little to learn about early-twentieth-century farm life that we need not discover how farmers went about their seasonal round? Town and countryside were very different places during the first three decades of the twentieth century, but has the town so triumphed that we are in danger of writing a "townsmen's history" of the farmers' lost world?

Written memoirs about Southern rural life are rich in the elements most scholarly histories neglect, the substance and daily details of farm families' lives, and we learn much from reading them. Ned Cobb, Ed Brown, Cecil Brown, Harry Crews, Troy Crenshaw, Claude E. Good, William A. Owens, Eddie Stimpson, Dorothy Howard, and George Lester Vaughn produced eloquent accounts, and in the Washington and Fayette County area, so did Robert Skrabanek, Kermit Fox, and

Mance Lipscomb.[12] For one thing, these memoirs show the universality of cotton culture across the South. What Harry Crews wrote of the south Georgia farm family he came from holds true in every word for the Texas farmers we interviewed. Cotton farming was a gambler's trade, and the role of luck was understood: "The world that circumscribed the people I came from had so little margin for error, for bad luck, that when something went wrong, it almost always brought something else down with it. It was a world in which survival depended on raw courage, a courage born out of desperation, and sustained by a lack of alternatives."[13]

This book describes the daily life of German-, Czech-, Anglo-, and African-American farm families as they went about their seasonal rounds during the late 1920s, on the eve of the Great Depression. Not that the great economic downturn changed very much for some of them. Robert ("Bat") Dement of Washington County often remarked to his sons: "There's not any Depression. Everybody else just got in the same shape I've been in all of my life, and they think it's a Depression."[14]

An ethnographic study of farm life might have been conducted in many locales across the eastern half of Texas or the American South, but in Texas a research area centered on Fayette and Washington counties had certain advantages. The area had been part of Austin's first colony, where Texas cotton agriculture began, the site of the state's initial cotton boom, and an important producer of the great staple crop well into the middle twentieth century. Culturally diverse, the area is environmentally diverse as well, a landscape of red-soiled alluvial bottomlands, blackland prairies, and sandy-land post-oak timber belts. As Jack Temple Kirby noted, before World War II there was not one agricultural South, but many: row-crop, black-belt areas where cotton dominated all; worn-out cotton areas retrograding toward subsistence farming; dairy product and livestock areas; and "the self-sufficient South," where free-range livestock and growing one's living on the farm took precedence over growing cotton.[15] Elements of all these "Souths" could be found in Fayette and Washington counties in the first three decades of this century, and afterward.

Furthermore, a strong case can be made that of all Texas cotton-growing regions, south-central Texas was where the beleaguered Texas yeomanry of hundred-acre cotton farmers made its last stand.

According to the U.S. Agricultural Census of 1964, Fayette County had more owner-operated farms than any other Texas county.[16] Kyle Wilkison has documented the decline of independence on farms in the eastern half of Texas, as cotton and renter status displaced subsistence crops and landownership, but in Fayette and Washington counties the tenant–landowner percentages remained for decades at only around fifty-fifty, and the subsistence farming economy—evidenced by farmstead production of hogs, chickens, potatoes, and dairy products—continued at the highest levels in the state.[17]

Clearly, the hundred-acre cotton farmers of the area did not want to quit farming, did not wish to leave the land, long avoided "living out of paper bags," and—at least some of them—refused to convert to tractors. As late as the 1950s, over one-third of Fayette County farms still used work stock in the fields, and stubborn farmers such as African-American Ed Lathan and German-American Herman Schoenemann still broke ground with mules during the late 1980s.[18] In 1974, the Farmers' Coop Gin at Burton ginned its last bale powered with the original 1925 Bessemer diesel engine—a bale hauled to the gin in an antique cotton wagon pulled by Gus Draeger's tractor. He explained, "We kept going, I just stayed with it that long, I don't know why, we just toughed it out."[19] Twenty years later, stubborn locals powered the Burton gin back into life as a living history exhibit, the only functioning gin of that vintage in Texas. By 1990, Houstonians had bought many area properties, and land values had risen until few families could afford to farm in these counties, but some, like the Roscher family of Fayette County, persevered. Eroy Roscher had been born on the farm as had his father and grandfather before him, and his family farmhouse was an evolutionary product of all those lives and years. "That kitchen and pantry there," he noted, "Grandpa always said they told him he was six years old when that was built, so that must have been about 1872. And this part here was added on later, I'm sure before 1900 because Mamma was born in 1901 and this was already here."[20] For many years, Roscher had won the "best corn" category at the Fayette County fair, and 1995 was no exception. According to records of the Heritage Farm Program of the Texas Department of Agriculture, over one-hundred farms in the county have been in the same family for more than a century, more than in any other Texas county.

No wonder, then, that in the old counties along the Colorado and

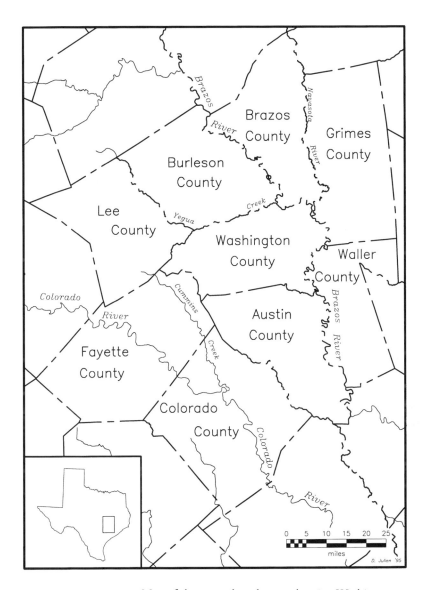

FIGURE 1   Map of the general study area showing Washington and Fayette counties and the counties bordering the Colorado and Brazos rivers. (Map redrawn from map by Dan Julien, Austin)

Brazos rivers, oral historians found many people with information about life on the family cotton farm. Much more than usual in grass-roots researches in rural social history, the authors benefited from interviewers who went before them. Using metal disks and the earliest sound-recording technologies, John Henry Faulk recorded the accounts of ex-slaves and Brazos valley sharecroppers during 1941—the earliest oral history recordings we have ever heard.[21] Oral historians collecting information for the Winedale Historical Center interviewed a score of Fayette County farmers and farm wives during the early 1970s on the topics of cotton, corn, and gardens, and at about that same time young Glen Alyn conducted his remarkable interviews with Mance Lipscomb, Lily Lipscomb, Bubba Bowser, Ed Lathan, and other black residents of northeastern Washington County.[22] Collecting information for his oral-autobiography of musician Mance Lipscomb, Glen lived in a teepee among rural black people until they finally got over their disgust at having a white "hippie" in their midst, became his friends, and told him what they really thought. Beginning around 1990, the Baylor University Institute for Oral History conducted a series of interviews with retired farmers living in the Burton area, and the Baylor interviews, as all the rest, became grist for our mill. Finally, forty-one additional individuals were interviewed during the research period of 1994–1995.

The voices of oral history give a different account of the small farmer's world from that given by the economic historians. "The hopelessness that permeated farm life" is little represented here. Instead, farmers tell a different story, and one followed—with qualifications—in this social history of the farming life in Fayette and Washington counties and surrounding area. As the oral histories and personal memoirs do, this book emphasizes farmers' pride of craft, their intricate farming skills, the importance of the subsistence side of farming, and farm families' humor and stoicism in enduring the vagaries of season and economics. We try to explain what Mr. and Mrs. Otto Fuchs meant when they proudly told that they "paid off their farm with five-cent cotton," the sentiments behind the Henninger parade, and why some area farm families are still on the land. "Dirt farmers," some might still call themselves, implying by that pride of craft, pride of knowledge about their personal pieces of ground. Even the structure of this book is grounded in the farmers' world. No pattern was so important to that world as the yearly agricultural cycle, the timeless drama of season from breaking the land to planting to cultivating to gathering to breaking the land once again. So is this book arranged.

CHAPTER 2

Texas Cotton

Sometime around 1926, young Cune Gutierrez helped his family clear "new ground" for a cotton farm on a high hilltop covered with virgin mountain junipers deep within the Texas Hill Country. This site at the Double Horn community of Burnet County seemed unlikely cotton land, but the Gutierrezes had seized an opportunity to become landowners and try the high-stakes game of cotton farming. A traveling "cedar chopper" by trade, Cune's father somehow acquired one hundred acres of cedar-brush hilltop from a local man, then cleared part of it for cotton. The big junipers presented formidable obstacles, as Cune noted, and beneath them the Hill Country soil lay thinly upon limestone bedrock:

> We couldn't grub up all them trees—big old trees—
> so we just cut 'em from the top down and started
> farming. The stumps is still there yet, and that's been
> a long time ago. For a while we made the best corn
> you ever saw, and then all at once Papa planted cot-
> ton. The first year we done a little bit of good. It's
> rocky country, it's real rough; sometimes you'd plow,
> you'd hear the plow hit something, the rocks were
> pretty close. You had to zigzag with that plow to
> miss them stumps.[1]

After a few years of cotton farming, Mr. Gutierrez gave up and moved his family back into the cedar-chopping life. Hauling household water four miles from Double Horn Creek had become tiresome, the subsistence crops of corn, pumpkins, and garden vegetables grew almost as poorly as the cotton, and even the family's "grasshopper turkeys," herded out each morning by Cune or one of his siblings to forage all day for insects in the tall grass, failed to bring in necessary cash income. After a hard try at the cotton life, the Gutierrez family moved on. For them, this attempt at dry-land cotton farming on a high hilltop, in the blue, arid, juniper-covered hills of backwoods Burnet County, had been a step too far.[2]

Others had the same experience during this final decade of a century and a third of cotton expansion. All across southern and eastern Texas during the 1920s, people cleared cutover pine forests, sandy-land hill-sides, and flood-prone bottomlands and broke the ground for cotton. The Gutierrez family's stay at Double Horn during the 1920s coincided with the all-time-high watermark of cotton culture, a precarious life-way based on the great staple crop that had been rolling inexorably west since 1793.

With the Gutierrez family contributing its small part, the last big expansion of Southern cotton came in Texas, where a record of 16,813,000 acres was plowed for cotton in 1929, and little Rockwall County on the Texas blacklands dedicated 85 of its total 147 square miles to this species of the genus *Gossypium*.[3] During that year, the value of Texas agriculture was over $11 billion—three times the value of oil, and cotton still remained the king. Texas far outdistanced all other southern states in cotton, producing over one-third of all the cotton picked throughout the decade of the 1920s.[4] By 1924, 56.7 percent of all Texas cropland—16,658,356 acres—was in cotton. Mississippi was next with 44.9 percent of its cropland in cotton (but only 3,011,444 acres).[5] Texas produced over 25 percent of the world's cotton each year, ginned it in nearly four thousand gins, and led all other states in percentage of gross income derived from cotton. One economist estimated that one-third of the total population of the state was direct-ly involved in cotton farming in 1929 and that many thousands more were involved in ginning, warehousing, merchandising, compressing, and transporting cotton, or in cottonseed processing.[6]

Small wonder, then, that Texas playwright Horton Foote's first childhood words were, "How's the cotton?" The question was on everyone's lips during the heyday of cotton agriculture, since the great staple was a gambler's crop, subject to the vagaries of wind, weather, soil, season, and world economics. Foote's father ran a mercantile store in Wharton catering to local cotton farmers while managing his father-in-law's cotton renters on the side, and the state of the crop remained much on his mind. In keeping with Foote's first words, Foote's first tottering steps followed his father outside on one of the latter's compulsive daily patrols to monitor the changing weather. Cotton people like Mr. Foote often gazed upon the fickle sky, whence came both the crop-destroying wind and hail and the saving rain.[7]

In truth, cotton farming was a gambler's trade, and every season was another roll of the dice. Economist Rupert B. Vance calculated the wild variations in average income for twenty acres of Southern cotton between the years 1914 and 1927 and found that it ranged from $1,212 in the best year to $298 in the worst.[8] Furthermore, these figures were *averages*; the actual incomes for any individual cotton farm varied far more dramatically than the figures implied. The value of lint cotton at ginning time ranged from 5 to 45 cents over the two decades after 1910, and every season the inexorable and unpredictable play of weather determined how much each farm family had to sell. In one season, a particular Fayette County farm produced 28 bales of cotton; in another, planting the same acreage on the same ground, it produced only 2.[9] Cotton farming, as Howard Davis told, was a "crap shoot."[10] Asked about the "average" year for cotton during his farming career, Teddy Keiler of Fayette County implied that the question was meaningless: "On the average, you could expect anything."[11]

In the play of weather, salvation and destruction often went hand in hand—two sides of the same coin. Sometimes the hit-and-miss thunderstorms of early summer bestowed much-needed moisture upon one's crops, then dropped a killer hail upon a neighbor's field only a quarter of a mile away; sometimes it was the other way around.

This dice roll of weather often took on statewide dimensions. Throughout Fayette County, Washington County, and the other counties that once had been part of Austin's Colony, where Texas cotton farming first began, farmers long pondered the dubious lessons of 1900. The growing season of that year had been hot and dry, and by most estimates the cotton crop looked in poor shape. Then came the

Galveston hurricane and torrential rains reaching far north through East Texas. A country editor recalled, "It was said that growing crops as far north as Temple were covered with a light salt film from the salt water blown that far by the storm." Deluged with moisture, around Paris the drought-stricken cotton began to grow, putting on many new bolls. The crop in northeast Texas ended up being very good, and as a measure of this cotton affluence, "Ringling Brothers Circus had to give three performances to take care of the crowds."[12]

The circus probably detoured around Fayette and Washington counties in that year, however; the hurricane that drowned six-thousand persons at Galveston and saved East Texas cotton roared into the counties along the Brazos and the Colorado rivers with tornadoes, thunderstorms, and high winds, destroying cotton, corn, gardens, and barns, and even sucking well buckets from wells.[13]

The gamble of cotton was an old story by 1900. A century before, Southern agriculture had already become different from northern agriculture and even more different from the agriculture of northern Europe. As geographer Terry Jordan has noted, it mixed and merged British, Native-American, and African-American elements "in a land climatically quite different from that of the ancestral homelands of the Anglo-Americans who practiced it, a land which could produce in abundance many of the staples of the tropics." One of those staple crops was cotton, and because of cotton, Southern agriculture in 1800 was poised "on the eastern rim of a vast, empty land into which it could spread. Expansion came suddenly, as though the long confinement in the narrow fringe of land along the Atlantic had built up an unbearable pressure."[14]

Eli Whitney's invention of the cotton gin triggered this explosive expansion to the west. Already, a society of planters, slaves, and yeoman farmers had evolved, focused on the labor-intensive, land-depleting cash crop of tobacco. The alternative crop of upland cotton did well across much of the South, but the lack of some device to separate seeds from lint blocked expansion until 1793, when a young Massachusetts schoolteacher named Eli Whitney invented a simple machine to accomplish this. Whitney's crude prototype cotton gin, invented on the Green plantation in Georgia, already cleaned from six hundred to nine hundred pounds of cotton a day.[15] A "Judge Johnson" of South Carolina, testifying later in Whitney's suit against copycat inventors infringing on his patent, observed about the effects of the gin: "The whole interior of the Southern states was languishing, and its inhabitants emigrating for want of some object to engage their attention and employ their industry, when the invention of this machine at once opened views to them, which set the whole country in motion."[16]

The judge did not exaggerate. From a high of only 6,276 bales in 1792, cotton production soared to 16,736 bales in 1794, only one year after Whitney's gin, to 115,063 bales in 1802, to 337,720 bales in 1820, on the eve of the settlement of Texas.[17] Southerners had gone "cotton crazy," the institution of slavery (which most thought necessary for cotton agriculture) had taken a new lease on life, and soon the cotton boomers moved west, launching a wave of cotton expansion that rolled westward through time and space to the 1920s and the Gutierrez family's high hilltop in Burnet County, Texas.[18]

The first cotton boom and Anglo-American colonization of Texas came very close together and probably were causally linked. Spanish Texas in 1820 was sparsely populated, with a total European population of only around 3,000.[19] San Antonio de Bexar had 1,814, Bahia (Goliad) had 600, and the area around Nacogdoches had less than 1,000. Other Hispanics lived along the lower Rio Grande in a series of scattered settlements and on the upper Rio Grande around El Paso. But for all practical purposes, Texas in 1820 was an empty land, an unguarded, vulnerable flank of Latin America.[20]

In this context, having not much to lose, the Spanish and, later, Mexican governments launched the *empresario* system for settling this troublesome northern province with hand-picked Anglo-American cotton farmers—registered, sworn to allegiance, nominally converted to Roman Catholicism, and hopefully indoctrinated against political insurrection. Moses Austin had acquired Spanish citizenship while living in Missouri, so he seemed safest. After his untimely death, son Stephen F. Austin began the actual colonization.[21]

Cotton—and wealth through cotton—was much on everyone's minds, Hispanic and Anglo-American alike. Moses Austin's original petition to the Spanish authorities in San Antonio emphasized that the proposed colonists would make their living by cotton farming. Austin implied that slavery would be necessary and in fact had a slave with him at the time of his petition. After Stephen F. Austin took charge, his detailed plan to the Bexar authorities proposed that 50 acres (later raised to 80) would be granted to settlers for each slave brought to Texas. Slavery was legal under Austin's first and subsequent contracts, since both Austin and the Hispanic authorities thought that slaves were necessary for large-scale cotton farming.[22]

Stephen F. Austin's journal, as his party traversed the Brazos–Colorado zone of south-central Texas searching for a base for his colony, revealed a man evaluating the landscape with a cotton-entrepreneur's eye. Austin commented on soils, vegetation indicating fertility, timber for building materials, access to rivers and the Gulf, and other things. The mixed landscape of prairies and woodlands, replete with "number-less clumps of grape vines," already looked like a cultivated place and presented a pleasing prospect. Soils were "productive beyond expecta-tion," rivers were "navigable" with "safe harbors," and even the wildlife riches of deer, turkeys, and wild cattle were seen as evidence of poten-tial productivity of the land—a landscape of "milk and honey," easily recyclable to cotton.[23]

Other Anglo-Americans took a similar view of the lands between the Brazos and Colorado rivers, which became the site of Austin's first colony, and of the countryside westward to the Guadalupe and east-ward to the Trinity. Traveler Benjamin Lundy found this country "charmingly diversified by the alternation of prairies and timbered land," and A. B. Lawrence noted that "as far as the eye could reach, there rose on the view a country magnificently checquered with alternate prairie and wood-land, like a region thickly settled with farms and plantations. Houses alone were waiting to perfect the resemblance."[24]

Austin had no difficulty recruiting American cotton farmers to his colony, though he perhaps attracted more small farmers and back-woodsmen and fewer large planters than he might have wished. Many big slaveholders considered relocating to Texas, but the Mexican gov-ernment's well-known ambivalence toward the institution of slavery kept some planters from bringing their valuable property to Texas before the successful outcome of the Texas Revolution in 1836.[25]

Alabama cotton planter Jared Groce chose to take the risk, however, and there were more like him. Groce was one of the new men, made wealthy by the cotton boom, and no sooner did he hear of Austin's Colony while on a business trip to New Orleans in 1821, than he went home to Alabama, sold his lands, and led a wagon train to Texas accom-panied by ninety slaves. Groce built a homeplace on a high point near present Hempstead and by grant and purchase soon claimed 44,000 acres in parts of what now are Waller, Grimes, and Brazoria counties. Cotton and corn went in the ground even as temporary housing went up, and though the corn failed from lack of rain the cotton prospered beyond Groce's wildest expectations. He marketed the first crop by wagon train to northern Mexico and subsequent crops by way of the Brazos River to New Orleans. By 1825 Jared Groce operated the Austin Colony's first cotton gin, brought from Georgia by his son Leonard, and by 1828 the colony boasted five plantation gins, which, as one contemporary said, soon "sprang up like mushrooms."[26]

Mexican authorities were both elated and alarmed by the boom in Austin's cotton colony and in that of fellow empresario Green Dewitt just to the west. Not only did cotton prosper abundantly along the valleys of the Trinity, Brazos, Colorado, and Guadalupe rivers and their tributaries, but its quality drew accolades from New Orleans buyers.[27] Five years after initial settlement, the population of Austin's Colony alone surpassed the total Hispanic population accumulated in Texas over the nearly three centuries before 1820. By 1830, the colony's population totaled over 4,000, by 1831, exactly 5,665. Settlement focused along the river valleys, especially on the "cane lands," which required only burning off and punching seed holes with an iron rod to plant in corn and cotton. By 1832, Austin's Colony had over thirty cotton gins, several gristmills, and a steam sawmill.[28]

In the spring of 1834, the Mexican government sent Colonel Juan N. Almonte to survey Texas, and he estimated a total population of 9,000 in the Department of the Brazos alone (Austin's Colony and environs), with some 1,000 of this number being slaves. The place was booming, and cotton was the cause. Almonte wrote, "In 1833, upwards of 2,000 bales of cotton weighing from 400 to 500 pounds each, were exported from the Brazos; and it is said that in 1832 not less than 5,000 bales were exported." Of total exports from Brazoria worth $275,000, cotton alone brought in $225,000. Moreover, Almonte reported, with the repeal of the law against Anglo settlement outside the empresario system in 1834, a large-scale influx of Americans had begun. Thousands had already arrived and untold thousands were on the way.[29]

Nearly 30,000 Anglo-Americans and their African-American slaves were in Texas by 1836, when Mexico's experiment with an American cotton colony ended with the Texas Revolution and the founding of the

Texas Republic, and many more came immediately thereafter. Earlier immigrants had come chiefly from the upper South, with Tennesseeans predominating; after 1836, the new republic having made the land safer for slaveholders, Texas attracted more settlers from the lower South, especially Alabama, and the proportion of enslaved Texans climbed to over one-fourth. After statehood in 1845, American farmers literally poured into Texas. By 1847, the Texas population reached 142,000, four times what it had been in 1835, then nearly tripled again between 1850 and 1860, topping 600,000 by the outbreak of the Civil War.[30]

Cotton agriculture both spread and intensified during these decades. As citizens of a Mexican province, then a frontier republic, then a new state of the United States, Texans raised cotton, talked obsessively to each other about cotton, and filled Texas newspapers with letters and editorials speculating endlessly about cotton. Cotton remained the main export by a large margin. Some 29,000 bales of Texas cotton passed through customs in the coastal towns during 1845, and many more thousands of legal and illegal bales went directly from East Texas into the United States. Cotton exported through the coastal custom-houses in 1845 was valued at over $580,000. Hides, the second most important Texas export, were worth only $17,500.[31]

The settlers who came to the new counties of Austin, Washington, and Fayette, formed in 1836 and 1837 from the core of Austin's first colony, typified the mix of farmers moving west with the Southern frontier. Soon, however, immigrants from Europe began to join them along the wooded creek bottoms, blackland prairies, and sandy-land post-oak uplands of this diverse landscape along the Brazos and Colorado. These foreigners from far away Germany and Czechoslovakia, after the swiftest of transitions, adapted the lifestyles of the southern cotton yeomanry they lived among.

The big planters with numerous slaves, who carved large plantations from cane lands and wooded river bottoms, always were in the minority. They settled along the rivers, while smaller slaveholders, often with a single family of slaves, settled farther upstream, along the tributary bottoms or, even, as time went on and the country filled up, the "upcountry" between the bottomlands. Most southern immigrants to Texas were farmer-stockmen who owned no slaves—part of a middle class of yeoman farmers in which ownership of a few slaves made little cultural difference.[32] William M. Rankin, who arrived in Austin's Colony from

Alabama in 1829, and who was still farming on the eve of the Civil War, typified the small, slaveholding farmers that practiced a diversified cotton and subsistence-crop agriculture, though many non-slaveholders lived much as he did. Rankin, who owned four slaves in 1850, produced ten bales of cotton on 100 acres of improved land on his 170-acre farm, but he also reported 900 bushels of corn, 200 bushels of sweet potatoes, 20 bushels of Irish potatoes, 500 pounds of honey and beeswax, 4 tons of hay, 40 milk cows, a hundred cattle, and a hundred hogs.[33]

Rankin fell somewhere toward the middle of an economic continuum ranging from the pure cotton entrepreneurs, most of them planters, at the one extreme, and the pure stockmen-backwoodsmen at the other. The latter often gravitated to the swampy bottomlands beyond the resources of pioneer cotton planters to clear and drain, or, perhaps more commonly, to the blackland prairies and post-oak uplands.

Early cotton farmers were stockmen, as well, and all of the lands between the Brazos and the Colorado were "free range" in the beginning. Big planters and one-horse cotton farmers built split-rail fences around their fields to "fence 'em out" in keeping with standard Southern practice and let hogs and cattle "run outside." Earmarked and branded, their animals mixed and merged with other people's livestock across many square miles of unfenced countryside. The cattle fed on upland grasses in the spring and summer and bottomland switch cane in the late fall and winter. The omnivorous "rooter hogs" foraged for many things in the lean season of summer, then fattened and prospered on the mast of hardwood bottomlands and post-oak uplands in the fall.[34]

Even the big slave plantations in the Brazos valley commonly ran their swine in the woods, and planters reported that the occasional failure of the oak mast caused as much distress as the rare failure of the corn harvest.[35] Hog-killing time on larger plantations reached epic proportions, as on the three farms of Tom B. Blackshear, who customarily slaughtered about 40,000 pounds of pork—some 180 hogs—every year.[36] Hogs, forest animals by adaptation, flourished in the virgin woodlands surrounding settlers' fields. Contemporary observer Mary Austin Holly noted: "In parts of Texas hogs may be raised in large numbers on the native mast— acorns, pecans, hickory nuts, etc.—with a variety of nutritious grasses and many kinds of roots, with an ample sustenance during the year."[37]

Since everyone had to fence cotton and cornfields against free-range livestock, suitable trees for split-rail fencing were a necessary and valuable resource of the landscape. Planters along the wooded bottoms had plenty of labor and plenty of trees. However, as the countryside filled up, it was a different matter on the upland prairies, and for a time before barbed wire fencing came in during the 1880s, poorer uplands well supplied with Virginia cedars and post oaks suitable for split-rail fencing sometimes sold for more than fertile prairie blacklands.[38]

A backwoods lifestyle of free-range stock raising, subsistence farming, hunting, and fishing typified the settlement phase of every part of old Austin's Colony, though it swiftly evolved into cotton agribusiness in the bottoms and, at a somewhat later date, into mixed cotton and subsistence farming on the prairie uplands. The backwoods farming lifeway, with the four "essential elements" of "corn, hogs, ax, and fire," lasted longest in the sandy post-oak uplands, which were ecologically well suited for raising free-range swine and turkeys and, in some places, had no stock law well into the 1920s.[39]

Backwoodsmen and would-be cotton entrepreneurs often were the same people, as in the case of Jesse Burnham on the far northwestern limits of Austin's Colony along the Colorado. In this frontier area, much bothered by Indian resistance in the early years of settlement, Burnham's family dressed only in buckskin, pounded corn to meal in an Indian mortar, and ate large amounts of venison dipped in wild honey. Nevertheless, the family and their slaves also raised a patch of cotton during their first year and often sat around at night in their locked and barred one-pen log cabin—blacks and whites together—picking seeds from cotton lint and singing to drown out the sounds made by Indians prowling around outside.[40]

Anglo-American settlers by long practice and tradition had accumulated many tricks of the trade of subsistence farming and backwoods lifestyle, no matter that they might plan a swift ascent into cotton farming affluence. Young blacksmith Noah Smithwick visited one such recently arrived family during the late 1820s at their small "pole cabin" in a small clearing where they had planted corn. Thomas B. Bell's family was of some gentility, but they were clearly both of limited means and possessed of a good measure of frontier ingenuity.

> The whole family was dressed in buckskin, and when supper was announced, we sat on stools around a clapboard table, upon which were arranged wooden platters. Beside each platter

lay a fork made of a joint of cane. The knives were of various patterns, ranging from butcher knives to pocket knives. And for cups, we had little wild cymlings [gourds], scraped and scoured until they looked as white and clean as earthenware.[41]

The first German settlers, arriving during the 1820s and 1830s, initially had no frontier skills to fall back on and a lot more to learn. Caroline Ernst came to Austin's Colony with her family at age eleven, when her father, Friedrich Ernst, formerly a professional gardener for the Duke of Oldenburg, first settled in what became the community of Industry in Austin County. A nearby Anglo-American family, people much like the Bells, invited the Ernsts to live with them for a time and helped them get started, but after a while the Germans were on their own. Friedrich Ernst soon posted glowing letters home to Oldenburg newspapers, praising Texas as a place of milk, honey, wild grapes, cheap land, and freedom, but his first couple of years in the wilderness were not easy. For a time the Ernsts had little to eat, making do only with cornbread cooked in a skillet, the only cooking utensil they possessed. Later, the Ernsts began to raise peas, providing a welcome supplement to their diet of cornbread. Meat remained in short supply, since Mr. Ernst lacked hunting skills, and the first house he constructed for his family also left much to be desired. Caroline Ernst remembered her first home in Texas as less than adequate shelter:

A miserable little hut covered with straw and having six sides which were made out of moss. The roof above was by no means waterproof, and we often held an umbrella over our bed when it rained at night, while the cows came to eat the moss. Of course, we suffered a great deal in the winter. My father had tried to build a chimney and fireplace out of logs and clay, but we were afraid to light a fire because of the extreme combustibility of our dwelling, so we had to shiver. Our shoes gave out and we had to go barefooted in winter, for we did not know how to make moccasins. Our supply of clothes was also insufficient, and we had no spinning wheel. Nor did we know how to spin and weave, like the Americans. It was 28 miles to San Felipe, and besides we had no money.[42]

Other immigrants had adjustments to make, as well. Driven by land hunger, economic hard times, and political unrest at home, Germans, Czechs, and other Europeans began arriving in the lands along the Brazos and Colorado soon after the Ernst family settled in 1832. Additional south Germans bought land from Friedrich Ernst and settled around him, forming the community of Industry. Others settled at Cat Spring in Austin County, at Hostyn, and at Fayetteville. One German pioneer of Cat Spring recalled the traumas of first arrival in the Texas wilderness, especially what had happened to her brothers. Having come to Texas to escape "the oppressions of Prussian society" and looking forward to a carefree life of romantic hunting expeditions, instead they found themselves clearing new ground, splitting rail fences, and laboring in the field, all "work which was entirely new to them." Only the advice and assistance of Anglo-American settlers in the area, ready to "share their last piece of bread" with the European greenhorns, lessened the shock.[43]

Czech immigrant Augustin Haidusek, who came to Texas at age eleven in 1856, told similar tales of frontier arrival and swift adaptation. His family and other Czechs founded the settlement of Dubina in eastern Fayette County, observed what nearby Anglo-Americans were doing, walked into the nearest settlement to buy axes, built log huts, and swiftly turned to fieldwork.

> With shelter provided, all began clearing the land, made rail fences, and prepared the land for tilling. In the fall, only one small bale of cotton was made by the whole group. It was loaded on a sled and pulled by oxen to La Grange, where it was sold. Indeed, this first struggling effort at making a living was filled with forebodings. By now the savings brought from Europe were spent, flour was twenty dollars a barrel, and an epidemic broke out, caused by hard work and contaminated water. It was truly a fight for survival, but God was with us. The following year crops were better, and with the kind help of those of English-speaking extraction we became firmly established.[44]

Four years after the Haiduseks arrived in Texas, a friend from Moravia visited them. After spending the night in their crude log cabin, the man told Augustin's father, "My dear Valento, you had a better pig sty at home," to which Haidusek replied, "I had rather live in this hut as an American citizen than to live in a palace and be under the Austro-Hungarian oppression."[45]

Like the Czech settlers of Dubina, no sooner did European farmers arrive in the new counties along the Brazos and Colorado than they built American-style log cabins, loosed hogs and cattle into the surrounding free range, and planted their fields in cotton and corn. German settlement in Texas spread out from centers around New Braunfels, Castroville, and Industry, and in the east—along the Brazos and Colorado—the European immigrants became cotton farmers almost at first arrival.[46]

Apprenticeships were short, and skills developed swiftly in the Texas wilderness; a decade or so after arrival, German and Czech log structures no longer seemed crude to anyone. The Legler house in remote Biegel's Settlement of southern Fayette County, for example, demonstrated full-dovetail corner notching of the finest workmanship.[47]

Germans (and probably Czechs as well) raised cotton with greater frequency than non-slaveholding Anglo farmers before the Civil War.[48] The Germans built typical Southern two-pen log houses with scattered outbuildings, consumed prodigious amounts of corn, sweet potatoes, and pork, just as the Southerners did, and supplemented their large gardens and full smokehouses with wild fruits and venison. After a decade or so, various mid-nineteenth-century travelers thought the diligent Europeans had better log houses, livestock, gardens, orchards, and cotton crops than the surrounding Anglo yeomanry.[49] By the 1850s, as geographer Terry Jordan has noted, these eastern Germans universally accepted cotton culture as the heart of their crop economy. "They became, first and foremost, cotton farmers. Approaching Cat Spring one traveler observed that numerous piles of cotton bales in the farmyards helped create the false impression from a distance that the settlement was one of considerable size."[50]

Unlike the organized beginnings of German settlement around New Braunfels and Castroville, the German and Czech settlements around Industry, Cat Spring, Hostyn, and Fayetteville grew informally from individual settlers' writing home, then aiding and encouraging other family members and friends from the Old Country to join them in Texas. For a century after 1832, Europeans continued to immigrate, and as the countryside filled up, they spread gradually northward. At many locations along the Texas blacklands, "Germans coming from the South" became an old story.[51] Newcomers often had their way paid by earlier arrivals, worked on their farms for a time paying them back with hard labor (and learning how to cultivate cotton and corn), rented someone else's cotton land for a few years to accumulate money, then bought their own farms. German and Czech land hunger was intense, as compared to that of Anglo-Americans accustomed to relatively cheap and available farmland. As Robert L. Skrabanek noted, Czechs came from a land-poor peasantry "in a country where land was at such a premium that it was almost worshipped," and Fayette County historian Julia Sinks observed that among local Germans "the love of the land fell like a benediction upon every heart."[52]

Early observers thought the Germans and Czechs were more social than the surrounding Anglos, helping each other more and sticking together better. Certainly, they were more inclined to organize. Soon after coming to Texas, the Czechs formed benevolent societies, insurance societies, and cooperative gins and stores, and the Germans organized these things, and more. Beginning in the 1830s, and demonstrating what students of German culture have termed a *Vereinswesen,* "an intense desire to band together," Texas Germans along the Brazos and Colorado swiftly united in farming, shooting, singing, dancing, literary, athletic, and mutual aid societies.[53]

Every settlement of European farmers had its own unique history. Snook, a Czech community just north of the Washington County line in Burleson County, began when a few families moved in, found Anglo-American stockmen selling blackland at bargain prices, and sent the word back by way of passing peddlers to friends and relatives in the Cat Spring area.[54] The Wendish community of Serbin began with the arrival at Galveston in 1854 of a congregation of about six hundred Lutheran Wends (a Slavic group of uncertain origin, living in eastern Germany). Following an unsuccessful search for land around Industry and New Ulm, the congregation purchased 4,000 acres of sandy-land countryside in Lee County and took up cotton farming.[55]

Biegel's Settlement in southern Fayette County began in 1832 when Joseph and Margarethe Biegel arrived at Austin's Colony to claim the league of land granted them by the Mexican government. Biegel soon wrote home to the Rhineland, and in time an international group of settlers arrived from the Rhineland provinces of Germany and France, Switzerland, and French Lorraine. As its historians have noted, the community "was a German settlement, though with a French flavor."[56]

The Meitzen family came to Texas to Biegel's Settlement in 1847, and their arrival typified that of many. They were among a boatload of immigrants who were dumped on the sand flats of Galveston Island in the dead of winter, crossed to the mainland, then climbed into a few ox wagons that afforded only room for the women and children. The men walked to Fayette County beside the wagons down roads muddied by torrential rains and scattered with dead oxen. One older woman had packed away a bundle of pine kindling before leaving the Rhineland and brought it along, much to the amusement of the rest of her party. Now, however, it allowed the desperately cold and wet travelers to kindle a fire at every campsite during their hard winter trek. The immigrants were on their way to distant Fredericksburg, but somewhere around Industry "old man Biegel" persuaded them to stop at his Fayette County settlement instead.[57] As a former Rhinelander, doubtless he reminded them of home.

Biegel's Settlement gradually accumulated around fifty families, a small crossroads store, a gin, a gristmill, and two syrup-making operations located in different parts of the settlement, but it remained one of those dispersed rural communities that a stranger could ride across without ever seeing that a community was there. Biegel's league was softly rolling blackland prairie bordered by post-oak-fringed ridges, with the valley of the Colorado to the south and east. Hogs and cows in the woods and bottoms, cotton and corn in the fields, and big gardens near the two-pen log cabins typified life at Biegel's Settlement, as they did everywhere else.[58]

After a while, Czechs began to join Biegel's Settlement. Lovers of blackland soils, the Czechs raised cotton, corn, cattle, and hogs like all the rest, differing only in their language and in a few cultural grace notes; they often whitewashed their two-pen log farmhouses and grew "double lavender poppies" in fall gardens to supply seeds for their traditional kolache pastries.[59]

A few Anglos with their black slaves lived in the area, and after emancipation the freedmen continued to live in Biegel's Settlement, often as "thirds-and-fourths renters" or "half renters," and working as day hands for Joe Tschiedel at his gin during ginning season. "These ancestors of

Fayette County black people raised cotton and corn, bought their supplies at Kroll's store, located in one half of his two-pen log house, and their ham, bacon, and sausage from the Scherers. Joe Polasek sold them sauerkraut for five cents a bucket." The black men worked for the Scherers and other families, and when they showed up early in the morning for a day's fieldwork, they would be served breakfast.[60]

Early social life at Biegel's Settlement revolved around the simple Sunday afternoon visit of one family to another family, and the occasional "house party." At the latter, dances were held wherever there was room, with music provided by a hand-turned organ made by a man named Schiller. Sometimes, both organ and organist would be put on an ox- or mule-drawn sled and followed by wagons of partygoers who sang as they drove across the dark countryside.[61]

In all these things, Biegel's Settlement closely resembled many other German, Czech, and Anglo-American farming settlements before the Civil War—"kinship communities," historians have termed them. An old Fayette County settler told historian F. Lotto around 1900 that in his youth many poor families had traveled to social occasions on sleds pulled by oxen, and that "People who came in wagons in those days were considered as putting on style." Boys danced at parties in "hickory shirts"—and barefooted on cleaned and smoothed ground, not on turn-of-the-century wooden dance platforms. "Each settlement formed one great family, and the settlers all considered themselves as brothers and sisters."[62]

As the upland prairies and post-oak belts along the Brazos and Colorado gradually accumulated farm families and communities such as Biegel's Settlement during the 1850s, down in the river bottoms cotton boomed as never before. Average production per Texas farm increased from 3.3 to 10.4 bales during the decade, and larger farmers using slave labor produced over 90 percent of the crop.[63] Cotton production in Washington County, for example, jumped from 4,008 bales in 1850 to 23,221 bales in 1860. Small, two-to-ten-bale cotton farms abounded in the land between the rivers, but slave plantations along the Brazos and Colorado produced most of the cotton.[64] As agribusiness boomed, some early backwoodsmen pioneers of the area picked up and moved west. Frontiersman Robert W. Chappel, who had come to Texas with his family and a pack of bear hounds in 1838, wiped out the local bears, shot the last Washington County buffalo in 1850, and relocated to Milam County, where there was more game, leaving only his name behind. Big slave plantations developed at the old hunter's Chappel Hill community, as they did upstream at Washington-on-the-Brazos.[65]

A traveler writing for *De Bow's Review* of 1855, described plantation cotton prosperity along the Brazos valley in glowing terms: "Above and below the thriving town of Washington On The Brazos, for many miles the cotton, corn and every vegetable substance seems to overload the earth, and when I viewed the fields and saw the corn and pumpkins rotting, and the hogs so fat that they could scarcely wallow, and passing the plump ears of corn without regarding them, I almost thought it a wanton waste of nature."[66]

As the boom 1850s progressed, planters along the Brazos and Colorado set about improving their lifestyles and creating homes more in keeping with their new agricultural prosperity. Thomas Banks of Washington County, whose plantation produced 750 bales in 1860, did this, as did smaller planter Tacitus Clay. Clay built one of the showplace plantation houses of the county, known as "Clay Castle" because of its large, glassed-in dance floor on the third story. Thomas Affleck completed his Washington County plantation, which he called "Glenblythe," in 1857, and proudly wrote of it:

> The dwelling-house is one of the most comfortable and
> commodious in the state; and situated in a very beautiful
> and elevated prairie valley, studded over with Live-oak
> and other groves. A fine cement cistern under house, affords
> abundance of delicious pure and cool water. The house
> contains six bedrooms, large and airy; dining room and
> parlour, two large and pleasant halls; dressing & bathrooms;
> kitchen; laundry room; etc.[67]

Glenblythe also featured enclosed galleries, a carriage house, a granary, stables, corncribs, "comfortable servants' quarters," an enclosed poultry yard, and even a "pigeonry." Located two miles away, the "plantation quarter and mill" included twenty slave cabins, overseer's house, church, hospital, storehouse, blacksmith's shop, cooper's shop, sorghum mill, and combined gristmill and gin mill.[68]

Not that the prosperous planters along the river valleys did not have their problems. The rich, red alluviums deposited by river floods along the Brazos and Colorado proved unmatched cotton soils, but every few years the floods returned at unpropitious times to drown crops in the field. Getting cotton to market was another problem. San Felipe on the Brazos and Columbus on the Colorado were the generally-agreed-upon heads of navigation for steamboat transport, which was dangerous at the best of times on these shallow, snag-strewn rivers.[69] Many planters preferred to ship their cotton to Houston by ox wagon on roads deep in mud and littered with the bodies of animals literally driven to death. By the 1850s, many up-to-date cotton planters had converted their agricultural operations to the use of mules, but sometimes only slow, strong, big-footed oxen could "pull the mud" into Houston—or even Washington-on-the-Brazos.[70]

As always with labor-intensive cotton farming, the work force proved another difficulty. Slaves frequently ran away—sometimes heading for Mexico, more commonly just staying in nearby woods and living off the land. Historian Abigail Curlee wrote, "Some left impulsively; others established a camp in the woods when the roasting ears and wild plums were ripe; still others timed their departures from the cotton fields by the purpling grapes, the silvering cane, and the dropping of the pecans." After two or three weeks, most of these short-range runaways returned, took their punishments, and returned to work, though "a few planters had Negroes in the woods all the time, particularly the woods around 'Peach Point' in the lower part of Brazoria County."[71]

When a slave returned, the planter felt himself torn between the desire to administer just retribution and the joy that an enormously valuable unit of agricultural machinery had been saved. As the cotton boom of the 1850s continued, the price of slaves grew accordingly. In 1859, the *Matagorda Gazette* reported that the prices for prime field hands had risen to unprecedented levels and ranged from $1,200 to $2,000—huge prices, which strongly suggested what might happen after emancipation to the persons who had indebted themselves to pay them.[72]

The Civil War destroyed the planters' prosperity. By 1865 things were going bitterly wrong for Thomas Affleck, the proud owner of Glenblythe plantation in Washington County. Now free persons, his former slaves also felt more free to express their opinions. Affleck wrote in a letter to the Galveston *Tri-Weekly News* in October of 1865:

> For my part, I will endure as patiently as I can, until better can be done. But, not one hour longer will I endure the impudent leer and lounging movement; the drawling, disrespectful manner; the neglect of duties; the want of care of stock, gates left open, fences laid down, and left down; horses and mules ridden off at night; the language used, even in the hearing of white females and children, which is of every day occurrence.[73]

As this passage implies, large cotton farmers had a labor problem after the Civil War, one that many of them never solved. Along the Brazos and Colorado, as everywhere else in the South, planters had been in no way afraid of debt and now faced the war's end with more than a third of their capital tied up in human property.[74] After emancipation, some former planters sold out almost immediately. Others, in attempts to pay off their creditors, struck various deals with their former slaves to try to keep them in the field, but with uneven success.

B. F. Elliot, of western Washington County, survived Reconstruction by executing labor contracts in 1866 and 1867 with his former slaves. They worked his farm for one-third of the cotton and corn, while he provided shelter, clothing, provisions, tools, teams, and access to a gin.[75] For a few years, farmers around Chappel Hill paid wages to freedmen but enforced conditions otherwise very similar to slavery.[76] John W. Lockhart was one of the men who did this, paying five dollars a month wages. As time passed and the Texas Freedmen's Bureau in the county seat of Brenham increased its power, the former slaves began to depart their semi-forced-labor situations on local plantations, and the planters grew increasingly desperate. Between 1871 and 1876, Lockhart and others formed the Washington County Immigration Society and through various agents tried to solve their labor problems by attracting Germans, "Polanders," and Anglo-Americans from Alabama, Georgia, and North Carolina to the area. This strategy did not work very well or for very long.[77] According to one account, 250 German settlers signed up, were brought from Germany, and went to work around Chappel

Hill. However, after assessing their situation, they saw that the landowners who had paid their way wanted only a permanent force of wage laborers, which was in conflict with their desire to obtain land. As soon as they could, they left the area.[78]

With inadequate or undependable labor, falling cotton prices, and rising taxes as the decade of the 1870s wore on, many big landowners began to sell out—often to Germans and Czechs, whose immigration had resumed after the war. As early as 1866 the Washington County Clerk commented that ninety parcels of land totaling over 10,000 acres had been sold to Germans in a six-month period.[79] Some former plantations were totally partitioned and sold. Other owners sold the unimproved parts of their properties to the Europeans and ran the original croplands with share-cropping ex-slaves.[80]

Some landowners, like the Routt family of Chappel Hill, hung on through the Reconstruction years until the violent reassumption of Democratic power in 1882. With political power came an increased measure of social and economic control over a black, mostly sharecropper, work force. In 1932, seventy-nine-year-old Joe Routt owned a gin and 1,300 acres of Brazos valley cotton land and well recalled his role in the Democratic takeover. According to a newspaper article, he told of being one of a "committee, a group of citizens who went abroad with their pistols, determining to kill off a group of men whom they knew were stirring up trouble with the Negroes." The newspaper writer explained, "Following the hanging of four Negroes, Mr. Routt had nine federal indictments hanging over him and was instrumental in the activities that caused a federal investigation. The precinct went Democratic in 1882, and the first box to report in was Joe Routt's Chappel Hill box." Intimidated by previous actions of the "committee," every black man in Joe Routt's precinct voted Democratic.[81]

After 1882, some big new cotton farms began to develop along the river valleys, often on previously uncleared bottomlands purchased cheaply from bankrupt planters. The new owners were business-oriented people—ginners, mercantile storeowners, and men inclined to take advantage of the railroads. The Terrell family fit this pattern, purchasing from the heirs of pioneer Robert Millican several thousand acres of mostly uncleared Brazos bottoms on the Grimes County side of the river opposite old Washington. During the 1890s, as the Santa Fe Railroad built westward, the Terrells began clearing and draining the swampy Brazos bottom and putting it into cotton. The bottoms were prime cotton land but hard to clear, hard to drain, hard or impossible to protect from periodic floods, and difficult to man with enough share-croppers to get the job done—but the Terrells persisted.[82] By 1920 their "Allenfarm"—much of it worked by black sharecroppers—rivaled the old slave plantations in size and complexity of social organization. Across the South, in the Mississippi Delta, the Arkansas Delta, and the Missouri "Bootheel," other major untouched bottomlands were cleared, drained, and developed for tenant plantations at about this time.[83]

On the other side of the Brazos, on the Washington County "Bluffs," an African-American community very different from the cropper community of Allenfarm had come into existence in the decades after the Civil War. This was the Mount Falls Settlement, a scattered community of freed slaves who had managed to purchase sandy hill land and clear fields from the virgin forest, and who now made a living producing cotton, corn, and whisky as independent small farmers.[84] At Flat Prairie on Yegua Creek forty miles west of Mount Falls, and at other remote locations between the Brazos and Colorado, farmers in other black communities lived similar lives—often as landowners, making the most of their poor sandy-land farms, trying to produce everything they needed on their places and in their communities, and attempting to stay out of the economic control of whites.[85] Sometimes referred to by Anglo-Americans as "independent quarters" and by African-Americans as "freedom colonies," these communities were part of the enormous social complexity of the Southern uplands after the Civil War.[86] Other former slaves worked on cropper plantations or dwelt among their former yeoman slaveowners at Biegel's Settlement and a hundred similar places across Fayette, Washington, and Austin counties.

Usually remaining far from the black independent settlements and the sandy hills, railroads followed the blackland cotton soils westward and northward across the area in the decades after the Civil War. During the 1870s and 1880s, the Houston and Texas Central Railroad built westward from Brenham to Austin, and the new towns of Burton, Carmine, and Ledbetter sprang up along the way. Farmers, many of them Germans, purchased railroad lands, and La Bahia Prairie and the country around the railroads filled up with cotton farms, gins, rural schools, and crossroads stores—the characteristic infrastructure of the Southern countryside.

Burton in western Washington County typified many such new towns. It had two gins, several mercantile stores, blacksmith shops, and various other businesses. Having created Burton from the blackland prairie, the Houston and Texas Central remained its lifeline.[87] In season, it carried hundreds of bales of Burton cotton into Brenham, and four passenger trains a day called on the town, two running east from Austin, two west from Houston. Florence Fischer recalled that everyone always went down to the depot to see who got on or off the train, and that someone in the employ of the Washington Hotel, two blocks away from the depot, always hung a special kerosene lantern on one corner of the building to show drummers arriving on the evening train where to go. Burton residents thought of the Houston and Texas Central as "their" railroad, and since its passenger trains commonly carried ten cars, they referred to the H & TC as "The Hen and Ten Chicks."[88]

The Houston and Texas Central crossed a corner of Fayette County on its way to Austin, and other railroads soon traversed the area, each spawning a line of railroad towns, including Schulenburg, Flatonia, West Point, Plum, and others. But even as they created these new towns, the railroads ruined the economic lives of dozens of bypassed communities. Rejected by the railroad, old Washington-on-the-Brazos in Washington County withered and died, and in Fayette County proud High Hill, where Texas's first cottonseed-oil mill had been established in 1867, was left high and dry and went into a long decline. "One of the most prosperous of German villages," High Hill in its heyday had four mercantile stores, three blacksmith shops, a brewery, a hotel, two private schools, a church, singing clubs, a town band, and an opera house, but when it missed the railroad none of this made any difference to its fate. It declined into just another sleepy crossroads burg.[89]

As the plantations sold their lands and the railroads built westward, opening up new farming areas, Germans and Czechs continued to arrive, work on other people's farms for a time, rent from someone, accumulate money, then buy their own land. They did this with a single-minded dedication that local Anglo-Americans sometimes found almost unsettling. People like John Skrabanek and his family "ate, drank, and slept farming" and pursued ownership of a blackland farm with religious intensity.[90] The family of Gilbert Buck's mother, the Hoppmanns, immigrated to the Burton area, lived with relatives, and saved every penny they could to buy land. On Sunday afternoons, Mr. Hoppmann traveled about to local properties he knew to be for sale to check them out. "He would take the walking cane and see how far he could stick it in the dirt, see how thick the dirt was, or where the rock was, see where he could farm and where he couldn't farm."[91]

Some came by themselves, with no possessions and no relatives before them. Albert Banik's father, for example, arrived at Galveston in the 1880s as a boy of fifteen, then set out on foot for the German country. Wagon freighters picked him up and let him work for his transport. Later, he worked as a hired hand near Nassau until he had accumulated money for his own farm.[92]

Many of the post-war German settlers had skilled trades that they used during their phase-in to the new land, or returned to later on. Ora Nell Wehring Moseley's grandfather William, arriving in 1882, practiced the cobbler's trade. Gil Buck's father was a skilled blacksmith and machinist. Robert Dement recalled old German immigrants from his youth who were millers, blacksmiths, carpenters, and furniture makers. He noted, "My grandmother said her daddy was a furniture maker, but he was also a farmer. He farmed for a living, but he made furniture."[93]

Memories of coming to Texas remained vivid and were passed down across the generations. Eddie Wegner's grandfather, Adolph Wegner, came from Germany on a sailing ship at age nine, just in time for a Galveston hurricane, and recalled to his dying day the ship being blown aground, the masts toppling, and sailors scrambling to chop the downed masts free before they capsized the ship.[94]

Even into the twentieth century, the Germans continued to come to the lands along the Brazos and Colorado. In 1909, the Oldenburg correspondent to the La Grange *Journal* wrote: "Dick Meinen and wife, and Mrs. Tiemann, went to Galveston Thursday to welcome another candidate for citizenship in the 'land of the free and the home of the brave,' their young nephew, who disembarked the day after their arrival. The party returned Sunday, and we all are glad to extend welcome to this bright, healthy, German boy."[95]

Through all the changes after the Civil War, cotton remained the king crop, the focus of all desires, the one great money staple that, if you were diligent enough, frugal enough, and lucky enough, could get you a farm. All this had its effects on cotton production in the counties along the rivers. By 1880, even with the increasing development of the pure blackland counties to the north and west, Fayette and Washington still ranked near the top among Texas counties in cotton and corn production. Fayette produced 25,000 bales in that year, tied for first place with Lamar County; Washington County ranked sixth with over 21,000 bales, down from first place before the war.[96]

CHAPTER 3

Lay of the Land

Forty years later, cotton still was king. In the late spring of
1920, after the rains slacked off, the roads dried, and the roadside grasses grew high enough to feed stock, the old scissors-
sharpener peddler, Bruno Huebner, readied his covered wagon
for his regular circuit of the Washington and Fayette County
countrysides. Model T Fords and other early automobiles had
been abroad for a decade, but most roads had yet to adjust to
their coming. Farms in the countryside remained remote, with
many farm families still visiting their county-seat towns only
once or twice a year. Peddlers like Huebner made a living by
braving black mud, deep sand, and flooded creek bottoms to
carry their goods and services into the deep countryside to isolated settlements and remote farmsteads.[1]

Farm families appreciated Huebner's services and looked
forward to his regular visits. He sharpened scissors, an essential tool of the farm women, who annually sewed canvas cotton pick sacks and most of their families' clothing except shoes
and overalls. Farm families wasted little, and after the bottoms
of the pick sacks wore out from the pickers' dragging them
across the ground, the tops were scissored apart and made into
blue-jean-jacket-like "jumpers," mattress ticking, girls' heavy-
duty work dresses, and a dozen other things. Shops in La
Grange, Brenham, and smaller market towns such as Burton

and Fayetteville stood ready to sharpen scissors, but transportation was slow, roads were bad, field crops required labor, and most families did not have the time for overnight expeditions to town that required camping out in the "wagonyard." Consequently, peddlers like Huebner brought goods and services to them.

Other peddlers, a few of them now in Fords, began to hit the roads at about the same time Huebner did. The Raleigh man, Watkins man, and "Red Ball" man carried condiments, spices, and various small luxury items; other peddlers sold patent medicines, canned foodstuffs, used clothing, shoes, fabric and sewing materials, and a great variety of other things, even including (in the fall after good cotton seasons) wood stoves, player pianos, and carbide lighting systems. The ordinary peddlers, like Huebner and the ubiquitous Raleigh and Watkins men, so commonly took housewives' chickens in barter for goods and services that some people called them "chicken peddlers." Whether they traveled by old covered wagons or customized Model T Fords, chicken coops hung everywhere on the peddlers' vehicles.[2]

Early one morning, Otto Huebner rolled through the quiet streets of Brenham, county seat of Washington County, and out into the open countryside toward the market town of Burton to the west. Brenham looked much like any Southern courthouse town of 1920, with its courthouse square, the big mercantile stores grouped around it, and the wagonyards on the edge of town—places where country people spent the night on the rare occasions they came into Brenham to sell cotton, pay taxes, or buy medicine. Often, only the fathers and older sons did this. Twenty miles out, many a rural child had yet to see the electric lights and other wonders of the courthouse town: its paved streets, giant cotton compresses and cottonseed mills, fall circuses and fairs, and wonderful department stores that whizzed customers' money in capsules along wires into high cages manned by men in green eyeshades, then whizzed the receipts back down.

In 1920, life in a place like Brenham, La Grange, nearby Navasota in Grimes County, or a thousand other Southern county seat towns, ebbed and flowed with the cotton cycle. For months of the year, streets emptied of farm wagons, store employees played checkers to while away the idle hours, and merchants anxiously watched the weather and monitored the development of local cotton fields from bud to bloom to boll. Then, sometime in August, someone brought in the first bale, and everything changed. The street parade to celebrate the first bale kicked off that year's cotton season, the wonderful months of cash-in-hand, payment of debts, fairs, circuses, and Christmas buying. As the wagons rolled into town, cotton buyers thronged the town square and stores hired additional employees—some as clerks, some to work the streets tolling in money-laden farmers to their establishments. Many a father marched his children into the mercantile store for a year's outfitting in overalls, straw hats, and brogans, with various luxuries and nonessentials purchased on the side.

On this late spring day in 1920, however, Brenham's streets remained quiet as Huebner's wagon headed out for the deep country-side. During this time of year, the vendor of goods and services had to seek out the buyers, rather than the other way around. Huebner's customers were out there, chopping and cultivating their cotton and corn from "can see to can't," as the farmers' old saying described their day-light-to-dark workday.

On the first day out, Huebner visited various old friends along the main road that ran from Brenham to Burton and on to distant Austin, ninety miles away, but his main customers lay well away from these centers where farmers could find other people to sharpen their scissors. In 1920, the thriving railroad market town of Burton prided itself on having two flourishing gins, a bank, several mercantile stores, a two-story hotel, a cotton warehouse, and virtually everything else that surrounding farm families might need. In the view of Burton merchants such as Thomas Watson, nobody had any reason to go to Brenham, twelve miles away, when everything "From the Cradle to the Grave" could be obtained within his establishment. Touting his store as the "Old Reliable," operating in terms of the Golden Rule, he claimed to have available inside "every item for the infant and adult from swaddling clothes to caskets." In truth, beside the "plain and fancy groceries," hardware, millinery shop, everyday clothing, furniture, wood stoves, and John Deere farm implements, Watson's store also sold cradles and caskets, noting: "The assortment of funeral supplies and fixtures is one of the best in the county, and two licensed funeral directors, morgue, and hearse-ambulance, are always at the disposal of those when life's darkest moment comes."[3] Furthermore, like most other mercantile storeowners, John Watson also bought local farmers' cotton, often making the best offers to individuals who owed him the most money.

In the late afternoon, Huebner the peddler turned south from Burton and the main road and headed down the dirt track toward Greenvine and distant Round Top in Fayette County, both lesser market towns, now somewhat on the wane with the coming of the railroad and the rise of Burton and Carmine. Here, Huebner began his calls at the usual farmsteads, and he found more farm wives who needed their scissors sharpened as he moved farther south and deeper into the countryside.

As the peddler went from farm to farm, people asked him for news from Brenham and about the state of the roads behind him. Rural telephone circuits were creeping out of places like Carmine and Burton at this time, but they went only so far and failed to reach everybody. Furthermore, many lines were cooperatives, maintained by amateur labor, and often broke down. A passing peddler might have interesting information about far-away events in the courthouse town, and he certainly knew the state of the roads he had just passed over, information of immediate usefulness.

Roads were much on Huebner's mind, as well, and he queried the rural mail carriers and other travelers he met coming the other way about the state of the roads in certain bottoms and creek crossings up ahead. In 1920 many rural lanes in Fayette and Washington counties still were ungraveled and ran torturous, winding routes across the landscape. They followed contours around hills, avoided steep grades and unusually muddy or sandy places that animals could not pull, and carefully picked their way across creek bottoms. These roads had been routed during a time of animal transport, when getting to one's destination at all took precedence over getting there quickly, and they maintained these characteristics into the automobile era.

A professional at driving the country roads, Huebner worried about deep sand, eroded ruts, fallen trees, and narrow wooden bridges, but his main concerns about these Washington and Fayette County roads were mud and motorcars. With a long slow rain and enough passing traffic to churn it up, a local road could turn overnight into thick, viscous, black mud that balled up on the rims of a wagon's wheels and crept up its spokes until they formed solid wheels of mud, finally stopping the team in its tracks. During part of the winter, no wheeled vehicles could run on certain of these rural roads, and travelers such as Huebner in other

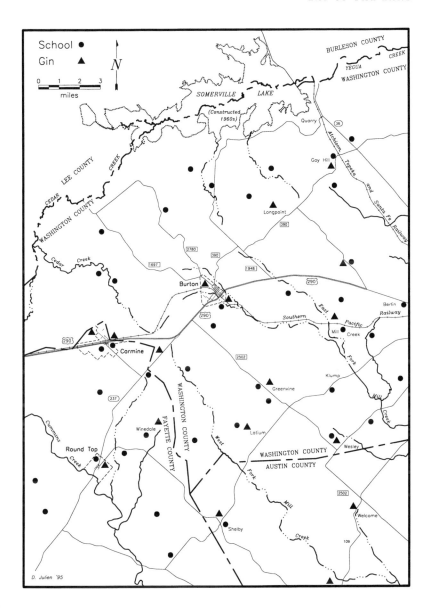

FIGURE 2   Current highway map of the Burton–Round Top area,
showing the cotton gins and schools of ca. 1927. In the years before
World War II, gins and schools were two of the most important
determinants of communities in rural areas. (Map redrawn from a
map by Dan Julien, Austin)

seasons always feared a sudden return to the full horrors of "mudtime."
Roads were narrow, unditched, and poorly drained, accumulating water
down the deep ruts, which were difficult to get one's wheels in and out
of, and which made it hard to pass the Model T Fords or other automobiles that ran the rural roads with increasing frequency. Huebner—
and his veteran horses—hated the automobiles and hated passing them
on the road, one wheel in the right-side rut, one wheel out on the narrow shoulder. The noisy chugging automobile passed very close to the
team during this maneuver, increasing the stress on the horses. Before
entering a boggy bottom with deep ruts, Huebner always stopped on
the slope above to listen for the sound of an oncoming car, and if he
heard one he waited for it to come through. Meeting and passing one
in the deep ruts of the bottom could be very unpleasant. Huebner's animals were controllable in these circumstances, but others' were not.
From 1905 to 1920, as the old peddler well knew, the pages of the
Brenham *Banner-Press* and the La Grange *Journal* had been full of stories about local stock–motorcar accidents, some of them fatal. A decade
after experiencing their first automobile, some horses and mules still
went berserk at the sight and sound of one.[4]

Periodically, Huebner passed through one of the small communities
scattered across the farming landscape a few miles apart, little urban
islands in a sea of countryside. Farmers disliked traveling the bad roads
for more than five or six miles to reach gin, store, and blacksmith, so in
time such places tended to grow up a few miles from each other. Many
had only the minimal community institutions of gin, store, blacksmith
shop, post office, church, school, and—in this heavily German and
Czech area—public dance hall. Once one element of this characteristic
assemblage established itself, the rest often followed. In times past,
crossroads communities often had included an informal race track
somewhere nearby for horse races on Sunday afternoons, but by 1920 a
community baseball diamond had become more common. This was the
heyday of mass participation in the national sport, and virtually every
community with nine adult males under the age of fifty fielded a team.

The larger crossroads communities, such as Round Top, had a considerable richness of economic and social life. More things might be
going on in Burton or La Grange, of course, but these places were
twenty miles of bad roads away and in certain seasons might as well
have been on the moon. Round Top had a gin, four stores, three saloons

(before Prohibition), a drugstore, a tinsmith shop, a blacksmith shop, a photo gallery, a shoemaker, and a cigar factory.[5] It also had a well-used dance hall, central gathering place of the Round Top *Schutzen Verein*, or "shooting club," and virtually everyone else. German and Czech dance halls had originated in shooting, gymnastic, singing, and benevolent societies, but by 1920 their functions as community center and dance hall predominated. Dance halls were huge, cavernous, barnlike, wooden buildings, with high roofs and big prop-up windows open to the evening breeze.

Round Top also had its own school, and Huebner passed the deserted campus on his way through town. Like the rest of rural society, country schools regulated themselves in terms of the cotton cycle, usually letting out early in time for the chopping season and starting up as late as possible in the fall to allow time for the harvest. At chopping time and picking time, cotton needed human attention the most, and servicing the great staple crop took precedence over education.

Children normally walked or rode horseback to these one-, two-, or three-room country schools established by the "common school districts" of the county school system. Networks of foot trails radiated out into the countryside in every direction from the schools, "beeline" trails that followed the routes of shortest distance from every corner of the rural school districts. A few lucky children might live just down the road from the school, but for most a cross-country route proved shortest. No one minded the scholarly trespassers across their farms, and some even built stiles over fences and foot logs across creeks to help them out. Adults also used these "near cuts" across the landscape and thought nothing about walking several miles from place to place. Farmers walked many miles every day they plowed the field and were well adapted to cross-country hikes.

Beyond each crossroads community and its hinterland and the hinterland of the next community lay the deep countryside, the realm of "settlements"—informal groupings of people united partially by scattered institutions of gins and stores, but chiefly by their belief that they belonged together. Biegel's Settlement, which Huebner knew well and after a time passed into, was one such. Biegel's Settlement had gin, store, dance hall, and school in widely separated locations, but the traveler might cross the area and not even notice that a community was there. However, as Huebner understood, a farm family in even the most remote farmstead always thought that it lived somewhere—that it was part of some community or settlement, no matter how faint or far away. Otto Huebner knew this, and he knew also that these dispersed settlements often harbored very different traditions regarding strangers (and peddlers) passing through. Biegel's Settlement was on his regular route, and he comfortably shifted from good English to fluent German to halting Czech as he called at farm after farm across the countryside. There were other, less friendly settlements, however, places where Huebner chose not to sharpen any scissors; in fact, he gave them a wide berth.

In truth, around 1920, the deep countryside in this farming landscape of blackland prairies, sandy-soiled post-oak hills, and wooded bottoms was a very complicated place; a person needed to know his way around, and in more ways than one. As farmer Eddie Wegner explained, "When it was horses and buggies, community life was very concentrated. Like the next town—ten, twelve, fifteen miles down the road, or whatever—it was kind of like another land."[6]

For decades before and after Otto Huebner passed through in 1920, each remote farm family in Washington and Fayette counties rose by lamplight each morning and went about their chores on the dark farmstead in the middle of a well-known landscape. Children milking cows readily identified neighboring farms by the sounds and directions of their crowing roosters and later by the smoke from their breakfast fires. If it was fall, the nearest communities also soon announced themselves with blasts from the whistles of their steam gins—some faint and distant, others close and clear—as the gins proclaimed to listeners for miles around that they were "hot" and open for business.

Some of these gins sounded from places the farmer's children had never seen. The farm family's world was circumscribed, the horizon line of its known universe did not reach out very far, but what the family knew it knew intimately, in depth and in detail. Family members knew the faint trails that radiated out from their farmhouse to the farmhouses of the nearest neighbors. They knew the drainage of water across their land, and most could call its flow downhill from small nameless branches to named creeks to larger creeks to yet larger creeks. And they knew their soil: the sandy spot at the back of the place that was good for watermelons or sweet potatoes and the sticky blackland areas in the cotton and cornfields that dried most slowly after rain. The family knew the wild verges of its farm, also: the bottom where red haws, mustang grapes, and dewberries might be had in their respective seasons; the deep creek holes that harbored perch and bullhead catfish; the pile of decaying tree trunks in the "new ground" where the "poke salad" grew; and the places in the woodlot and along the fence rows where the turkeys and guineas liked to hide their nests.

During the 1920s, thousands of farms, large and small, were scattered across the landscape of Fayette, Washington, Austin, and the other counties that had been part of Austin's Colony, as the Texas cotton-farming world reached its greatest extent and complexity.[7] Frontier lifestyles of free-range herding and mixed subsistence and cotton farming persisted in the sandy-land post-oak belts, where land was cheap and settlers still were moving in to clear new ground from the virgin woods.

Born in 1900, Lydia Domasch of the Warda community in Fayette County grew up on such a farm and recalled a lifestyle that might have come from a century before. Her family lived in a two-pen log house, walked everywhere they went barefooted or wearing homemade wooden shoes, tried to produce everything they needed to eat on the farm, and even made their own furniture, "shuck mattresses," and wooden plates and spoons.[8]

Families such as Lydia Domasch's often took advantage of their locations in the post oaks to fatten hogs and turkeys on the fall acorn mast, watching the progress of acorn development beforehand as anxiously as farmers on the blackland prairies a few miles away watched the progress of their corn. The stock law arrived piecemeal in these counties, and as late as the 1920s areas in the post-oak precincts still were free range. Herman Schoenemann of Sand Town in Washington County lived in another of the post-oak, free-range areas. He raised so many semiferal turkeys in the woods around his cotton farm one year that he cleared $1,800 from their sale just before Thanksgiving—several times what he received for that year's cotton crop.[9]

Grover Williams's grandfather at the African-American Flat Prairie community in the Yegua Creek bottoms also practiced a mixed farming and herding lifestyle that took advantage of the nearby bottomlands. Flat Prairie farmers also raised turkeys as a money crop, and they followed a local practice of penning hogs and cattle during the year, then opening the gates after harvest to let them roam far and wide to fatten on crop stubble, switch cane, and wild acorns and pecans. Sandy Yegua bottom soils also were good cotton land—if the floods did not get the crop; Williams's grandfather made twenty-three bales in his best year.[10] Ed Lathan grew up in a similar black community in northeastern Washington County, where local farmers did all these things and made whisky besides, specializing in old-fashioned, high-quality "double-run" moonshine to be sold in Brenham, Navasota, and the nearby Brazos bottoms.[11]

Free-range stockraising was not just a practice of black or German farmers. North of Yegua Creek in the Snook community, Robert Skrabanek's Czech family rented, then owned, a fifty-acre farm on the dense blacklands. A zealous row-crop farmer who could not abide a weed in his fields, Skrabanek strove for blackland landownership through cotton profits. However, a few miles away the family had another very different piece of ground also important for the house-hold economy. This was their fifty-acre, sandy-land, post-oak "pasture," which served as the home base for important hog- and turkey-ranging operations. Taken to the pasture in the fall, hogs and turkeys roamed about over an area of several square miles, passing in and out of fences and fattening themselves on the mast. Like East Texas free-range stock-men, the Skrabaneks and their neighbors earmarked their hogs and toe-marked their turkeys, calling the animals up from time to time to check on them and dole out small amounts of corn to keep them partly tame. Since free-range livestock wandered about, mixing and merging, on anyone's land, each family normally cooperated in keeping other families apprised of their animals' whereabouts.[12]

Far from post oaks and bottomlands, farmers on La Bahia Prairie and other blackland areas placed greater emphasis on the row crops of cotton and corn, though they strongly maintained the subsistence sides of their farms, as well. Both Germans and Czechs preferred the black-lands, and by 1920 most ran their blackland cotton-subsistence farms in much the same way. Most farms averaged around a hundred acres in size, of which perhaps twenty-five would be in cotton, twenty-five in corn. Farmers fertilized their fields with barnyard manure and rotated cotton and corn every year. Cotton and corn acreages varied partly with the size of the farm, partly with the size of the farmer's family, and partly with the individual farmer's willingness to get out on the precar-ious limb of cash-crop cotton agriculture. The larger the family, the more mouths there were to feed (and shoes and overalls to buy with hard cash), but also the more "hands" there were to help in the cotton field. Most blackland farmers and their wives opted for large families.

Robert Dement's home farm out from Burton was typical in its mix of cotton and subsistence farming and its emphasis on self-reliance, recycling, and frugality. Robert's father, Bat Dement, usually raised about twenty-five acres of cotton and thirty-five acres of corn on this hundred-acre farm, and steadfastly maintained around forty acres in pasture, vegetable garden, and large potato patch. Robert Dement noted: "Half of that field is going to be for feed; that's corn, because that's the kind of feed we raised. The other half was cotton; that's your money. That's the way everybody else did." The Dement family's cotton land raised about half a bale to the acre, year in and year out, so:

> Even if the price was twenty cents a pound, that was a hundred dollars a bale—five hundred dollars. That was his cash money. He could pay his taxes and buy his clothes. That five hundred dollars was his cash money because he was living at home. He wasn't spending much in groceries. Mama made all our clothes. I told somebody not long ago, "I was grown before I had any underwear that was bought at the store."[13]

Dement kept his food purchases to a bare minimum of flour, salt, sugar, and coffee, and his clothes purchases to overalls, hats, coats, and shoes. And when anything on his farm "wore out," it had attained a true state of rags and tatters. Otherwise, it was fixed or recycled as something else. Bat Dement even owned a last and knew how to put half soles on worn-out shoes. Older children "handed down" clothing to younger ones, and Mrs. Dement made girls' dresses and boys' shirts (and underwear) from feed sacks and practiced many other household economies.

The cotton crop brought in the money, but the half-acre garden, large potato patch, several milk cows, and varied flocks of domestic fowl drew almost equal attention from the Dement family. Robert Dement explained, "Papa fed all his corn up. He had a pen out there with five or six hogs in it. We started feeding those hogs, and as soon as fall of the year come—say, November first norther come—he'd kill one." Soon, the main hog-killing time arrived, and the Dements' smokehouse filled with hams, bacon, and sausages, which were consumed through the next summer until the pork got wormy and mouldy and Robert's mother would "go out there and get that ham and slice that off and throw that away—it had good lean meat in the middle, you know." The family's next most important corn-fed domestic animals were their many chickens, whose eggs provided enough "egg money" during the course of the year to pay most grocery bills. As the year wore on and the smokehouse pork diminished, chickens came to the fore as a meat source. Mrs. Dement often prepared fried chicken for breakfast and commonly caught, killed, plucked, cleaned, and fried a breakfast chicken in the short time it took Mr. Dement to milk the cows.[14]

Some miles away to the east, but likewise on the blacklands, Herbert Wegner's family farm also grew cotton but practiced even greater subsistence frugalities. The 101-acre Wegner farm had 15 acres in cotton, 15 in corn, several acres in old-style "red top cane" (grown as a feed crop), a full-acre garden, a half-acre potato patch, a woodlot, several rows of molasses cane, a "cow pasture" and a "calf pasture," eight milk cows, and many chickens, turkeys, geese, and guineas. Like Bat Dement, Mr. Wegner sent most of his children to college on the scant cash income from his usual eight to ten bales of cotton supplemented by money from cream and eggs sold in nearby Brenham, but to accomplish this Wegner ran a tight ship. Breakfast for the Wegners was composed of corncake and molasses, only, with each family member getting but one wedge of the cornbread "wheel." And since every possible egg needed to be sold, each morning corncake had but one egg in it.[15]

On poorer soils and more hilly lands miles to the northeast, black farmers in the Mount Falls Settlement on the Washington County Bluffs nevertheless lived similar lives to the Wegners. However, every morning well before daylight they heard the wake-up bells ringing at Allenfarm and other big plantation farms on the Grimes County side of the Brazos bottom, where a very different sort of cotton farming life held sway.

The rich, red, alluviums of the Brazos valley produced cotton at the rate of a bale an acre, or better. Brazos valley cotton plants grew so tall that small children could climb up in them, and so big around at the bottom that farmers often had to use special steel-tipped sleds to cut the stalks, some of which were three inches in diameter. Brazos valley cotton farms varied in size, but most of them were large and owned by absentee owners, people who lived in nearby Navasota, Brenham, or other towns, and they were worked by sharecroppers under close direction of white supervisors variously referred to as "overseers," "foremen," or "pushers."

As this revival of the old nomenclature suggests, what historian Pete Daniel termed the "shadow of slavery" lay heavily upon the Brazos Bottoms.[16] Sandy-land farmer Herman Schoenemann, before he bought land in the post oaks, had grown up on a rent farm around Gay Hill, and he knew what life was like on the big bottomland plantation farms. Asked about how they operated, he pursed his lips in distaste and said little, only repeating the harsh Southern motto of the decades after the end of slavery, "Kill a mule, buy another'n; kill a nigger, hire another'n."[17]

Although obscured by the U.S. Census takers' unrealistic insistence on counting every twenty-five-acre cropper plot as an independent farm, big agribusiness plantations had been reforming in the last decades of the nineteenth century and the first decades of the twentieth, in Texas as elsewhere in the South. North of Corpus Christi, for example, rangeland had been converted to cropland by the thousands of acres on the huge Taft Ranch cotton farm, which included three company towns, several gins, and hundreds of sharecroppers and wage hands.[18] The Brazos valley had its own agribusiness giants, however; one of the bells ringing across the river from the Bluffs was at the Allenfarm community owned by the Terrell family.

At Allenfarm, some sixty to seventy African-American sharecropper families lived in two-room or four-room cropper shacks scattered across thousands of acres of bottomland. At the farm's center was all the infrastructure of a small company mill or mining town of 1920, including a company office, two commissaries, a gristmill, three gins, two blacksmith shops, a barbershop, a two-story cattle loading facility on the railroad, three saloons (before Prohibition), a school, two churches, and the farm's own spur line and railroad depot.[19]

A huge bell located near farm headquarters drove the daily schedule at Allenfarm, as had similar bells on slave plantations before 1865. The first bell meant "wake up," the second meant "eat your breakfast," and the third meant "be at the central mule lot to draw your work stock for the day." Hands did this by lamplight, since they were expected to be at their work sites—sometimes miles distant—ready to start plowing when it got light enough to see.[20] Sharecroppers' individual family plots on some of the big Brazos valley farms were virtually fictional, since most plowing, chopping, and other agricultural labor was done by gangs of laborers, who moved together from one field to another and worked all fields the same—the so-called through-and-through system. As was the case for the German family farms on the uplands to the west, Allenfarm and other Brazos valley plantations had no bell for quitting time, since it was not needed; quitting time came when it got too dark to see.[21]

Besides the re-establishment of agribusiness plantations, other changes were afoot in the rural world of 1920—not just in the counties formed from Austin's Colony, but all across the South. From 1900 to 1920, more and more land was put into cotton, rural population grew, land values (and taxes) increased, and so did the frequency of rent farming. Landownership remained the goal of every young farm family just starting out, but the so-called agricultural ladder—the climb from half tenant, to thirds-and-fourths tenant, to cash renter, to landowner—was not working well anymore; a lot of farmers now stalled out in the rental life. To climb the ladder you had to accumulate wealth to purchase work stock, farming equipment, and land that grew more costly all the time. Meanwhile, the price of cotton showed no such steady increase—far from it, in fact; from 1914 to 1926 it fluctuated wildly between 5 to 45 cents a pound.[22]

Large families served the economic interest of the individual farm couple, since the more hands in the field, the more cotton at the gin, and the more money in the bank. By 1920, however, Southern farms had been divided and redivided until they often were marginal in size to support a family. Invariably, most of a farm couple's children had to leave to find their own farms, usually by renting from someone else. Some farmers fell into hard times, lost their farms, and sank into rentership, but far more commonly it was their sons and daughters who became the new renters. Although farm ownership remained the ideal, by around 1920 the new standard of minimal respectability had come to be renting on thirds and fourths—share tenancy—where the farmer brought work stock and farming implements to the deal with the landowner and paid him for use of his house and farm with one-third of the corn and one-fourth of the cotton produced.[23]

Fayette and Washington counties shared in the general trend. Between 1880 and 1920, the percentage of Texas farms that were rent farms rose from 38 percent to 51 percent. In the latter year, 49 percent of Fayette farms and 57 percent of Washington farms were occupied by renters.[24] As elsewhere, thirds-and-fourths renters farmed most of the rental acreage. In 1925, Fayette County landowners farmed 100,725 acres, thirds-and-fourths renters 72,616 acres, sharecroppers 10,065 acres, and cash tenants 4,203 acres. In Washington County, landowners farmed 62,335 acres, thirds-and-fourths renters 51,172 acres, sharecroppers 14,207 acres, and cash tenants 3,930 acres.[25] The census categories concealed enormous differences in renter status and lifestyle in the countryside and on the farm.

Cash tenants, a relatively small group, paid flat rents per acre for the corn and cotton land they farmed. Thirds-and-fourths renters supplied stock and equipment and paid the landowner one-third of the corn and one-fourth of the cotton—often just putting every third wagon of corn in the landowner's corncrib and giving him every fourth bale of cotton. The half-tenant status concealed two types of relationship to crop and landowner, though in each case the rent farmer paid the landlord half his cotton and half his corn for the use of land, house, work stock, and farming equipment. "Half tenants," usually "whites," were in a higher status; like thirds-and-fourths renters, they were share tenants in the crop, and they normally sold their own cotton. "Sharecroppers" ("halver-hands"), usually blacks or Mexicans, were classed as wage hands being paid with a portion of the crop and normally had their cotton sold for them by the landowner.[26]

From 1910 to 1914, worried by rising land taxes, some landowners on the major blacklands to the west and north of Washington and Fayette counties had tried to increase their incomes by charging "bonuses" for use of their lands beyond the usual thirds and fourths, or by downgrading their renters' statuses from thirds-and-fourths renters to half renters, or from half renters to true sharecroppers, and at the same time replacing troublesome Anglo-Americans with more tractable (and politically powerless) Mexicans and blacks. Much hard feeling resulted from this. Rent farmers tried to organize, landowners in Travis County received envelopes in the mail filled with matches and Johnson grass seeds (suggesting what might happen to their barns and fields), some Anglo-American rent farmers attacked black rent farmers in an indirect assault on the big landowners who employed them, and in the midst of the troubles the federal government came down to investigate landowner-renter relationships and the abuses of the farm credit system.[27] In the end, nothing much had changed, and everyone soon became happier after cotton prices shot up following the war-crisis year of 1914. During this time of troubles, most renters and landowners in the older cotton counties along the Brazos and Colorado chose not to become involved.

In Fayette and Washington counties, as elsewhere, the complicated landowner-renter relationships depended on many things, including who rented from whom. Howard Matthies's father owned a fifty-eight-acre blackland farm in Washington County, but—since he stubbornly maintained part of it in pasture land for his milk cows—he did not have enough cropland to support his growing family (or to keep them hard at work). Consequently, he rented several more acres from a neighbor as a cash renter and another several-acre plot on thirds and fourths, and in this way produced enough corn, cotton, and cash income to meet his needs. Thus, Matthies was landowner, cash renter, and thirds-and-fourths renter, all at the same time.[28]

At the Salem community, a few miles away from the Matthies family farm, Robert Wilhelmsen's father rented on thirds and fourths from *his* father, and relationships were amicable between father and son. The Wilhelmsens divided cotton money as each bale sold, while every third corn row harvested became the landlord's and was carried by wagon to his corncrib by his son and grandson.[29]

Like many farmers on the blacklands around La Bahia Prairie, farmers with more cropland than they needed (and enough pasture) often rented part of their farms to thirds-and-fourths renters, who were sometimes relatives, sometimes fellow Germans, and sometimes local blacks. Eddie Wegner's father rented at various times to Germans and to African-Americans, and on more or less the same terms.[30] Ora Nell Jacobs Fuchs's family owned a 151-acre farm, farmed 40 acres of it, and rented 30 acres to a succession of tenants, one of them her father's cousin. The Jacobs family regarded this latter arrangement as both "trying to help family out" and getting a renter they could depend on.[31] Henry Fuchs's family owned a larger-than-average 300-acre farm a few miles away from the Jacobs, farmed about 50 acres, and rented out about 100 acres on the thirds and fourths to a family with two big sons, good work stock, two riding cultivators, and other up-to-date equipment. This family farmed more cotton and made more money than their landlord, paying him a fourth of their cotton income and a flat rent of $5 an acre on their land in corn.[32]

Some thirds-and-fourths renters were even better off. In the "Mud City" (Dunlap) community along the Colorado, Howard Davis's father had six strong sons, a wife that worked in the field like a man, eight big 1,000-pound "cotton mules," several walking cultivators, and 180 acres of prime bottomland to farm. His landlord "furnished" him at the Mud City store the landlord owned—provided him with a line of credit to draw monthly groceries. Before all his sons got old enough to work, Davis had sub-rented part his of rented land to "halver-hands"—sharecroppers—two black brothers in one season, two Mexican brothers and their families in another. The croppers brought nothing to the deals but their labor and that of their families, received half of the cotton on their 15 or 20 acres, helped Davis on his land when he needed help, and "ate out of the Mud City store" using part of Davis's furnish allotment from his landowner-storeowner.[33]

Near Snook, in 1924, just north of the Washington County line, John and Frances Skrabanek still rented a blackland farm from fellow Czechs on the thirds and fourths. The Skrabaneks had begun married life with nothing but a wood stove. Neighbors contributed the rest of their furniture, and their first landlord had let them farm his land rent-free the first year "in exchange for breaking a pasture and making it into land for crops." This deal to pay no rent but to clear and cultivate so many acres of "new ground" was not uncommon. The family lived on three different farms as half renters before accumulating enough money to buy their own work stock and farming equipment to rent their blackland farm on thirds and fourths. By this time, the Skrabanek's also owned fifty acres of sandy post-oak land a few miles away from the Snook community, but to blackland "dirt farmer" John Skrabanek, this sandy-land acreage did not even count. (In 1924, the family's first blackland landownership still remained four years away.)[34]

In the Colorado bottoms, the landlord of Howard Davis's father preferred to rent his several-hundred-acre bottomland place to several Anglo thirds-and-fourths farmers such as Davis, but other big farms in the area hired only black or Mexican sharecroppers, issuing each family twenty-five acres, two mules, and a "cropper cabin" in the field with cotton growing right up to its walls.[35] On a 630-acre farm in Fayette County near Warrenton, sharecropper Johnnie Loud had a better deal. The owner was an unmarried German lady, a Miss Miners, who lived on the property with her croppers. Miners treated her halver-hands as independent farmers who knew what they were about. She let them run their own farms and sell their own cotton; then she took her rightful half. When a policy decision about farm operations needed to be made (for example, whether to purchase riding cultivators to replace walking ones), owner and black renters held a conference about it. Miners allowed her renter families to have two cows, as big a garden as they wanted, a watermelon patch in the field, and "hogs—that was your business."[36]

Cropper-landowner relations varied also in the Brazos bottoms, but Mance Lipscomb's family never struck a deal as liberal as this. After Mance's father, Charlie Lipscomb, "took off," his mother ran the family and soon promoted Mance, age eleven, to head plowboy. Every cropper family had to have a male plowman, even ones headed by so formidable a field hand as Mrs. Lipscomb, who could out-chop and out-pick most men. So, at this early age, Mance dropped out of school and began to plow, even though he had to reach up higher than his head to grab the handles. Black sharecroppers in the Brazos bottom did not sell their own cotton—ever, under any circumstances—nor did they dare to dispute the owner's or overseer's word at fall "settlement time."[37] One year the Lipscombs made thirty-one bales of cotton and were told by the landowner that they had exactly broken even.[38] Black people could not even be seen on the streets of Navasota with a cotton sample in their hands, as Bubba Bowser recounted:

> Uh uh! You could work like the devil and raise it, but now you come to town toting a cotton sample? Uh, uh, Lord! They'd kick him. Let the white man tote that sample and sell the cotton and give you what he want out of it. And sometime nothing. We made 120 and 130 bales of cotton, and the white man get ready to sell it, say, "Hey, Joe, you like to come out, you liking a hundred and something of coming out." That was working his land. See, he kept books, and he'd feed us and claim we took up all that stuff, you owed it to him. And when he'd sell it, he'd say, "You get $20, Joe."

Well, you had to take his word for it. You didn't know what
he got for the cotton or what he got for nothing. All you
got to do is take his word.[39]

Willie Davis affirmed, "All up and down the bottoms, you couldn't sell
no cotton. But out on the hills with the Germans and all like of that,
some of 'em would let you sell the cotton, if it your cotton."[40]

Whether from "down in the bottoms" or "out on the hills," the social
landscape looked different to African-Americans in 1920. In a white-
dominated society, "slings and snares" abounded for black people, and
not just at settlement time. For two decades after 1900, the La Grange
weekly newspaper always carried at least one account of a lynching or
burning of a black man. The editor, who clearly regarded these
accounts as helpful warnings to local African-Americans, got his stories
from Texas if at all possible, but he went as far afield as needed across
the South to include the weekly lynching. For example, on March 11,
1909, the La Grange *Journal* noted that Andrew Ellis, a black man living near Rockwall, Texas, had been identified by his rape victim, tied to
an iron stake, and burned alive. A mob had "overpowered" the jailer,
taken his keys, and secured Ellis. "He was tied to a large iron stake driven in the ground. Cordwood saturated with kerosene was piled all
around him. In the presence of Mrs. McKinney, who fully identified
him as her assailant, the torch was applied and in nine minutes life was
extinct. Over 150 people witnessed the burning."

Black men such as Mance Lipscomb in the bottoms and Bubba
Bowser, Davis Washington, and Ed Lathan on the nearby Bluffs looked
out on a different world than did Germans, Czechs, or Anglo-
Americans. In the countryside, there were communities black people
could freely visit, others they passed through quickly, and still others
they avoided at all cost. There were whites known to treat black people
fairly in economic dealings, and others known as social predators,
cheating blacks at every opportunity and taking full advantage of their
inability to dispute a white man's word.[41]

Courthouse towns also developed very different reputations
among African-Americans, and Navasota in Grimes County had a
bad one. Not only could blacks not be seen there with cotton samples,
but they needed to show up dressed as honest field hands or face the

consequences. Wearing upscale clothing in the streets of Navasota invited public attack. Willie Lipscomb recalled: "You go there with a silk shirt on, they'd tear it off and spit on it—tear that shirt off you! You couldn't wear a silk shirt to Navasota, and you couldn't wear nothing during the week but blue duckings or khakis and a straw hat. You get out with a white Stetson on and you'd come back with it all flopped down round your head."[42]

Mance Lipscomb, Willie's older brother, concurred in his opinions about Navasota. Mance did not like Hempstead, the seat of Waller County, which many blacks called "Six Shooter Junction" because of its tradition of violence, but Navasota had an even worse reputation, and Mance knew it well: "Navasota—a dog call that a dirty hole—that's what I call it. That's the dirtiest place there in the world, Navasota. More niggers killed there'n any place in the world, specially if a man try to stick up for his rights."[43]

For black people in 1920, life in the bottoms on the big plantation farms and life in the hills as a small landowner or thirds-and-fourths renter for Germans could be very different. One strategy was to farm your own soil—poor though it might be—to produce everything you needed on the place, to keep economic dealings with whites to the minimum, and to try to stay out of debt to them. Ed Lathan of Mount Fall did this all his life, noting that: "I never got that big, and I always spent wise, renting the other fellow's land. I's born a free man, you understand what I mean? I ain't never been under slavery, no white man riding up and down the middle behind me telling me what to do in my crop, like a lot of them people. That's what I mean, free."[44]

Economic transactions with whites could not altogether be avoided, and when they occurred even independent black hill farmers dealing with Germans and Czechs paid a certain price. When Grover Williams's grandfather sold virgin cedar off his place to a nearby "peckerwood" sawmill for a portion of the sawtimber, the boards he got back included but little of the best quality "heart" wood, and he felt he could say nothing about the matter. On another occasion, when he sold an agreed-upon number of cedar posts from his farm to a local German, the man cut more posts than he was supposed to and again Williams's grandfather could say nothing.[45] Nor did black people's cotton always bring quite as high a price in nearby Burton as "white man's cotton."

For black sharecroppers in the bottoms, however, things could get a lot worse, but it all depended on the white landowner and what he or she required. Jeff Lott's big farm in the Brazos bottom hired only black thirds-and-fourths renters and treated them well. Lott came up from Navasota every two weeks to check on them but otherwise let them run their own farms.[46] For most, however, life as bottomland renters included cropper-shack housing, gang labor, close supervision by overseers, no gardens, a poor diet drawn from the commissary store and comprising mostly the "three M's" (meat, meal, and molasses), no control over one's cotton sales or the "settling up," and the threat of violence. Bubba Bowser of Washington County described the Moore family of Navasota, all large landowners:

> They was just rich white folks, they was the law. An American white man, he is the law. A American white man is Uncle Sam. I say something about the law to Mr. Tom [Moore], he say, "Hell, Bubba, we the law, me and the white people is the law. We Uncle Sam, we make the laws and break em, we the government." This here's American-white-man country, and he rules it, just what he say go. Mr. Tom used to tell them old niggers, "Now, you can go out and raise all the hell you want, kill who you want, just so you don't get killed. All you got to do is make it back here, back to my place."[47]

For a few years during and after World War I, the "American white man" troubled local German and Czech cotton farmers, as well. As Bowser observed, "I seen the time the Germans, they would be scared to meet a white man. They'd get out [of the way], just like you would." During the war, some area Texans of German descent considered to be opposed to the war effort suffered tar and featherings by mob action. One such mob sought out a German farmer picking cotton in the field but retreated when they found he had thoughtfully included a shotgun in his pick sack.[48] Most people simply became uncomfortable about speaking German in public where Anglo-Americans might hear them. Howard Matthies's mother, who spoke little English, cut down on her visits to Burton stores. She frequented only certain establishments and preferred to wait to conduct her business until only the German store operators were present and "the air was clean."[49] A few miles away, another family stopped singing traditional German songs at night in fear that passers-by on the road might hear them.[50] Most families made sure they had their Liberty Bond posters prominently displayed in their front windows to show patriotic fervor. Country schools ceased teaching in German during the war, and at the school Leola Tiedt attended, the patriotic teacher directed her students to pick peach pits from hog droppings at the farm across the road. No one was quite sure what the peach pits were to be used for in the war effort; at the time Leola thought they were for "poisonous gas."[51]

The war had been an uncomfortable time for German farm families in Fayette and Washington counties, and when word came over the telephone on November 11, 1918, that the war was over, many communities erupted in impromptu celebrations. As Kermit Fox recalled, "Most of the family immediately stopped work in the field. With our touring Buick loaded we all headed for Round Top and there participated in an impromptu victory parade and celebration. I recall undue noise and jubilation. Where I got it I don't know, but I was using a heavy wooden whistle with which I was trying to do my part."[52]

The celebrations began a little too soon, however; the wave of nativism and antiforeign sentiment stimulated by the war effort took a few years to ebb away. On May 21, 1921, some four hundred members of the Houston Ku Klux Klan rode into Brenham on the train and paraded the streets (gaily decorated for the German Mayfest) clad in white flowing robes, pointed caps, white face masks, and a red circle with a cross on their uniforms. The KKK men carried signs that read, "Our fathers were here in '61, and their boys are here in '21," and more to the point, "Speak English or quit speaking on the streets of Brenham." Local people soon had a mass meeting and resolved to use only English at soldiers' funerals, to discontinue teaching the German language in the schools, and to bring local Lutheran ministers into town for intensive instruction in spoken English.[53]

In Washington and Fayette counties in 1918, as elsewhere in Texas, the patriotic fight in the "War to End All Wars" got all tangled up in people's minds with getting in the bumper cotton crop of that year. Cotton picking became equated with patriotism, rural youths not in uniform flocked to the fields, and woe to those "town blacks" who failed to do their duty. In some places local lawmen arrested black men on the streets for vagrancy and forced them to pick cotton.[54]

Throughout the years between 1914 and 1925, the great gamblers' crop of cotton continued its wild fluctuations up and down. At odds about other things, the Anglos, Germans, Czechs, blacks, Mexicans, Poles, and Wends of the counties of Austin's Colony were of one mind about cotton. All, or nearly all, depended on cotton for their livelihoods; their fates were intertwined in the same dice roll of season, and landowners' daughters and sharecroppers' sons all hoed or picked down long cotton rows from "can see to can't." Cotton farming was a great equalizer. The farmer launched into each season with no way to predict the price he would receive at the end of the year for whatever cotton the fickle weather allowed him to produce. As a country editor noted, the cotton farmer was like Columbus, who did not know how to get where he was going and did not know where he was when he got there.[55] Cotton farming took a gambler's nerve—hedged as much as possible with gardens, hogs, and subsistence farming support on the side, just in case the dice turned up "snake eyes."

In many ways, farmers' risks went up during the first two decades of the twentieth century, as farms grew smaller, renting became more common, and landowners forced their renters to raise more cotton and less corn and subsistence crops. The renters' gardens, potato patches, milk cows, and hogs did their landowners no good at all; landowners, who had financial problems themselves and worried about losing their farms, wanted their rental land planted in cotton and only cotton, and since the renters badly needed cash money, few of them complained. If they complained too much, the owner simply put them off and got other tenants. One landowner bluntly explained, "I tell em to plant cotton, and they plant cotton."[56]

As historian Gilbert Fite has noted, many Southern farmers had become caught in a vicious cycle, a kind of "cotton trap." The smaller their farms, the farther down the ladder of rentership they sank, the greater their seasonal indebtedness to landowners, credit stores, or banks, the more desperate their circumstances, then the more they needed to plant cotton. Growing too much cotton had brought them to where they were, but no other Southern cash crop could save them.[57]

Agricultural experts, government officials, country editors, and the writers of *Progressive Farmer* and *Texas Farm and Ranch* preached endlessly to farmers to grow less cotton and more subsistence crops, to produce more food at home, to diversify to other cash crops, to mechanize their operations, and to practice "scientific farming," but these voices generally fell on deaf ears. The La Grange *Journal* editor, for example, was one such voice crying in the wilderness. He hated cotton, buried each year's "first bale" story in his back pages, and went on endlessly about the wonderful merits of blackeyed peas, peanuts, pecans, tomatoes, cucumbers, and every other crop but cotton, but to little avail.[58] A bit later, in 1925, then again in 1930, the editor would say (although discreetly), "I told you so!"

In the fall of 1924, area farmers could look back over the past decade for guidance about how much cotton to plant and not come to any clear conclusions. The year 1914 had presaged great things, and Southern farmers produced a huge crop of 16.1 million bales, but then came war in Europe, disruption of world cotton markets, and the fall of cotton to just over five cents a pound.[59] Made desperate by their debts and losses of the season, all across Texas cotton country owner-renter relationships turned ugly. One Brazos valley landowner recalled, "In the weeks following the beginning of the war, when cotton dropped so low and credit was being cut off right and left, a common saying among white and negro tenants in this neighborhood was: 'If my landlord won't feed me I'll take my gun and go after it—and I'll get it.' I personally know that this sentiment was general." [60]

Prices rose to normal and social relationships improved during 1915 and 1916, though boll weevil outbreaks hurt the crops, and in 1917 cotton jumped to 28 cents a pound. Farmers planted more cotton in 1918 and even more in 1919, when they were rewarded with 35 cents a pound and the South's first $2-billion-dollar cotton crop. Many farmers responded by buying their first Model T Fords in this "tall cotton" year and by otherwise living "high on the hog." Across the South, many a new farmhouse was begun with 1919 cotton money.

Many repented of last year's extravagances during the post-war depression year of 1920, when cotton plummeted to 13 cents a pound. In some places farmers tried to force others to join them in holding their cotton off the market until it climbed back to 35 cents, but most could not afford to do this. There was some violence, a few gins were burned, renter-landowner conflicts and black-white conflicts increased in frequency—the usual social phenomena following a bad cotton year. The number of lynchings also went up.

Many voices urged crop reduction in 1921, and farmers across the South did cut their acreage 5 million acres. This was, however, only about the average reduction after a bad cotton-price year. Farmers in these days paid little attention to the opinions of "book farmers" and editorial pundits. Cotton prices and acreages crept upward in 1922 and 1923, and in 1923 the 37.1-million-acre cotton crop, a new record, brought an average of 30 cents a pound.

Emboldened, in 1924 cotton farmers threw caution to the winds and planted a record 41.3 million acres in cotton from which they harvested 13.6 million bales, no less than 4,856,142 bales of which were Texas cotton. Increased production drove prices down, but cotton still brought an average of 23 cents a pound. Falling prices ignored, in 1925 farmers increased acreage by 5 million acres and harvested a huge crop of 16.1 million bales, equaling the previous record year of 1914.[61]

Not much of this 1925 cotton came from Washington, Fayette, or other counties of south-central Texas, however. There, farmers had broken ground for a record acreage of cotton like all the rest, but the worst had happened. In 1925 the dice roll of season brought disaster.

In the counties that had been part of Austin's original colony, the year began with an unusual rash of unexplained barn burnings that had some farmers shaking their heads.[62] The weather prophets who counted the number of stars inside the ring around the moon, or watched the behavior of cows in the field, or calculated the season's coming weather from close analysis of the first twelve days of the new year, had nothing very encouraging to report. On Sunday afternoon, February 26, 1925, dark rain clouds rolled in, but lightning and a few thunderclaps were all they produced. Thunder in February predicted a killing frost exactly sixty days later, some believed—April 22 to be exact. Later, others remembered this as the first of many occasions during 1925 that clouds strangely withheld their rain.

By May, correspondents to the La Grange *Journal* began to complain of drought, although they also complained of plagues of grasshoppers and mites. One correspondent noted of the hoppers, "It is just another detriment this section of the country has to contend with, the drought not being enough. The fields are alive with these pests."

By May 14, the Winchester-area correspondent reported that the time for planting corn had passed but that "very few people have a stand of it" because of the unusual lack of rain. Grasshoppers were on a tear around Winchester, and some farmers sat around complaining and beating their breasts in the usual way, while others took arm against the hoppers with bags of poison dust and gasoline torches. The grasshoppers roosted at night on the grass of the turnrows and sat mesmerized by the light until it was too late to escape. Farmers crisped them by the untold thousands using "pear-burner" torches.

Late in May and early in June a few passing thunderstorms went by but did little good, and for the first time a real note of desperation began to creep into the weekly writings of the correspondents. Dick of High Hill reported that young cotton that had managed to come up was dying in the ground, and he had other bad news: "Dick Schenck of near Schulenburg made the statement that he was tired of living and carried out his threat to end it all. He was found hanging to a rafter in the corncrib by his son as he entered to feed the stock." However, on June 25, a good local rain fell on poor High Hill, and Dick observed that "readers of the good old *Journal* may as well know that we were glad that the Good Lord has not deserted us altogether." But the rain that saved also was the rain that killed. Black farmer Eddie Smith died when struck by lightning while walking through his cotton field carrying an axe.

By mid-July, no significant rains had fallen in Fayette and Washington counties and the summer "dog days" lay heavily on the land, a time of weird events made worse by the drought. A "sandstorm" hit Winchester on July 9, and on that same day several of a local man's cattle, starved for feed, broke through a fence and gorged on a stand of Johnson grass, then died mysteriously. Had the drought somehow turned grass to poison, the correspondent wondered? On July 16, more strange events occurred. M. B. Harris, noted local greyhound breeder, while at a meet at Lexington, had three of his hounds develop hydrophobia during the fifth race. This led to a long cross-country chase after the afflicted animals (and greyhounds are hard to catch). Farmer Henry Krause also reported that sparrows just destroyed a half-acre patch of cane he had been saving as foodstuff. The sparrows stripped the cane of all seed, something never before seen. The correspondent noted that "even the birds of the air" seemed crazed by the heat and drought.

Their own corn dead in the ground, on July 23 local farmers read a news story predicting a national record crop for this year. Other notes would follow in August and September providing more details about the wonderful U.S. corn and cotton crops of 1925. What the farmers thought of these may only be imagined.

On July 30, Dick of High Hill surveyed the disaster: "Last week was a hot, dry, and a fair week, excellent weather to kill the grass and what remains of the crop. In some places the army worm has appeared and is ravaging the cotton. Dick took the time last Sunday to give the crops a fair lookover. The condition is one that we have never before seen in all our lives." Cotton plants were only about six inches high and were trying to put on bolls at that height. Cornfields, gardens, potato patches, and feed crops all were dead.

On August 6, a large ad from the International Press Club of San Antonio appeared in the La Grange paper, as in other regional papers. The drought was a blessing in disguise, it told, because "Boll weevils are catching hell! Billions are dead or dying!"

This terrible scourge of area cotton fields was being eradicated by the drought. This was the farmers' chance to get ahead for good. "Buy farms, houses. Stick! Our bankers and merchants are going to stay with the fellows who have sand in their craws. Stick! Tell the merchant you owe, 'I am going to stick to my former business. I am going to pay my debts.'"

The *Journal* printed this without comment, but rural correspondents in the same issue told of land so dry that farmers were carrying water to wet the ground before digging fence holes, and of other farmers near La Grange who were so desperate for cattle feed that they were cutting fences and letting their stock graze on the Southern Pacific right-of-way, taking their chances that trains would run them down.

September brought no rain and little cotton to be picked. Dick of High Hill told that "Hopes for rain have almost been abandoned." A few lightning storms passed by, with bolts that ignited several barns and farmhouses, but they dropped no rain. Farmers that had the money to do so joined together to order several railroad cars of hay, corn, oats, and sorghum to try to get their stock through the winter. After October 1, no further mention was made of crops and drought in any of the correspondents' columns, and for good reason: the game was lost, all of the corn, and most of the cotton crop, was dead. The "gin reporter" reported on September 17 that 2,590 bales had been ginned in Fayette County prior to September 1; last year by that date there had been 12,713 bales.

Across the drought-stricken area, farm families struggled to get by. Robert Skrabanek of Snook and his sister drove their cows several miles each day to water at the closest "spring creek." Fodder was so lacking that their cattle grew weak and sickly. Cows about to calve became unable to stand and were hauled to the barn on a sled to receive special care.[63] Robert began attending Merle School that fall, and school started three weeks earlier than usual, there being no cotton to pick. The school cistern was so low and stagnant that it got "wiggletails," and school trustees poured in kerosene to kill them. Students still had to drink the water, so for Robert Skrabanek the drought year of 1925 had the oily taste of kerosene.[64] Leola Tiedt left her renter family in Fayette County to pick cotton in one of the parts of Texas spared by the drought. Her family got so low on food that they lived for some time on a big bucket of cherry jelly, used to fill doughnuts, which had been contributed by an uncle who worked in a grocery store. When Leola got her first teaching job that fall, she bought two heifers and two pigs for the family with her first paycheck.[65] Henry C. Jaeger recalled that "It Ain't Gonna Rain No More, No More," a song popular in rain-plagued 1924, was no longer played in any of the German dance halls. Nobody dared: "They didn't want to hear it, cause they needed rain so bad. It made people mad to hear it."[66] All over the area gardens had failed, and in early fall the two Colored County Agents of Washington County traveled the countryside giving demonstrations teaching black families how to "can their beeves in order to have something to help tide their families through the winter." L. E. Lusk and John Lusk showed farmers how to process their "dried-up" milk cows and drought-sickly steers into Number 2 cans of stew, chili, and potted meat, as this terrible year wound toward an end.[67]

Only the Brenham semipro baseball team had succeeded in 1925. While the crops failed, the gardens dried up, and the wheels fell off the local cotton economy, the Brenham nine defeated team after team in the statewide semipro competition, finally beating China Grove for the state championship. Beginning with the entire back page of a four-page daily paper, baseball coverage expanded to engulf all of the *Banner-Press*. There was, after all, nothing good to print about the cotton.[68]

Then, on October 23, Dick of High Hill's prayers finally were answered, and the rains came—too late and too abundantly, however. Sixteen inches of rain fell, washing out roads, carrying away bridges, drowning cattle, eroding upland fields, destroying miles of fencing, and cutting the Southern Pacific tracks. On Herbert Wegner's farm east of Burton, gullies eroded the blackland fields to chalky subsoil down the lines of cracks formed by the summer drought.[69]

As fall turned into winter, farmers went about their yearly round, bedding up corn and cotton fields in preparation for the next crop year. Farmers were gamblers, and every new season was another game. Some despaired, but most were stoic, and some even viewed the events of 1925 with a kind of dark humor, noting that at least they were beginning 1926 after a good rain. By early in that year, a new record of 17.7 million acres of Texas farmland was in cotton, 40 percent of the total U.S. cotton acreage.[70] Robert Skrabanek's rural school let out a month early in 1926 for spring cotton chopping; this year's crop could not afford to fail.[71] At the Czech community of Hostyn in southern Fayette County, Catholic Czechs reacted to the drought of 1925 by building "Our Lady Shrine," a replica of the grotto at Lourdes, France, near their parish church, concluding: "We will make an offering to God thanking him for past blessings and asking that such a drought would never reoccur."[72]

CHAPTER 4

Midwinter

During the early winter of 1926, as in so many other years, farm families rose each morning in darkness and went about their chores by lamplight. Coal-oil lamps provided but feeble illumination, and overhead the constellations hung close, bright, and familiar. Farmers watched the sky both by day and night, and they well noted the shifting arrangements of the stars as the year turned toward cold and dark.

Young Robert Skrabanek normally awakened to the sound of his father, John Skrabanek, starting the wood stove in the next room. The elder Skrabanek scooped out the dead ashes, added newspaper and corncobs as tinder, put in the stove-wood, splashed on a little kerosene, and lit the fire to heat water for his whisky "toddy," ritual beginning of the day's round of chores and fieldwork from "can see to can't." Miles away across the dark countryside, Howard Matthies's German grandfather, Ed Lathan's African-American father, and many other men of John Skrabanek's generation rose from their beds and did the same. Whisky before breakfast was an old Southern tradition for adult males, as was cotton farming.

After his toddy, John Skrabanek came into the boys' room, lit the lamp, and told them to get up and do their chores so they could eat breakfast and be in the field before sunup. Knowing that "Papa meant business" and that a second wake-up call must be avoided, John, his brothers, and his sisters immediately rose, dressed, splashed cold water into their faces on the back porch, and hurried about the morning chores. Robert's mother cooked breakfast and made preparations for the noon and evening meals, his sisters made the beds and put the house in order, his father readied things for the day's work (checking harness, filling water jugs), and Robert and his brothers went out to milk the cows and feed the stock.[1]

Forty miles to the south, on La Bahia Prairie, the sons of diligent farmer Bat Dement did the same. Some farmers penned the cows and ranged the calves in the field at night; others did just the opposite. The first task of the Dement brothers was to find the calves in the dark pasture and bring them in to the cows. Unfortunately for the Dement boys, the pasture was large, the night dark, the lantern inadequate, and the calves illusive. Often, the cows began bawling and their calves came in to them before the Dements found the first calf. As J. M. Dement remembered: "Those old kerosene lanterns—well, about all you can do is keep from stepping on a prickly pear, or something. And walking around out in that old high grass, and dew all over it, and you get cold and wet. And after a while you hear the calves bawling at the house." The Dements sometimes argued with their father, suggesting that they wait for daylight and let nature take its course, only to be told that if they could not find the calves they should get an earlier start.[2]

Robert Skrabanek and his siblings rarely won arguments with their father, either, and morning chores were part of the iron law of the daily round, not matters to be questioned. While the girls put the house in order, the boys went forth to feed stock and milk cows. Unless there was a moon, all was still completely dark. Chickens were just fanning out in the yard from their house, and penned and hungry calves were straining to get to their mothers just in from the field. Robert and his brothers let the calves suckle briefly until the mother cows "let their milk down," then tied them up and began the morning's milking. Occasionally, they squirted milk at each other or at the faces of attendant cats. Robert liked this early morning darkness in the summer, but by November the air had become cold, and the lot lay six inches deep in blackland mud, cow manure, and cow urine. He waded this mess in rubber boots, but his main problem with milking was the risk of getting slapped in the face with the filthy, mucky cow's tail. In the dark, you could not always see it coming, and sometimes it got dung in the

milk bucket.[3] Some miles to the southwest, at the Flat Prairie community of Washington County, barefooted Grover Williams milked each
cow over the place where she had been lying down and warmed his feet
on the ground previously heated by her body.[4]

Morning chores done, the Skrabaneks, Dements, Matthieses,
Lathans, Williamses, and thousands of other families of the counties
along the Brazos and Colorado came inside to their lamplit kitchens
and sat down at their board tables for breakfast. Women ruled the
kitchens, places of light and heat and centers of farmstead life, but men
dominated the mealtime rituals. Three meals a day normally were
eaten here, two of them in the dark. Now fiercely radiating heat, the big
wood stove nearly filled one end of the room. Nearby were the kitchen
table, with chairs at the ends for the farmer and his wife, and benches
on each side for the children. Kitchen furniture was sparse, with a large
work area preserved for the chores of cooking, ironing, and food
preservation. Most kitchens also had a kitchen cabinet, a punched-tin
"safe," wall shelves for storage, and an evaporative "cooler," or perhaps an
ice box. At the Skrabanek farmstead, the family seated themselves at
their accustomed places after all had gathered and John Skrabanek sat
down. Mr. Skrabanek then served himself from each platter of fried
eggs, bacon, ham, and biscuits and passed it around the table. Children
ate what they put on their plates—all of it—and if they finished early
they sat there until John Skrabanek bade them leave, usually giving
work orders for the day before he did so.[5] In many families, and perhaps also the Skrabaneks, male heads signaled the end of mealtimes by
ritually crossing knives and forks on their empty plates.[6]

Not all breakfasts were as substantial as the Skrabaneks' and not all
kitchens and farmhouses so well equipped. Bubba Bowser's mother
still cooked "ash cake" and other things in their open fireplace in nineteenth-century fashion. The Bowsers "had a cross piece up on top of
the fireplace, had a chain over it with a hook. Mama put on a big pot of
peas or spareribs and things, she just hang it up over that fire until it
get mushy done."[7]

In the winter of 1926, Washington and Fayette County farmhouses
ranged from sharecropper shacks (where cooking sometimes still was
done in open fireplaces), to board-and-batten renter houses in various
stages of repair, to well-made, substantial farm homes like that owned
by the Otto Fuchs family near Carmine. The smaller of the cropper

shacks more resembled children's playhouses than structures intended for adult habitation. Long before 1920, the Allenfarm plantation had construction of its two-room and four-room cropper houses down to a pattern. The Terrells knew to the board foot how much lumber they needed to build one, and would drive east to the nearest sawmill to pick up necessary planking, then nail together the shack in a day or two.[8] The approximately fourteen-by-twenty-two-foot Allenfarm cabins often had no front windows, since their front doors took up too much room in the wall.

Cropper houses often had no porches, ceilings, sealed walls, screens, or glass windows, and after they got a little "run down" they developed cracks in the floors and walls that allowed the occupants to keep sky and earth under continuous observation. One Alabama man noted that his family had "laid in the bed and seen the stars through the cracks in the house. But it was a healthy place to live cause you got plenty of air, didn't never get too hot. It wasn't hardly possible chance of you catching a cold cause you didn't sweat in the house and go out and hit the air—you was already cold in the house."[9] Elnora Lipscomb tersely described similar housing along the Brazos in these few words (there not being much to talk about):

> Some had two rooms, some had three. And nothing but
> wooden windows, and they opened from the outside and
> shut from the outside. You have to pull em in and latch
> em with latches, didn't have no glass windows in those days,
> no porches, nothing. We set out in the yard, that was our
> porch. Sometimes you'd catch a few houses with trees in the
> yard, mighty seldom. And the walls, just one piece and
> some of em had cracks in em big enough to put your fingers
> through it. Just tape em with newspapers, help stop up
> the cracks.[10]

Landlords intended cropper shacks for the use of black or Mexican "halver-hands," and most would have felt uncomfortable putting "whites" in them. However, some "houses built for a rent house" used by thirds-and-fourths renters did not improve on these in anything but floor space. As landowner's son Eddie Wegner admitted, such places "were nothing extraordinary."[11] One blackland renter wrote to

FIGURE 3   A Waller County sharecropper home of the 1930s.
Such houses often were sited in or near the main fields, with little
or no room for yard or garden space. Images of such homes are
rare, since landowners generally preferred not to have them pho-
tographed. (Special Collections, Manuscripts and Archives, Sterling
C. Evans Library, Texas A&M University)

University of Texas researchers just before World War I to describe his current home in words that well depicted many such places up to World War II.

> I am going to give you a description of the house that I am in while I am writing this letter. It is a four-room shack, two big rooms 14 by 14; two little side rooms, 8 x 14, just boxed and stripped; no overhead ceiling; no shutters inside; no strips inside; three windows, 8 x 10 light; no porch and there is plenty of cracks in the outside walls that a half-grown rat can run through.[12]

As this renter noted, a common mark of a carelessly made rent house was the necessary repapering of inside walls with newspaper or Sears and Roebuck Catalogue pages by successions of rent families—this to cover the cracks large enough for the "half-grown rats" that also let in the north wind. Many families did this as a matter of course immediately after they moved into a new place.[13]

Landlords offered brisk rebuttals to any criticisms of their rent houses, however. Families often abused and neglected their properties, they claimed, and generally lived in them "like renters." Feckless and improvident renters kept their places in a constant state of disrepair, and under the circumstances they could not afford to erect better housing.

Very often, the better sort of rent house was a house built by a former landowner who had moved off the place or built something better.[14] Relegated to renters as they aged, and rundown though they might become, the marks of better days were on such places—peach trees in the yard, galleries across the front, breezy dog runs up the middle, inner ceilings and walls, and siding instead of board-and-batten construction. A renter's son recalled his parents' delight in coming on a farm where "the well curb, windlass, and shelter, were in good shape. So was the smokehouse and the garden fence. Furthermore, there were rose bushes and other flowers growing in the yard, and a dozen bearing apple trees, and several healthy peach trees." This simple list gives an idea of what most tenant farms lacked.[15]

Renters like this family took pride in the care they gave to the various places they rented and contradicted by example landowners' stereotypes of "careless croppers." They believed that a well-cared-for farm advertised for the farmer, and for the bad farmer "all his surroundings proclaim the verdict against him—his horses, cattle, wagons, plows, fences, fields—even his wife and children bear silent but unmistakable evidence against him."[16] Cotton renter's son Robert Skrabanek seconded this, believing that "a man's worth was judged by how well his farm was kept."[17]

Around 1900, an old Fayette County settler told historian F. Lotto that the farmhouses of his youth had been made of logs with their cracks covered with slabs, and that "they were generally on the edge of timber or in the timber and close to a creek." Some people still lived in some of these log-pen structures in the winter of 1926, but most had been covered with siding or relegated to a lesser use as barn or storage building. Lotto described the typical turn-of-the-century farmstead as a substantial, simple, one-story frame building with a gallery in front, facing southward to catch the cooling summer breeze. The most popular style of building has in the middle a large hall with two rooms on each side of it. One of these rooms with rocking chairs, carpet, pictures, a few tables with albums and bric-a-brac is the stateroom that is generally entered only on festive occasions. The other room and "upstairs" (usually the attic) are the dwelling and sleeping rooms of the family and contain simpler furniture—beds, a few tables, and wooden or raw-hide chairs. A kitchen and dining room are generally apart from the house, but connected to it by a gallery.[18]

Except for the separate kitchen-dining room, which had generally moved inside the house by 1926, Lotto's description still held true for most owner-operated farmsteads a quarter of a century later. His mention of an "upstairs" to a "one-story" house probably referred to the common practice of using attic space as a rustic sleeping area for family youths, especially the males. Bedroom space often was at a premium in large farm families—for example, that of Frank Janish, who had 14 brothers and sisters.

The first home of the Otto Fuchs family on La Bahia Prairie approximated Lotto's general description, but by winter of 1926 the family lived in a large, white, two-story farmhouse perched near the crest of a long ridge that sloped for many miles west and north to Carmine. The Fuchs family took justifiable pride in their big farmhouse, built in 1913, with its five bedrooms and four wrap-around "galleries" that allowed porch-dwellers to adjust their positions to wind direction and angle of

FIGURE 4   The Squire Reeves family poses for a formal portrait
outside their Fayette County farmstead, ca. 1900. (Percy Faison
album, Fayette Heritage Museum and Archives, La Grange)

the sun. Visible from miles around, the Fuchs farmhouse made a statement. The house was crowned with an array of tall, glass-ball-topped
lightning rods linked by twisted copper cables to ground stakes that
the family swiftly watered at the approach of summer thunderstorms.
(This to increase conductivity, should lightning strike.) Though still a
far cry from Antebellum plantations such as Thomas Affleck's
Glenblythe, grand farmhouses like that of the Fuchs showed how far
cotton, hard work, and frugality had brought some area families in the
half century since the Civil War.[19]

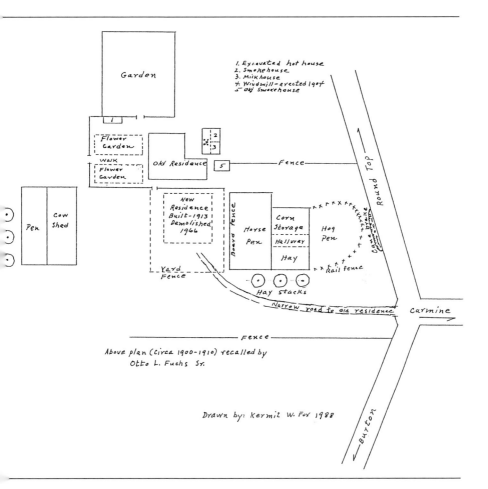

FIGURE 5   Site map of the Lorenz and Otto F. Fuchs homestead
east of Carmine, Texas, ca. 1910. (Drawn by Kermit W. Fox, M.D.,
with assistance from Otto L. Fuchs, Sr., 1988)

During this early winter of 1926, poor black sharecropper families
along the Brazos bottoms and well-off German farm families on La
Bahia Prairie had important things in common, since certain hardships
of the rural world affected everyone alike. Problems of heat, cold,
insects, lighting, mud, and water access plagued everybody, at least to
some degree, on farmsteads of the 1920s.

The relentless heat of Texas summers affected everyone, rich or
poor, just the same, and farmhouses were so desperately adjusted to the
heat they froze their inhabitants in the winter. Breezy galleries facing
the prevalent southeast wind, "sleeping porches" built into the house,

dog runs up the middle, high ceilings (and heat-buffering second floors), and even the loose, board-and-batten construction of rent houses attempted to counter the heat of summer. The Fuchs home in particular was known as a "cool house," but in winter this meant it was a cold one. Only the kitchen remained comfortably warm in the early winter of 1926, and when the Fuchs children filed upstairs to bed in the unheated second floor they carried foot warmers in the forms of well-wrapped stove lids or sad irons, then covered themselves with feather comforters, gritted their teeth, and waited for the beds to warm up. Kermit Fox (originally Fuchs) recalled, "The accepted technique of approaching such a cold bed was to dress in a flannel gown and socks, and then curl up into the smallest cocoon possible, until you dared slowly to unwind into that frigid fringe all around you."[20] But at least the Fuchs family had a second floor to sleep in; many a farm child in lesser dwellings awoke one morning in frigid attic spaces under quilts dusted with dry snow that had sifted through the board roof.

Kerosene lamps illuminated the Fuchs's home, the Lipscomb family's cropper shack, and all the rest. Normally, one or two lamps burned all the time after dark, in situ, while family members carried others around as needed. On trips outside, they were the best lighting available—and none too good, either, as many pre-dawn calf hunters and nighttime travelers testified. Howard Matthies recalled, "Used to, when the neighbors would visit each other at night, Papa would lead the parade with the lantern, and we'd follow like geese."[21] Even moving around the house with a kerosene lamp took a certain care. Kermit Fox recalled: "We as children were frequently admonished but also taught how to carry a burning lamp correctly. To keep the draft from extinguishing the flame, one walked shielding the advancing edge of the top of the chimney with a hand, but not so close to get burned."[22]

Kerosene lamps and lanterns had their drawbacks. They provided, at best, minimal reading light, they required daily attention for wick adjustment and chimney cleaning, and they could burn your house down. Occasionally, a lamp's flame moved down its wick into its glass-globed fuel reservoir, burned for a time, then exploded, splattering fiery kerosene all around. The pages of the Brenham *Daily Banner-Press* and the La Grange *Journal* often reported such incidents. If the family was lucky, someone was present when the kerosene lamp or lantern began its metamorphosis into a firebomb, noticed the strange initial decrease in light intensity, grabbed the lamp off table or shelf, and threw it out the doorway to explode in the yard.

No wonder, then, that better-off farm families such as the Dements, Wegners, Matthieses, and Fuchs gradually replaced their home kerosene lamps with lighting systems using carbide gas from tanks or electricity from batteries and generators. In the dark barnyard and on the path to the neighbors, however, "coal oil" lamps and people following each other "like geese" remained the norm.

Insects were another common hardship of area farmsteads. However, in most years, as in the chill early winter of 1926, the worst of the "bug season" had passed by November. Most homes remained unscreened, and in the worst of summer heat even homeowners who possessed screens, such as Otto Fuchs, often removed them to facilitate the entry of every passing breeze. Since most houses went unscreened and were relatively porous, with various cracks and fissures, insects entered freely, and farm families fought internal wars against them. The wooden legs of kitchen tables and safes often stood in dishes of kerosene to keep ants from climbing up; housewives covered dinner tables, carefully laid out for the next meal, with porous cloth designed to keep off insects; and "fly strips," covered with sticky, bug-attracting adhesive, hung about to trap airborne pests.

Actually, most people were used to their in-house, flying and crawling menagerie of insects and paid them little mind, but there were exceptions, and especially at night. Mosquitoes could be so numerous as to threaten sleep, and many families resorted to "smokes"—smoldering buckets of dried cow dung, burlap sacks, or other substances—strategically positioned upwind to drift mosquito-repelling smoke across the sleeping family in bedroom or gallery. Mosquito "bars," or netting, had long been available to drape beds, but most regarded this option as insufferably hot. Given the choices between heat, mosquitoes, or dung smoke, most families chose the smoke. Choosing another unpleasant option, others smeared their skin with kerosene at bedtime to try to keep off the bugs.

Unfortunately, kerosene did not much deter bedbugs, which presented a recurrent problem for many families in this era before effective pesticides. Resembling a "little pine cone," bedbugs lived in bedding, creeping out for a blood feast only after lamps were out. Stealthy, they usually bit you before you detected them, then scampered back into corn-shuck or hay mattresses long before you frantically lit the kerosene lamp to take counter measures. The approved response to a bedbug bite was to leave the bitten limb in place while stealthily sliding a hand over to catch the blood-sucking bug still in position. Then, as Grover Williams told, "You didn't have to light the lamp to see whether you broke him; you could smell him." The next day you would get up and find a bloody streak on your arm or leg where you had killed the "cinch bug."

Bedbugs sometimes made people rise from their beds and sleep outside with the mosquitoes on the porch or in the barn. On a good, warm day, however, Grover Williams's family often carted springs, mattresses, and other bedding out to some ant mounds near the house and left them there a few hours for the ants to do their work. At the end of the day, they brushed off the ants and moved the beds back inside the house, usually free of bedbugs.[23]

After lamps were extinguished across the dark countryside, farmhouses attracted more night visitors than common insects, and many more things wandered up central dog runs besides the dogs. Despite such customary "barnyard police" as barking canines, honking geese, and clattering guineas (the last of these sounding the alarm at every passing shadow), many a farmer rose from the bed for a trip to the side yard at night to find a possum or skunk exploring his dog run. People often took a live-and-let-live attitude toward these nocturnal visitors, especially the striped and spotted skunks, animals especially common around prairie farmhouses.

Animals not cheerfully tolerated were the often-glimpsed rats, capable of increasing their numbers until they made drastic inroads into the family's field corn stored in the corncrib. During the nineteenth century, agricultural society meetings had often discussed the rat problem and someone's proposed new solution to it—some ingenious new sort of trap or new kind of poison. However, the rats remained, and in 1926 many farmers controlled their rodents by judicious administration of poisons such as "Rough On Rats" combined with biological controls. Eddie Wegner's farm and many others maintained a semiferal cat population (their diet supplemented with excess milk) to keep down the rats, and some liked to catch and release king snakes to assist the felines. Most farmers regarded king snakes in the corncrib as a good thing to have, despite these reptiles' occasionally startling appearances in smokehouses and outdoor toilets. Not only did king snakes catch rats, they preyed on other, less welcome, reptiles, especially "chicken snakes."

Getting sufficient, good-tasting water for household and barn use could be another problem for farm families. Farmers were almost water-obsessed, and the ones lucky enough to have a good spring or well often bragged about how tasty, abundant, cool, and ever-flowing it was. Pioneer settlers of the nineteenth century often had located their farms with a keen eye to nearby water sources, including springs, "spring creeks," and easily accessible groundwater. Springs often passed through several stages of human use, from natural pools, to deepened pools protected by "spring boxes" of cedar timbers, to covered "spring houses," sometimes arranged to double as cool boxes for preserving milk and butter.

By 1926, however, farms had spread across the landscape of Fayette and Washington counties, and not all locations had good springs or accessible, good-tasting groundwater. Every "dug well" that went down in an area provided data about water-bearing strata for surrounding farmers, and sometimes the news was not good. At Turner Farm upstream on the Colorado, and in places on the Washington County Bluffs, groundwater lay too deep, and families relied on cisterns to capture rainwater from their roofs or used home-made wooden "slides" or "sleds" to haul water from river or spring. Farm families at Turner Farm got murky water in barrels from the nearby Colorado, and Olivia ("Chang") Ewing on the Bluffs dragged water from a "never-failing spring" used by local African-Americans since slavery times.[24]

At Turner Farm, young Nona Mae Tatum hitched a mule to a wooden slide, pulled a fifty-five-gallon wooden barrel to the river, filled it with a bucket, then dragged it home as a daily chore—a practice that left her disinclined to waste water. In truth, extreme water conservation was the norm at all farmsteads. At most places, used dishwater became a component of the daily "hog slop," and lye wash water from Monday washdays helped scour wooden floors. Nona Mae recalled, "After we washed our clothes, we took that good soapy water we washed with, [and] we scrubbed the floors. And you talk about clean floors!"[25]

In Fayette County, Frank Janish's family had a "weak well" but practiced water austerities equal to the families at Turner Farm. The Janish's 120-foot well provided barely enough water for this large family and its stock, and the time and exertion required to lower and raise the well bucket reinforced conservation measures. No water could be spared for the Janish's garden, and they often watered their mules at a local spring creek.[26]

Robert Wilhelmsen's family, near the Salem community in Washington County, had good water—at least most of the time. The excellent well at their original homeplace had been found by a "water witch," one of the part-time specialists often involved in the mysterious and chancy business of water finding and well digging. Most water witchers used a wooden wand or forked stick of some kind to find water, but not this man, who probed for unseen water sources with his bare feet. Robert's uncle, Albert Wilhelmsen, recalled that, "He pulled his shoes off, and he walked around there. Then he stopped, he said, 'You got a peg here somewhere?' He had big toe on his foot, he had it right there, and he kept it there. He said, 'Get me a stob.' He said, 'You got it, it'll be twenty or twenty-five foot to the next big stream.'" Then the man dug the well, and his estimate proved correct. Water from this well turned out to be especially copious, good-tasting, and cool, "just like it come out of a refrigerator."[27]

Farmers were pragmatic about the powers of the water witch; water was terribly important, and what worked to locate it simply worked; you really did not need to know why. Albert Wilhelmsen himself admitted to having some water-witching abilities and well recalled the day a peach-branch wand turned so strongly in his hands that its bark twisted off. Oliver Whitener described the practices of another Washington County witcher, who, "After he located the underground stream, would let the forked stick turn around and around in his hands—each turn would mean five feet—and when it had turned the correct depth the stick would jump straight up."[28]

Preoccupied with both water sources and soils, farmers such as the Wilhelmsens, as time passed, came to know their farms not just on the surface but for "a hundred feet down." They recognized how the soil changed from place to place across their fields—here shallow "watermelon sand," there "mixed soil," and somewhere else deep "black waxy." Likewise, they knew the various water-bearing strata beneath the soil zone and the characteristics of each—how deep they were, the kind of dirt they appeared in, how productive of water they were, how their water tasted, and how dependable they were. No less than five water strata lay under the Wilhelmsen farm, the last one a step too far, "rotten egg water."[29]

Farm families that had good water often made the most of it. Albert Wilhelmsen's father eventually erected a windmill on the cold-water well the water witcher had found on his place, and so did Robert Dement's father. At the Dement's farm on La Bahia Prairie, the windmill pumped water up to a cypress cistern, which fed the kitchen by gravity flow. Eddie Wegner's mechanically inclined father went even further. At the Wegner place, a galvanized cistern positioned on a wooden tower caught "soft water" rain from the roof, then fed it by gravity into the kitchen and laundry, where the "power washer" ran off a small, one-cylinder, Witte gasoline engine. Periodically, Wegner redirected the faithful Witte to pump drinking water from his "hard-water" well to the cypress cistern that stood side by side on the tower with the galvanized one and also fed the kitchen by gravity flow.[30]

Although modern economic historians sometimes have termed the farmers of the 1920s unskilled laborers, farmers of 1926 regularly adjusted and repaired complicated machinery, did a lot of their own blacksmith work, and adapted so swiftly to the coming of internal combustion engines and automobiles that they repaired their Model T Fords virtually from the beginning. A lot of practical ingenuities went into their design and use of water-delivery systems, as well. If the Dements wanted cool drinking water in the summer, they "drew it out of the north corner of the well." If they wanted warm water for the Number 3 galvanized tub for a winter bath, "We'd run out to the horse trough out there and get us a bucket of that water that was in the pipe. That would be warm water, see; we could get the first bucket."[31]

Good water sources, however, did not mean the end of water conservatism. With water piped directly to the back porch, the Otto Fuchs family nonetheless recycled dish water as hog slop like all the rest, and the Fuchs, Dement, and Wegner children took their once-weekly baths in the usual way in cramped Number 3 washtubs. Eddie Wegner described the process:

> The way we learned to take a bath in a Number 3, you sit
> frog style, you know. You crossed your legs, the lower part of
> your legs, and sat down in the tub and then bathe from the

top on down. And then the last end, your feet and legs, you washed them while standing in the tub. Then, you walked out on the towel and dried off.[32]

On the farmsteads of 1926, the weekly chores of cleaning house and washing clothes fell heavily upon the farmers' wives and daughters, with rich and poor suffering nearly the same. The underlying problem among "dirt farmers" was dirt—or, in this rainy season of late 1926— mud. In blackland areas, mud balled up on people's feet and had to be laboriously scraped off at the doorways. Commonly, as at the Fuchs farm, housewives stationed a dull knife beside the back door so people might finish off the job of cleaning their feet. But despite that, so much mud was tracked inside some farm homes that the women began their weekly floor cleaning by scraping the floors with cotton hoes. As Nona Mae Tatum Gilley told, the cleaning occurred normally after Monday washdays, so that the women could scrub and scour the wooden floors with recycled lye-soap water from the big black washpots.

Farm families' clothing got excessively dirty in line of duty and needed strong measures to come clean. Although men and boys often drew water for the tubs and built fires under the big iron wash pots, women ran the washing and ironing regimens. They "battled" clothing on rub boards and boiled them in pots of lye-soap water, then rinsed them in tubs.

Every household did things a little differently, but most housewives were especially concerned about their "whites," which flew as emblems of family cleanliness on clothes lines for all to see. Otto Fuchs's mother "was aware that it took just the right amount of bluing to make the white pieces flapping on the clothes line look whiter than white."[33] Often required to help with Monday washdays, Howard Davis well recalled his mother's high standards on these matters.

Mama was very particular. We was very poor, but there wasn't a piece of dirty clothes in that place, and she looked them clothes over when we'd get through washing them sheets. [She'd say] "Ain't nobody gonna pass by our house and talk about my clothes being dirty!" And boy, if they wasn't white, she'd come back and throw em in your tub; they had to be clean. She'd say, "Nothing wrong with being poor, you may have raggedy clothes. But there's plenty water and soap, you can go clean."[34]

Some women even hung their whites out to dry on berry bushes and broom weeds in the belief that clothes dried on these turned out whiter than those dried on picket fences or barbed-wire fences. In any case once clothes had dried, iron-day Tuesday relentlessly followed washday Monday, with more hard labor in hot circumstances. Most women ironed with several solid metal "sad irons," successively cycled back and forth from hand to top of hot kitchen stove. Mrs. Otto Fuchs had a new-fangled gasoline iron with which to do her weekly ironing, but her advantage was dubious; the hot, hissing, and dangerous object was not beloved.

On the well-equipped Fuchs farm, the back steps served as a transitional work area between the kitchen and the kitchen-focused outbuildings beyond—the smokehouse, milk house, chicken house, and potato-storage area. Fuchs children often sat on the steps to churn milk, shell peas, and perform other assigned chores. An array of outbuildings surrounded the farms in the counties along the Brazos and Colorado, each with specific, vital functions.

Many of these outbuildings were linked to the subsistence side of the farm and tended to disappear, one by one, as the families descended the agricultural ladder from landowners to cash renters to thirds-and-fourths renters to sharecroppers and became more and more focused on growing cotton. Large tenant farms seldom had individual outbuildings at each cropper shack, since owners kept work stock, feed corn, and farming equipment in centralized mule lots and barns, and for toilets "the brush" sufficed. On smaller, more loosely run sharecropper farms, families often managed to have a small garden, a hog or two, and some chickens. The Lipscomb family tried to stay on these sorts of places, where they could at least have a "small smokehouse."[35] Thirds-and-fourths renters such as Howard Davis's family and Leola Tiedt's family had more hogs and larger smokehouses than did croppers, but they also suffered under landowners' constraints. Their gardens, milk cows, and hogs were limited, and they rarely raised watermelons, peas, cantaloupes, potatoes, or other subsistence field crops, only a little

FIGURE 6   This typical backyard farm scene (ca. 1907), the working area of the J. J. Stalmach farmstead in Nelsonville, Austin County, includes a smokehouse (left), blacksmith shop (center), sharpening stone, wine press, wagon, and a bale of cotton. Farmers often stored bales on their farms in speculation of higher market prices. (Winedale Museum Photo Collection)

"high gear" for feed. As Davis recalled, "Most of the time that landlord said, 'Plant your cotton and corn.'" Farm families regarded syrup as a staff of life, but thirds-and-fourths renters such as the Davis family rarely raised any cane to make it. Instead, they bought many gallons of commercial "Brer Rabbit Syrup" out of landowner "furnishing" money at the Mud City store.[36]

Rent farms such as those the Davis family stayed on usually had a pared-down array of outbuildings, including a mule lot, cow pen, small barn, corncrib, smokehouse, and some sort of "potato bank." The Davises kept four or five hogs but had no pen for them, using instead the mule lot, and their landowner may or may not have approved of this. A constant scuffle between renter family and landowner over such improvements was not unusual. The renter families wished to improve their lifestyles and hedge their bets by having more hogs, more chickens, larger gardens, watermelons in the field, and more of the accouterments of a subsistence farm, and their landlords simply wanted more cotton. In truth, a natural conflict over these matters was built into even the most cordial of renter-landowner relationships; from the owner's perspective, his renter's subsistence activities took valuable cropland and valuable work time best used for cotton. Over time, conflicts over these and other matters tended to develop and caused the renter family to move on. Moving was virtually a way of life for many Texas renters by the 1920s, approximately one-third of which changed farms every year. These frequent moves also discouraged renters' subsistence farming, since any hogpens, chicken houses, smokehouses, or other improvements they might have made on their rented places had to remain behind.

Owner-operated farms in Fayette and Washington counties were far more complex, and this complexity was manifested in an array of outbuildings. Fayette County historian F. Lotto observed in 1900:

> The reader has not seen the farm if he has not looked at the barn. The barn is a large building, generally painted red, built in most different styles, the approved one is with thoroughfare in the middle and stables on either side of it. At one of the ends are rooms for corn and rooms for sheltering farm utensils. In the loft under the roof is the store place for hay. A cow pen at the end of a pasture, a hogpen, and a smokehouse filled with bacon complete the surroundings.[37]

To this list might be added some sort of Irish-potato and sweet-potato storage facility (a teepee-shaped, earth-covered temporary "potato bank" made of cornstalks in the yard, or a more permanent storage arrangement under the farmhouse), a well house covering the "dug well," a chicken house, an outdoor toilet, and perhaps a milk house.

Milk houses were insulated "cool houses" for preserving milk, butter, and other dairy products and were not found on every farm, although area farmers kept a lot of milk cows and many families had them. The Fuchs's milk house had thick walls insulated with cotton burrs, and the Remment family near Nelsonville used a hewn-log milk house inherited from former slaveholders. A shed that housed a large trough chiseled from a solid log stood between milk house and kitchen on the Remments' farm. Puzzled by this feeding trough used by the former plantation's nursery, the family recycled it for salting down meat before hanging hams and bacon in the smokehouse.[38]

Outdoor toilets were present on most landowner's farms by the early winter of 1926, although women and girls used them much more than men and boys and not everybody thought they were preferable to the brush. The porcelain "chamberpot" by night, the brush by day, men and boys to the left, women and girls to the right, remained the practice at many isolated farmsteads. Despite regular applications of lime or wood ash, pit toilets stank and attracted such vermin as flies, red wasps, snakes, and even bats. Encounters with something unpleasant in the outhouse were common. As Robert Skrabanek recalled, "Flies seemed to get special pleasure out of stinging us on the exposed parts of our behinds."[39] However, by 1926 some progress had been made in the dimension of "toilet paper," if nowhere else, since on most farms the corncob era had evolved into the Sears and Roebuck era. Town merchants, chafing at the expansion of their hated mail-order competitors, must have taken some small satisfaction from this.

By this time in the late fall of 1926, "hog killing time" had come and gone, and farm families took comfort in their smokehouses full of meat but perhaps even more satisfaction in their full corncribs. Either as separate outbuildings or as special rooms in the barn, corncribs were large, sturdy, wooden bins with gaps between their boards so that air could circulate and delay arrival of the inevitable corn weevil. When the first field corn of the year matured in the field, a family often picked a few bushels, dried it on a metal roof, and took it in to the local grist mill to be ground for the first fresh cornmeal of the autumn. As Robert Skrabanek observed, "Humans and animals deserved a break from last year's crop, which had a few weevils." After this "break," however, "we finished all of the corn with weevils in it until it was all used up before the next year's crop was put in the barn."[40]

Most area farmers used all the corn they produced on the farm—for human consumption, as "fuel" for the work stock, and as feed for a menagerie of domestic animals of vital importance to the household economy. When the farm family's corn crop matured to the point that ears were "made" and at least a minimal crop was assured, all breathed a huge sigh of relief. In Fayette and Washington counties, as everywhere else in the South, corn played a critical role in human diet and was consumed as "roasting ears," mush, hominy, grits, and a variety of breads.

Farm families fed dried field corn on the cob to mules, horses, and hogs, and fed shelled corn to chickens, ducks, geese, turkeys, and guinea fowl.

Farmers were particular about their corn—especially the seed corn saved for next year. When Robert Skrabanek's family "pulled corn" in the field and threw it into the accompanying wagon at harvest time, each person wore a special sack in which to place the champion ears encountered. John Skrabanek kept this corn separate in wagon and barn, shelled and screened it for size as planting time approached in the spring, then planted only the largest, best-formed grains for next year's crop.[41] Others selected their seed corn for next year during the daily husking of corn for the stock during the winter, perhaps throwing it into a certain barrel near the corncrib, as Henry Jaeger's family did.[42] Eddie Wegner's father had a special formula for selecting his seed corn, believing that: "the diameter of the cob should be no more than the length of the two grains across. And when it came to planting time, it was taboo to shell it on the machine sheller. He said it broke the tip too bad. He would knock off the ends, and the middle was always hand shelled for planting." Like many others, Wegner also had a system for selecting corn for different purposes. "Nubbins," poorly developed small ears, went to the hogs; "the nubbin type, but soft cob, went to the work horses and mules"; and the best ears were hand shelled for human consumption, chickens, other domestic fowl, and seed corn.[43]

Farmers prided themselves on using "all of the hog but the squeal" and all of the corn but the bottommost stalk and roots. Families began pulling "suckers"—offshoot stalks—for fodder as they developed in the spring, and they cut "tops" for fodder after the ears had matured around July 4. As soon as the corn developed but the kernels were still soft and milky, farmers pulled "roasting ears" for human consumption and sometimes grated the corn with a grater to make a kind of sweet, moist cornbread. Shucks from ears of corn shucked daily for mule and horse feed were not discarded, but were carried in "shuck baskets" to feed cows and calves (also primary recipients of the corn-top fodder) and saved for shuck mattresses and "cotton-cloth ticking comforters." Shelled corn went to feed flocks of domestic fowl, which on well-regulated subsistence farms often numbered in the hundreds. Farm families saved their corncobs to recycle as cook-stove tinder, iron-wash-pot fuel, water-jug stoppers, fishing corks, outhouse toiletry, medicinal sulfur-and-kerosene-impregnated amulets for mange-afflicted dogs, and other things. As Robert Skrabanek recalled, he and his brother also used corncobs for silent, pre-dawn "corncob fights" while ostensibly milking the cows. Corncobs discarded from whole ears neatly nibbled by horses and mules were recovered by the Skrabaneks, and only the cobs fed to the hogs were lost. Hogs tramped these down into the mud and excrement of the hogpen beyond the point of reasonable recovery, and even John Skrabanek had to draw the line somewhere.[44] After families had gathered the corn crop, they let cows, horses and mules into the field to feast on the remnant corn leaves, stalks, and any weeds that had grown up since "laid by" time. Finally, farmers chopped the stalks and plowed them under to serve as fertilizer for next year.

Corn and domestic fowl stood in close relationship on the farmsteads of 1926. Irwin Blume of Fayette County recalled of his grandfather's home place near Walhalla, "The split-log corncrib, with hand-operated corn sheller to provide much feed for hundreds of brown leghorns that roosted in the nearby big live oak trees, flying down like birds."[45] On the Blume family's farm, as on all the rest, concentric rings of fowl ranged out from the farmyard each morning at first light, all getting some of their sustenance from the daily feedings of corn and scavenging for the rest in farmyard, fencerow, pasture, and woods. Domestic fowl differed in how far they roamed, how dependent they were on corn, and how much protection they needed, but all were more resourceful than modern birds, and some—particularly the guineas and turkeys—were at least semiferal. Geese played a minor role in most farmstead economies, but many families tried to keep enough around to provide feathers for pillows, comforters, and "feather beds," and to be sacrificed for the traditional Christmas roast goose. Farm women plucked female geese (not ganders) several times a year as they began to moult and saved the soft, downy feathers. Often, the intent was to produce enough feathers so that each child of the family could be issued a goose-down feather bed and set of two pillows when he or she married. Geese had other uses, as well. They joined the noisy guineas as "barnyard police," honking the alarm when any strange person or animal happened close by, and occasionally farmers made serious use of flocks of geese to weed their cotton fields. Geese loved to eat new grass and hated the taste of little cotton plants, hence the practice. Unfortunately, this only worked for the cotton, since geese found new corn to be very tasty. At Christmas, weddings, and other times, excess ganders provided roast goose for celebrations, as well as the traditional goose-blood-and-prunes pudding, much favored by the Germans.[46]

"Yard chickens" roamed at large at virtually every farm in the counties along the Brazos and Colorado—even those of sharecroppers, who might have no other domestic fowls, little or no corn to feed them, and not even a milk cow. Resourceful, roosting in nearby trees if no chicken house was provided, chickens fanned out at first light searching for insects and other edibles. Every farm had a few chickens, most had several score, and by 1926 some had two or three hundred. Chickens were the business of the farm wife, who managed them for maximum eggs and egg money. As at the Fuchs farm, wives usually sought to generate enough cash to pay for family groceries with some left over for sewing supplies and barter with the passing chicken peddlers, and they usually accomplished this. Cotton money from last fall went a long way if chickens bought all the family's groceries until the next cotton crop came in, and for many families this indeed was the case. Families ate eggs and excess roosters throughout the year, and old hens that stopped laying also became expendables. As Howard Matthies said, "Mother would get an old hen and she'd cook noodle soup—homemade noodles and chicken broth—there was a lot of noodle soup eaten in the old days."[47]

Yard chickens took occasional losses from predators, work stock, bad weather, and other acts of God, but these were to be expected. Usually, the natural increases of the flocks more than made up for them, and various countermeasures were taken. Eddie Wegner's family often set out glass eggs, both to encourage hens to lay and to function as anti-chicken-snake devices. Snakes swallowed the glass eggs, broke them by constriction, then suffered the consequences; Wegner often found the snakes dead. Hawks caught a few chickens, but the Wegners and others followed a practice of erecting a tall cedar pole on the edge of the barnyard with a board nailed across the top, leaving it there for a few days until the hawk got used to perching on it, then setting a small steel trap on the top.[48] Another method was to sit still with a shotgun near the hen yard and keep a close eye on the roosters, who always saw and reacted to the hawk's approach before you did. Chicken houses protected the flock from nocturnal threats, skunks and roaming dogs, and from unusually cold winter weather—if the chickens used them. Grover Williams's family had some chickens who refused to roost in the hen house and consequently "were doomed" in a bad cold snap. Williams found some of these wild tree-roosters lying on the ground the morning after, rather like the "frozen Butterball turkeys" of later years. "He was just hard as a rock, and you could tell when he froze and hit the ground. It was just like somebody throwing a rock out there. You get up the next morning and go out there, and there he is."[49] The Williams's flock took other losses that were compensated for by their natural increase. Snakes and chicken hawks got a few, mules stamped some chickens to death as they tried to get spilled corn next to the trough where the work stock was eating, and hogs caught and ate a few. Chickens also got in the hog trough, and a hog might fight to keep them out, catch one, and discover it was tasty. "Then, from then on, that hog had tasted that blood, and he would catch chickens when he wasn't eating."[50]

Neglected by historians of the farming life, "free range" turkeys sometimes brought in more income to area farm families than their cotton crops of the year. By the late fall of 1926, the old days of free-range hog and cattle raising had ended in most areas with the coming of local stock laws, but such statutes did not apply to turkeys. Virtually every farmer raised some "grasshopper turkeys," which roosted in trees at the farm each night, then roamed for miles across pastures and woodlands, scavenging for grasshoppers and insects in the spring and summer and fattening on natural mast—acorns and pecans—in the fall. Grover Williams's household at Flat Prairie was in prime turkey habitat, near prairies and the wooded Yegua bottoms, and Williams recalled: "We had the black ones and Mrs. Amanda Perkins, she had brown turkeys. Everybody else had the black turkeys with the psychedelic colors on their wings. Everybody had domestic turkeys, and had long lines of turkeys going back and forth. They didn't mix. If they mixed, then they went to fighting, and when they got straight they went on to where they were going."[51] Mercantile stores at crossroads towns served as collection points for area turkeys just before Thanksgiving and Christmas. Merchants at Burton sometimes kept well over a thousand birds in semiconfinement near their stores, while they fed fattening corn to them at the rate of hundreds of pounds a day. Turkeys periodically escaped, some to roost on the top of the Burton gin, but they always came back to be fed. Just before the holidays, the merchants shipped them to New Orleans "where they didn't care if they were grasshopper turkeys." Storekeepers made money and so did the turkey raisers. An old bachelor farmer of the area told Howard

FIGURE 7   Children, not dressed for chores, pose behind the
family turkey flock on a Fayette County farm. (Fayetteville Area
Heritage Museum, courtesy of Louis J. "Buddy" Polansky)

Matthies that one year he had made $2,000 from the sale of turkeys
that had cost him only a little supplemental corn to raise.[52]

Farm families "free ranged" turkeys exactly as earlier generations had
ranged hogs. Turkeys were marked, fended mostly for themselves,
ranged freely across property lines, mixed and merged with other families' flocks, were kept semitame with supplemental feedings of corn,
then fattened themselves for market on the natural mast fall of the
autumn woods. Matthies noted, "Them turkeys get under a pecan tree,
they'll clean them up."[53] As had been the case with free-range hog raisers, turkey raisers cooperated with each other, feeding other families'

birds when they found them mixed up with theirs, notifying other turkey raisers about the whereabouts of their flocks, and scrupulously separating the marked birds as Thanksgiving approached. Turkeys, like hogs or cattle, could even be driven to market for considerable distances, as a yearly five-day, fifty-mile, five-hundred-bird drive from Johnson City to Austin repeatedly demonstrated. Harold Davis sometimes herded his family's wandering turkeys back from a neighbor's "high gear" field along the Colorado, recalling that he "drove em back with the horse, you could drive em bout as good as you could cattle, or better."[54]

This sort of turkey raising was a strange enterprise. Each family began the season with only a few hens and a turkey tom or two. Turkeys were wild and had to be allowed to "steal their nests" in the nearby woods. Someone among the children, often a boy, had the job of shadowing the hens until they made serious nests and began to lay. Ed Lathan, designated turkey stalker in his family, recalled, "It was fun to me, like when we's kids playing hide and go seek. Old turkey, she'd fool you, too. She'd act like she's making a nest here, and if you turn your head she's way down yonder somewhere. I always played safety first, I'd bell that heifer, put a little turkey bell around her neck, and more or less I could always find her."[55] Grover Williams had the same job. He stalked each turkey hen in turn until he found her nest, then marked the location with a strip of sheet or old ironing board cover tied nearby. This was not easy, since the hen seemed aware of you watching her and would slip off "like a ghost" the moment your attention wavered. Williams, too, relied on a bell of sorts. "It might have been a Carnation can with the top cut out of it with a strap and a little piece of wire with a little nut in there for a little tapper, something like that. We didn't have too much store-bought stuff."[56] After they found the nests, Williams and Lathan removed turkeys and eggs to pens back at their farms, hatched the eggs under mother turkeys or "broody hens," and gave the young turkey poults over to the care of the turkey hens.

At this point, the hens began to lead their broods out from the farm each morning to forage in nearby pastures and woods, then back home to roost and a feed of corn in the evenings. Ed Lathan often saw the young turkeys "running grasshoppers like a dog running a jackrabbit,"[57] and farmers sometimes turned these voracious feeders into the cotton fields to combat "army worms." By this time the turkeys were all marked to distinguish them from neighbors' birds. Local farmers often consulted about their plans, as Howard Matthies recounted: "They'd ask the neighbors, 'This year, what gonna be your mark?' They'd say, 'We gonna cut off the right middle toe.' Then we would cut off the left middle toe."[58] Others marked turkey poults by dabbing paint on their wings, notching their gullets in a certain way, or punching a hole in each poult's left or right foot with a paper punch.

Sometimes the semiferal turkeys came home in the evening as they were supposed to do, and sometimes they did not. In that case the designated turkey stalkers sprang into action. Both Robert Skrabanek and Mance Lipscomb's mother had trained their turkeys to come to call for a handout of corn (again, just as East Texas stockmen trained their "rooter" hogs), but Ed Lathan relied on the bell. "I'd come out of the field, I'd run down through them woods a half a mile or a mile. You'd hear that bell on the mother hen, and I could course myself to em and drive em home."[59]

The diversified hundred-acre farms of Fayette and Washington counties, with their array of domestic animals, gardens, subsistence crops, and cash crops, were complicated operations. Asked to label her "occupation" back in the 1920s, Annie Schmidt of the Round Top area could give no simple answer, responding: "Well, our occupation was of all sorts—farming and raising cattle, chickens, and eggs, and gardening, raising hogs and pigs and making sausage in wintertime. Never had no other job than just around the home, sewing, cooking, baking, maybe quilting, stuff like that."[60]

By early winter of 1926, perimeter fences of barbed wire surrounded almost all area farms. Fencing had been a problem in earlier times, and farmers had used cedar, split-rail, zigzag fences to bar free-range hogs and cattle from their cultivated fields. A little later, they experimented with stake-and-rider rail fencing and bois d'arc hedges to accomplish the same thing. After barbed wire became available during the 1880s, farm families fenced their fields, then began to fence the perimeters of their farms, sometimes recycling their old rail fencing and mature bois d'arc hedges as fence posts. Other fence posts came from the farms' woodlots, and both Virginia cedars and post oaks had their advocates. By 1926 the only rail fences still in use fenced in hogpens and hog pastures. "Hogs in the meadow and cows in the corn" (or chickens in the garden) were not things the farm family could afford to let happen, and only effective internal fencing could prevent them.[61]

Area farms presented a complicated mosaic of land use, usually including garden plots, potato patches, orchards, cotton and corn croplands, subsistence croplands, pastures, hay meadows, and wood-lots. Farmers used all of these parts of the farm in their yearly rounds, and if they lacked something deemed essential they arranged to get it somewhere else. Verlie Wegner's and Howard Matthies's families did not have enough cotton and corn land, so they rented fields from neigh-bors. Robert Skrabanek's and Kermit Fox's families needed woodland for stove fuel and (in the Skrabaneks' case) pasturage, so they rented and purchased it elsewhere.

Characteristically, the cotton-deficient Wegners and Matthieses refused to put their permanent pasture land and native bluegrass hay meadows into additional field crops. The pasture and meadow sup-ported family milk cows and work stock and so played an important role in the farm's economy; converting these to cotton was unthinkable. Besides, where else would the "grasshopper turkeys" find their grasshoppers?

Most area farmers wanted enough land in cotton and corn, but only that. Ratios of cotton to corn in major cropland varied from farm to farm, but were usually somewhere between one to one and two to one. One advantage of the one-to-one ratio was ease of rotation of crops every year, cotton land to corn and corn land to cotton. Rotation often was less than precise, however, because farmers cultivated not by acres but by fields, and fields varied in size. The more cotton and less corn the farmer planted, the greater the chance he took; corn was the "safety first" crop. On a smaller-than-usual farm of 75 acres, Verlie Wegner's family cultivated about 20 acres in cotton, 20 in corn, rotating the crops every year, and many other small landowners maintained about these same acreages. On a much larger, 380-acre Fayette County farm, Kermit Blume's family put only about 45 acres each in cotton and corn and used the rest for cattle and hog pastures and subsistence field crops.[62]

Farmers often grew other things in their fields beside cotton and corn, but if they had room for only one other crop, it was likely to be some kind of syrup cane. Most families felt they needed at least a few rows of molasses, "red top," or "ribbon" cane to cut in the fall and haul to the nearest neighborhood syrup mill for processing into syrup. An open gallon bucket of syrup stood on many dining tables during all three meals of the day, and large farm families' yearly consumption of this dietary staple often exceeded fifty gallons. Syrup served as the high-calorie survival food of the Southern diet, providing concentrated calories for dawn-to-dark days in the field. Farmers poured syrup on their cornbread, punched holes in their "cat head" biscuits and filled them with it, and even poured it on their fried chicken. Farm women often used syrup (and honey) in cooking as substitutes for store-bought sugar.

Other commonly grown subsistence field crops were field peas (often interspersed between rows of corn), grain sorghum grown for animal feed, and watermelons. If the farmer had a patch of sandy land anywhere on his farm, he planted the land in watermelons, peanuts, cantaloupes, or sweet potatoes. Any of these subsistence field crops might produce far in excess of the farm family's needs, but nothing was wasted. Edibles produced in excess or spoiled for human consumption became hog food, hence were recycled into valuable pork. Rotten watermelons, soured honey or syrup, sprouted potatoes from last year's crop, suspect canned goods from years past, food scraps, and even dish-water went into the hog slop.

Large fall gardens, separate potato patches, and small orchards sur-rounded most family farms during this fall of 1926. Even Brazos valley sharecroppers often managed to find room for a small garden some-where close to their houses. The natural conflict between the renter family's desire to improve its diet by means of subsistence activities and the landowner's preoccupation with cotton led to various renter sub-terfuges—a half row of watermelons secreted in the far corner of the cotton field, black-eyed peas twining up the cornstalks after "laid by" time, a peanut patch hidden in the thicket, or even a few unmarked hogs roaming the nearby creek bottom. Thirds-and-fourths renters such as Howard Davis's family usually negotiated better deals for garden spaces and potato patches, but their gardens often were poor affairs compared to the gardens of many landowners' families. The Davises—and many others—ate a lot of Brer Rabbit Syrup from the store.

Some of the fall gardens observed by passers-by in Fayette and Washington counties during 1926 reached epic proportions. Kermit Blume's mother masterminded her family's two large gardens, each a full half-acre in size. As Kermit told, "The garden was worth money, because it saved buying your groceries." Near one of the gardens was a separate, one-acre Irish potato patch, which produced several wagon loads of potatoes each year. Fences surrounded the Blumes' gardens as they did all the rest—one-inch chicken wire at the bottom to keep rabbits out, two-inch wire above that for "chickens and whatever."[63]

A few miles away, Helene Bothe Eichler, wife of ginner-farmer Herman Eichler, ran an even larger garden—heavily into fall cabbages, second-crop potatoes, and other cool-weather crops this autumn of 1926. Helene Eichler fed many mouths from her garden—herself, her husband, eleven children, various visiting grandchildren, her husband's four hired hands, and any farmers whose wagons happened to be in line for ginning off or corn grinding when the noontime whistle blew. An hour before noon shutdown, Herman Eichler sounded the steam whistle one toot for every farmer then in line so his wife could calculate her dinner preparations.

All knew the menu would be varied. Helene Eichler's garden featured seven kinds of beans and nearly every vegetable that grew in La Bahia Prairie blackland. Large quantities of "hog beets," green cabbages, peanuts, and potatoes grew in the large separate garden plot called the "potato land." The main garden produced in season (besides the seven kinds of beans) snow peas, English peas, cauliflower, kohlrabi, white squash, New Zealand spinach, mustard greens, Swiss chard, Chinese cabbage, eggplants, shallots, red onions, white onions, several varieties of tomatoes, radishes, carrots, peppers of various sorts, cucumbers, okra, and more. Two sorts of "tame" table grapes twined the garden fence in season, and dewberries, various kinds of peach trees, pear trees, plum trees, and Herman Eichler's tobacco patch grew nearby. When the local photographer came around for a family portrait, Helene Eichler had someone drag her pride and joy, two lemon trees growing in half barrels, around to the front of the farmhouse and placed beside her for the family portrait. And her seasonal food preservations matched the epic proportions of her garden. Granddaughter Leola Tiedt recalled, for example, that *Grossmutter* Eichler normally pickled several multigallon crocks and over one hundred quart jars of cucumbers every year.[64]

Renter families wagoning household goods to new places this late fall of 1926 had no gardens or fruit orchards to look forward to, though children soon might explore the nearby creek bottoms in a search for wild pecans, black haws, persimmons, or late-crop mustang grapes. For many Fayette and Washington County farm families each year, the first activity after cotton season was moving on. Leola Tiedt's family moved almost every year after her father's mercantile store in Carmine failed, and Robert Skrabanek's family moved several times during the 1910s and 1920s. The Skrabaneks had moving to a new place down to a formula, though a painful one, especially for Mrs. Skrabanek. Having found what was to his satisfaction better land, a better farmhouse, a more reasonable landowner, and a better chance to make money next year to buy blackland property, John Skrabanek announced to his family that they would go somewhere else in the Snook community for the next year. In the late fall, the family first moved its farming equipment across, then the work stock, then—with help from neighbors from the old place—household goods in wagons. Robert Skrabanek's mother hated all of this: the move into a "dirty house" without time to clean up; the immediate set up of the cook stove wherever the stove pipe hole happened to be (no matter if she would have preferred it elsewhere); the immediate preparation of a meal, since Skrabanek males "were not in the habit of eating cold food at our house"; and the annoying jumble of household possessions piled by sometimes-careless neighbors on the front porch.[65]

The new farm often had a name derived from a previous renter family—the "old Johnson Place," or some such; the names lasted longer than the families, and in truth the Johnsons might be even then transporting their worldly goods toward the "old Skrabanek Place."[66] But the Johnsons and Skrabaneks were not alone. One-third of Texas rent farmers, nearly 150,000 families, packed up and moved to a new farm every year during the 1920s.[67] As Howard Davis recalled, beginning in late fall you saw farm wagons going down the road, husbands, wives, children, domestic fowl, and total possessions piled inside. Renters traveled light: "They didn't have much furniture, just an old wood cook stove and a bed and a few things like that—like myself!"[68] Contemporary Rupert B. Vance observed, "After the cotton harvest is over, one meets them at every nook and corner of the rural South, driving along the country roads with their scanty household goods exposed to the gaze of an indifferent world. They move from a pillar to post from year to year. They are a migratory type of farmer, cursed with the reckless foot of the wandering Jew."[69]

Farmers developed their own grim humor about this annual event, which usually involved moving from place to place in the same general locality. An East Texan recalled, with only a little exaggeration, that one tenant family moved so often that the father had only to back the wagon up to the house and "all the chickens automatically crossed their legs to be tied and the cow and hound dog quietly fell into line."[70]

Moving from sharecropper farm to sharecropper farm in the Brazos bottoms involved additional considerations for black renters, which helped to explain why African-American families moved less often than Anglo-American ones. Moving might be easy, or it might be difficult; it all depended on the landlord. Sometimes, the better a cropper family farmed, the more cotton it produced, the more valuable it became to the landlord, and the more he desired that the family remain on his farm. Unfortunately for the croppers, the best way to accomplish this was to keep the family in debt. The belief that too much cash in hand ruined black labor was an old Southern rationalization; landlords in the Mississippi Delta, for example, informed sociologist John Dollard that black families often moved because they had "made too much money that year."[71] Consequently, hard-working families often failed to come out in the black when the landowner added things up at settlement time, and often were told that they had to stay on the place next year to work off their debts.

The cropper's only recourse was to secretly arrange a position on another white man's farm, then move in the dead of night and allow the new landlord to protect him from the old one. Lily Lipscomb explained, "Say, if I lived on your farm, and you and I didn't get along, I left. And I done made a leave overnight—slip off, on midnight, middle of the night—and go live on another farm. And you [the old landlord] go to John B. Quinn, and John B. Quinn say, 'You better not bother him,' you ain't gonna bother him." Willie Lipscomb, Lily's brother, put even ruder words into the hypothetical landlord John B. Quinn's mouth: "Now, that's my nigger, don't you mess with him. He'd go anywhere he want to go, he's at liberty. But don't you mess with him, you take it up with me."[72]

For Brazos valley blacks, sometimes the only alternative to a move from one exploitive white landlord to another exploitive white landlord was a relocation to Dallas, Houston, or some other place far from the Brazos bottoms. As former slave Charlie Lipscomb advised his son Mance, "If you can't pay a man in full, pay him in distance."[73]

For renters and landowners alike in the old counties along the

Brazos and Colorado, this late fall of 1926 after cotton season was a time of hard work, not leisure. A lot of activities took place right on the farm, as families busied themselves clearing new ground, cutting wood for winter heating and cooking, repairing fences, making clothing and quilts for the new year, mending harnesses, and getting plows and work tackle ready for bedding up the fields. Early winter also was the time that part-time specialists in many farm families cut fence posts, made syrup, cut and hauled firewood, carpentered, blacksmithed, water-witched, gathered pecans, made illegal whisky, and seized upon any means at hand to make a little extra money.

No sooner was the cotton picked, ginned, and sold, than Frank Janish and his fourteen brothers and sisters began clearing new ground on the family's sandy-land farm out from Fayetteville. The numerous Janishes needed more crop land, so every winter they fell to work with grubbing hoes and axes putting new land into cultivation the hard way. As in other sandy-land areas, part of this farm never had been cleared, and dense virgin woodlands of post oak, elm, and other trees stood thickly on the land. The Janishes first cut the yaupon underbrush, then the larger trees, leaving the stumps to rot in the new field. In earlier times, area farmers had only girdled the larger trees, leaving them to die, stand in the field, drop their limbs, fall, and rot; not only was this the easiest way, but farmers believed this made better farmland.[74] In several weeks of hard labor before time came for bedding up the old fields each year, the Janish work force usually cleared two or three additional acres of new ground.[75]

Thirty miles northwest at the Sand Town community of Washington County, Herman Schoenemann also cleared virgin post oaks on a sandy-land farm during this early winter.[76] Old ways lasted longest in the post-oak uplands, some precincts of which still were free range for hogs and cattle in this winter of 1926. Land was cheaper here, and few families rented from others. When families cleared new ground, sometimes neighbors pitched in to help, carrying, piling, and burning the downed timber in a traditional Southern "log rolling," one of several communal work events that were also social occasions.[77]

Sometimes families cleared land for other farmers for so much an acre—usually only a few dollars, though the work was the hardest agricultural labor anyone could do. Many landowners allowed renters to clear new ground for the privilege of raising crops on it rent-free the first year. Along the Brazos, Bubba Bowser's father sometimes did this. Mr. Bowser was a thirds-and-fourths renter from the Moores and a hard-working and ambitious farmer; if he failed to raise a hundred bales "he said he had a short crop." Bubba recalled, "When we moved in Moore bottom, when you get through picking cotton, Daddy would put us out in the woods cleaning up land—piling up brush and cleaning up land. And Mr. Walker Moore would let us [work] all the land we clean up and burn the brush off—he'd let us work it the first year, didn't have to pay no rent. We clean sometimes fifteen and twenty acres of land, and Daddy would put corn there."[78]

Late fall after cotton season also was the time for farmstead repairs and refurbishings, all the things that had been neglected during the relentless labors of the crop cycle. Robert Skrabanek recalled that his family "fixed fences, built or repaired storage sheds and barns, got all of the plows in shape and plowshares sharpened, replaced old double- or single-trees and outworn harness parts, repaired wagon beds, and made wood for our stoves. Papa had a forge and blower at home, so we did a lot of our own repair work instead of having to pay for it."[79] Most other small farmers did much the same, often making every effort to effect repairs before taking items in to the full- or part-time local blacksmith. Like John Skrabanek, Robert Wilhelmsen's father had his own small blacksmith shop, sharpened the family's plowshares, and did other minor work. Wilhelmsen also designed a special, heavy-duty, two-row stalk cutter and a unique root-cutting extension for his bedder plow, then took his plans to the Salem blacksmith to execute.[80]

Others, such as Grover Williams's grandfather, possessed fewer mechanical skills and often tried to keep vital machinery going by the strategic application of baling wire. Big tangles of baling wire hung on barn walls and fences at most farms, and periodically farmers snipped off pieces to jury-rig a repair to the walking cultivator or even the Model T. Farm families recycled baling wire for every conceivable purpose. Often in winter, Grover Williams and his brothers wore homemade canvas jackets—"jumpers"—made from the tops of old cotton pick sacks; sometimes these fastened at the front with proper buttons and sometimes with short, twisted lengths of baling wire.[81]

For small-scale repair that baling wire could not accomplish, Williams's grandfather often took his problem to a nearby Flat Prairie farm that had one of the "government balls." Somehow, several black farmers had ended up in possession of heavy iron balls still connected to telltale chains and ankle shackles, and local people often used these as makeshift anvils. Williams explained, "If you hit a stump and bent the point on the plow, you didn't bring it all the way to town to straighten it, you just took it there to that government ball and beat it back straight."[82]

If such home remedies failed, broken objects might still be taken to professional blacksmiths in Burton, Brenham, and every crossroads community. Local blacksmiths of awesome skill still struck sparks from their anvils in the winter of 1926. Part-time specialists such as Gus Keiler of Round Top abounded. A cotton farmer with not enough land, Keiler blacksmithed and carpentered "between plowings" to generate additional cash.[83] Born in 1911, Carmine blacksmith Joe Knutzen worked at his trade all the time, although, like other professional blacksmiths, he had branched out into auto mechanics.[84] At Burton, blacksmith Christian Buck doubled as master gin mechanic. The slight, wiry, Buck could fix anything except a broken heart, people said, and he worked fast—if you knew enough not to request that he do so. Pressured to complete a job, Buck went very slowly indeed. Twelve miles to the east in Brenham, master blacksmith August Schoenfelder approached the end of a fifty-year career as professional. Born in Germany, Schoenfelder's father had required that he and his brother make twelve horseshoe nails before leaving for school each morning, and the rigorous apprenticeship had paid off. Early blacksmiths often built wagons and other farming equipment from the ground up, and Schoenfelder recollected that he had made 5,870 middle buster plowshares, 6,950 sweep-stock plowshares, and hundreds of wagons during his long career.[85]

While men and boys mended fence, wagoned in stovewood, and readied farming equipment for bedding up the fields, farm women often patched old clothing and made new clothing for next year. Considerable sewing was always necessary, though families kept this to a minimum by recycling older children's clothing for younger ones. If you were a younger child like Howard Matthies, this meant that your clothing might have been worn by not one but several brothers. Matthies remembered, "All we wore in the country was hand-me-down.

FIGURE 8   Teenager Ida Hoffman carding cotton on the back
porch of the Recknagel home in Round Top, Fayette County,
ca. 1907. The process of carding, or combing, the cotton prepared
the fibers for spinning. (Winedale Museum Photo Collection)

One brother wore a suit, I wore it, next brother wore it, and the next
year you got it. It went down the stairs till there wasn't no frazzle left.
New clothes, that was a luxury."[86]

Some clothing always had to be made, however, and in most families winter was the sewing season. Ready-made dresses, shirts, and
underwear cost several times more than such items made at home, so
many a seamstress purchased her own cloth from the local mercantile
store or the passing peddler. A housewife with several children might

buy an entire bolt of fabric at cotton-pay-off time, then sew new clothing until Christmas. Often, the only clothing items purchased in the
store were men's denim overalls, straw hats, and work shoes.
Unbleached cotton muslins provided the cheapest cloth until around
1920, when printed flour and feed sacks began to appear. Women used
this free fabric to make dresses, underwear, shirts, sheets, and pillowcases, often swapping sacks with each other to get enough of a certain
pattern for an item of clothing. Approximately three feed sacks were
needed to make a dress, for example.[87]

Rich and poor, landowners' wives and sharecroppers' wives, all
joined in the fall sewing spree, though some chose to delegate these
tasks to their oldest daughters. William Terrell worked in his family's
commissary at Allenfarm as a teenager, and he recalled that a good
many of the sharecropper families preferred to make their own clothing. A surprising number of renter families and landowner families
owned sewing machines, often purchased in cotton season from traveling Singer men, one of a group of luxury-item peddlers that hit the
roads in the fall after cotton had been sold. A farmer or his wife might
never travel to the county-seat town to buy a player piano, carbide
lighting system, or Singer sewing machine, but sometimes when one
turned up at their door, the product proved irresistible.

Most of the sewing of early winter was of utilitarian wear—women's
work dresses, sunbonnets, underwear, and quilts. Women wore sunbonnets to protect themselves from the sun and to prevent the tanning
that marked them as field hands. Bonnets worn in the field, "slat bonnets," often had wooden staves inserted in them to keep them shaped
up, and "slit bonnets" could be stuffed for warmth in the wintertime.
Women often made more decorative and elaborate sunbonnets to wear
to church, and at one point the minister at the Wendish settlement of
Serbin had to consult with his church elders about this practice. These
Wendish bonnets had become so large, deep, and dark that the minister could not discern the women's open mouths wherein to place the
communion wafers.[88]

Seamstresses often recycled the tops of worn-out cotton pick sacks
as boys' jumper jackets, heavy-duty "hoeing dresses and picking
dresses" for girls, hand towels, sheets, and pillow tickings. One woman
described the cotton-sack dresses her mother made as having "butterfly
sleeves, just a slip-on, just a common, plain dress."[89] Nearly every year,

families bought some cotton canvas and sewed a few new pick sacks, nicely adjusted to the size and personal preferences of each family cotton picker. Sacks abraded on their bottoms as pickers dragged the heavy seed cotton across the ground, but farm seamstresses always repaired them or—if beyond repair—recycled them as something else. To keep a sack going, the bottom might be replaced, its top and bottom might be reversed (with the strap repositioned at the other end), or the sack might be patched. Pickers became attached to their personal, custom-made, just-right-fitting pick sacks and sometimes repaired them until they had patches upon their patches.

Winter quilting usually went on at every farmstead, since in the drafty, ill-heated farmhouses quilts functioned as necessary insulation for family bedding. Some women liked to piece, some liked to quilt, and some liked none of quilt making, but all had to do it; quilts were a basic resource for the farm family. Quilting might be done alone, with immediate family, or in "quilting parties," a communal work occasion involving extended family and neighbors.[90] Social quilting varied in frequency from community to community but still remained common in the old counties along the Brazos and Colorado.

Some farm seamstresses, especially those lucky enough to own sewing machines, made men's shirts and girls' cotton dresses for other families, often charging less than half of what the store-bought item would cost. Trying to make a little extra money in early winter was a common practice, as every rural family fielded one or more part-time handymen, and a variety of rural specialists roamed the countryside. A few cotton pickers still worked northern cotton fields along the distant Red River valley during this late November, though they soon would return. At La Bahia Prairie south of Burton, young Lawrence Schmidt chopped wood and hauled manure to the field for a one-armed neighbor for one dollar a day; Schmidt's father felt some responsibility for this man, who had severed his arm at the elbow in a Greenvine gin accident while processing the Schmidt family's cotton.[91] Thirds-and-fourths renter's son Johnnie Loud and his brothers did various "winter work" for their Fayette County neighbors, cutting and hauling loads of cordwood in their ox wagon and cutting and splitting cedar posts "by the hundreds." Loud's grandfather, who lived with them, had made rail fences and split-oak cotton baskets as winter work in decades past.[92] Other men, women, and children foraged for wild pecans along creek and river bottoms and sold their windfall to mercantile stores, which bought them for so many cents a pound.[93] In times past, other people's land had been "free range" for this sort of activity, but newspaper notices declaring individual farms off limits for pecan gathering, hunting, and general trespass were appearing with increasing frequency.[94]

Other part-time specialists offered their services in this agricultural slack time of early winter: blacksmiths, carpenters, stock doctors, chimney builders, well witchers and diggers, syrup makers, and moonshiners all plied their respective trades. Farm families tried to do everything for themselves that they could, but large-scale carpentry jobs, chimney building, well digging, and other tasks often were beyond their skills. Various neighbors specialized in these things part time and sometimes were hired. Brick-chimney building required considerable skill, and as one woman observed, "Everybody had to have a chimney."[95] Well digging (and water finding beforehand) also required special skills; not everyone felt comfortable working sixty feet down in a "dug well," either to dig it or clean it out, and most farmers believed these tasks to be too dangerous for their families to attempt. In many localities, the well digger and water-witch were one and the same. Traditions of water witching had been carried across from Germany and Czechoslovakia, as well as learned from Anglo- and African-American practitioners in Texas.[96]

Stock doctors also called on farmers who believed they needed outside help, though most men were like John Skrabanek and felt capable of curing their own mules of "the bots," "the colic," or whatever else ailed them. A properly administered Nehi soda-water bottle of strong medicine forced down the ailing animal's throat soon had Skrabanek's mules healthy, fat, and flatulent (the saying was, "a farting mule is a healthy mule"). Farmers like Skrabanek regarded these part-time "horse doctors" with some suspicion, and perhaps rightly so. A man in the Serbin community treated mules by walking around the afflicted animal several times, making the sign of the cross, praying for the beast in the name of the Father, Son, and Holy Ghost, then pulling on its tail.[97] A German farmer near La Grange, who had called in a black "horse doctor" to diagnose a "fractious" mule, soon found himself paying for a more general problem the specialist had discovered—magical objects supposedly buried around his farm by a vindictive neighbor, which the stock doctor helpfully located and neutralized for $25 each.

Two other sorts of rural specialists set up small processing sites at semipermanent locations in early winter and let the farming public come to them. Every little rural community supported one or more farmer–syrup makers to process their neighbors' yearly molasses. Very possibly, the same thing might be said about Fayette and Washington County whisky makers, though by necessity they were more secretive in their operations and never stood up to be counted by the U.S. Census taker.

Virtually every landowner family, and many renter families, raised a few rows of some kind of syrup cane. Families kept their own cane stocks across decades and generations, and syrup makers had to deal with many varieties of cane, each requiring slightly different processing. Eddie Wegner's family cut their cane with a sickle, used their gloved hands or special stripping sticks to strip it of leaves in the shade of a nearby oak, then hauled it four miles to the syrup mill of a man called Gonke, who cooked people's syrup for a portion of the finished product. At this operation, families pressed their own cane in a mule-powered syrup mill and strained the juice through a burlap strainer into barrels, then carried these to the cooking pan, where the experienced Gonke took over. Gonke poured the raw juice into one end of the compartmentalized cooking pan, cooked it, skimmed it, and supervised its gradual movement to the other end "where there was not so much fire." The Wegners relied on Gonke to get the syrup just right; syrup cooked too fast became scorched and tasted bitter, syrup cooked too slow often soured and spoiled. Syrup makers such as Gonke used all their senses to make sure nothing went wrong, noting the color and consistency of the syrup from time to time during processing, watching how it slid off the testing ladle, smelling it, and occasionally tasting it. The Wegners stored their syrup in wooden kegs in their basement. These had swing spigots, and when the Wegners needed syrup someone went downstairs and drew a pitcher.[98]

Otto Fuchs's family near Carmine raised cane in much the same way and, like the Wegner family, could choose among several nearby syrup mills for processing. Syrup makers always were farmers, too, and processed people's syrup only as late fall and early winter sidelines. Dozens of ricks of people's cane stood around on wooden sleds surrounding the cane press and cookers in the Fuchs's favorite syrup mill at Carmine, and "since the pressing of a freshly stored stack was usually

FIGURE 9   Harvesting and stripping cane in a Fayette County
field adjacent to a cotton patch in flower. (Photograph by O. B.
Pokorny, courtesy of Kermit W. Fox, M.D., Austin)

delayed by days, cane straw was liberally used to shelter these yet
unpressed stalks from drying out in the Texas summer sun."[99]

The Hoermann, Ebner, and Frenzel families all operated syrup
mills within wagoning distances of the Fuchs farm. After the untimely
death of Mr. Hoermann, his family continued to raise cotton but

increasingly specialized in syrup making for the Carmine community. They raised cane on their own farm, and occasionally sold it in fifty-gallon barrels to stores, but spent most of their time making syrup for neighbors.[100] Edwin Ebner's family near Round Top did much the same, alternating syrup making with cotton picking until just before Christmas, when all the cotton had been "scrapped" and all the cane "cooked off." Many people brought their cane to the Ebners, some of them in ox wagons, and the Ebners processed cane to syrup at a standard rate of thirteen cents a gallon. The Ebners' syrup mill was close to their house, which made it easy for the family to move back and forth between farmhouse, mill, and fields.[101] The Ebner family made syrup the old way, but some miles away at Walhalla, Alfred Frenzel's syrup operation had modernized beyond mule power and wood combustion. Frenzel's cane mill ran off a Model T engine and his juice cooked over a butane fire. Processing over four thousand gallons of syrup in some years, Frenzel did mostly "customer work" for local farmers at twenty cents a gallon or a toll of two-fifths of the finished syrup. Ricks of cane on wooden sleds, each one numbered, littered Frenzel's farmyard at the height of the syrup season. Many sorts of cane grew in the area, including "Texas ribbon cane," "oldtime gooseneck cane," "orange-top common cane," and "red-top common cane," and in season Frenzel saw them all.[102]

Whisky makers produced another desired commodity during this late fall of 1926. Fayette and Washington counties had been reluctant participants in the National Prohibition officially ushered in on January 1, 1919, and people's general sentiments about alcohol made local whisky men hard to catch and even harder to convict. The 1911 vote on a statewide constitutional amendment for prohibition called forth a huge Anti-Prohibition League picnic at La Grange, and the amendment, which narrowly lost statewide, went down seven to one in Fayette County. Before, during, and after National Prohibition,

FIGURE 10   Molasses-making time in Austin County, ca. 1910. Pictured is the family of Willie Wienke (center, with mustache and hat) by the syrup press and in front of the family gin near the New Bremen community. During the cotton off season, the gin house area was frequently used for the production of other commodities. (Winedale Historical Center Photo Collection, Winedale)

most local farm families made beer and wine for home consumption, and anyone who wanted whisky usually knew where to get some. Harold Matthies recalled a local man who made whisky in twenty-five gallon lots for sale in San Antonio, in this way paying off his farm, and Oliver Whitener and others reported encounters with stills, set up and running, in local woods.[103]

However, moonshining of more epic proportions went on at the black "independent quarter" of Mount Fall on the Washington County Bluffs during this winter of 1926. Ed Lathan vividly recalled the practice:

> Everybody round the country made liquor, that's right! Cooking whisky, homemade whiskey—they had more barrels and distilleries on branches and little thickets. And man, those folks get right out behind my smokehouse in the broad daytime and cook that liquor and sell it. And they had money in they pocket. They'd work a little cotton or a little corn, raise the hogs, had cows, chickens, turkeys. And they'd feed them turkeys and chickens on that mash.
>
> People over here made whisky for big white people, and they bootlegged it like the black folks, and lot of em drank it. The law wasn't prevalent, then. They'd get right out there in any kind of little thicket and set em up two, three barrels, and kick that liquor off, and take out there to Washington or Navasota and sell four, five gallons for three or four dollars a gallon. That's big money, you can buy yourself some groceries in them days. And that's the way lots of people survived and fed the kids.[104]

Elsewhere across the South during 1926, moonshiners increasingly used dubious speed-up methods involving excessive sugar in their mash, "thumper" kegs to produce strong whisky in a single "run," and even chemical additives such as lye or battery acid, but Mount Fall moonshiners remained true to tradition. They put corn chops, water, and yeast in barrels, fermented it until "ripe," distilled this "mash" in copper-pot stills to produce first-run whisky ("blucher"), then cleaned out their stills and ran the whisky again. This time it came out 180 to 190 proof—"hot whisky," some called it—ready for diluting with spring water, tinting brown with a little scorched sugar "to make it look like old-time whisky," and selling in town.[105] This classic "double-run" method dated back to family "pot distilleries" of the sixteenth-century Scottish Highlands.[106]

Ed Lathan got his details on Mount Fall moonshining by word of mouth and close observation of neighbors, not by direct participation. Lathan's trade was corn and cotton farming, and he followed mules down rows on upland fields for over sixty years. As time for bedding up approached in the winter of 1926, many men across the old counties along the Brazos and Colorado readied plows, harness, and work stock for the first tasks of next year's crop cycle—"knocking stalks," spreading barnyard manure, and plowing the fields into new rows in preparation for spring planting. A few tractors broke the land in 1926, but not many. Most area farmers were die-hard horse and mule men and would remain so for a generation.

Some of Ed Lathan's earliest and most pleasant memories involved work animals. "I always did love stock, horses and mules and things," he said. Woodcutters often cut oak cordwood for steam gins across the road from Lathan's home when he was a boy, and he heard them "hollering at mules and popping their whips and whooping and hollering, they getting that wood out there with them wagons hauling it to the ginhouse to get up steam to gin cotton." These men "specialized to drive four mules with them big old long wagons, and they'd be out there hollerin. Man, they's happy as larks. Might be raining, but they singing or poppin them mules. And I'd try to mock em, I'd be at home, I'd get up in my Daddy's wagon, have a rope tied to the end of the tongue, little boy just shouting!" Lathan's mother told him on one of these occasions, "You never will be worth nothing, you like horses and mules too well."[107]

A lot of people shared Lathan's love of work stock in 1926 and to a person could give detailed descriptions of every animal they had ever plowed behind, ridden, or driven—ox, horse, or mule—from childhood to the present. Farmers and work stock grew intimate over long hours and close associations in the field, and they walked many miles together. According to Robert Wilhelmsen's estimation, every crop season he and his father and the family work stock logged over seven hundred miles up and down the rows of the family's twenty-acre cotton field.[108]

Farmers knew work stock and felt comfortable using them, but to Robert Wilhelmsen's father, Otto Fuchs, Ed Lathan, and others, hard economic calculations entered in to their decisions to stick with mules and horses. Tractors were costly, often required the family to go into debt, and seemed technologically inappropriate for hundred-acre cotton farms. Unlike tractors, mules helped grow their own "gasoline" in the form of corn, and penned in the lot at night, they recycled the corn as manure for the fields. Sterile hybrids, mules did not reproduce themselves, but most mule farmers kept a mare or two around for periodic breeding to someone's donkey "jack" to create replacement work mules, another trick tractors could not duplicate.

Most area farm families owned both horses and mules. Normally, families thought they needed a riding horse, a buggy horse, and two to four good field stock for a basic complement of work animals. Even among the zealous mule fanciers, few people chose to ride mules or use them to pull buggies, since they traveled too slowly and presented an inappropriate public image. The proper place for showing off the family's matched team of fat and shiny work mules was on the wagon. Poorer people made do with what they had for transportation, despite appearances; Howard Matthies recalled one Flat Prairie farm family that came to town pulled by the only stock it owned, a sorry-looking mule and the family milk cow.[109]

Partly by purchase, partly by selective breeding, farmers tried to match their work stock to their needs. If they wanted a fast-stepping buggy horse, they bred their mare to a stud horse of these traits; if they wanted a work mule, they bred her to a jack, perhaps the famous "Aggie jack," whose services were provided at five dollars a contact by Texas A&M College. Farms on different soils called for different work stock. A pair of small 600-pound mules might be all a farmer needed on an easy-to-plow sandy-land farm, while another farmer on the dense "black waxy" a few miles away needed big Missouri "cotton mules" of 1,000 to 1,100 pounds, bred from large jacks and 1,300-pound Percheron mares. When a farmer changed farms, he often changed work stock as well; work stock needed to match your "place." When your mare gave birth to a new mule colt, you already could estimate how big it would become. Farmers measured "hands from the hoof to the knee" then multiplied that by three to calculate "how many hands high" for the adult animal.[110]

Work stock chosen from a family's available animals also needed to match the task at hand, and, if more than one were used, they needed to match each other. A light, fast task, such as stalk cutting, went better with faster animals, whereas deep, slow plowing into rows with a "lister buster" required power over speed. Some animals pulled heavily loaded wagons without a murmur, others refused to pull them even when nearly beaten to death. Ideally, the team chosen for a particular task matched the needs of the task; matched each other in size, speed, strength, and disposition; and also matched the plow person. "Plowing with mules wasn't like just turning a key," one man explained, it included a lot of intangibles tractor operation did not involve, as well as companionship in the field. A slow animal beside a fast one might require the plowman to place the slower of the two on his good right hand side so he could "punch him up" and "feed him some gas" by judicious administration of a stick.[111] A big animal beside a small one required a lot of adjustments to doubletree, singletrees, and harness for both to pull their share of the load. Animals well matched for speed, size, and strength still might not work well together because they did not like each other. Eddie Wegner's "Spanish mule" Jeff had an obnoxious habit of rocking from side to side when stopped that Wegner's other work mules found intolerable.[112] Furthermore, many work stock, especially mules, played favorites, working well and obediently for one person while balking and misbehaving for another. Mance Lipscomb's mule Caesar, for example, worked well only for him, and tried to bite or kick anyone else who came near.[113]

Mules (and horses or oxen) had individual personalities, as Robert Skrabanek well described:

> In some ways our mules were like people. Some would lead, while others would follow. Some would balk and shirk, but others would overdo. One or two would dominate the rest, driving them away from the feed, water tank, or salt block. Some would kick and nip, but others had such friendly dispositions that even a small child could walk around or under them with the greatest of ease. It did not take long to find out what type a new mule would be, and we quickly learned how to behave around her.[114]

For a variety of reasons, purchasing or trading for new work stock, which all farm families periodically had to do, remained fraught with peril. "Let the buyer beware" held true with a vengeance in stock deals, and few farmers escaped an occasional bad purchase. Everybody knew stock, but you could not always examine an animal up for sale or trade and detect its invisible behavioral flaws, nor could you exactly trust your eyes; mule and horse traders had tricks beyond the ken of ordinary farmers. In Grover Williams's opinion, his grandfather was "shafted all the time" in stock transactions with certain Burton mule men. Old "smooth mouthed" mules might have their teeth altered with files and hot irons so as to pass for much younger animals. Caved-in spots in old used-up animals might be injected with something to fill them out and make the animals appear young and muscular. Lethargic animals might be stimulated to spirited new life by "doping" or by irritating substances placed behind their hooves or inside their anuses. Cautionary tales abounded. Albert Wilhelmsen's father purchased a nice-looking horse from a dealer after first trying it out by pulling a half-cord of stove wood, but "three weeks after that, that horse wouldn't pull your hat off your head."[115]

Even the shrewdest stock purchaser often could not detect an animal's invisible behavioral flaws: one mule hated bedder plows, often kicking at them as they lay in the field; a second had been used only to go round and round at a syrup mill and so became uncontrollable at the end of every crop row; a third proved an incorrigible escape artist—until the night he skewered himself trying to jump out of a cedar-pole pen. One man sold a neighbor a milk cow without telling him of her one fault, which the purchaser discovered after the cow attacked his wife and nursing infant on their front porch; the cow loathed children and tried to kill them at every opportunity.[116]

The farmer obtained new work stock from neighbors, part-time dealers, traveling "road traders," sale barns in town, or occasional auctions held by big-time stock men down from Fort Worth, but all deals were buyer beware. Stock entrepreneur Ray Lum from Mississippi had his Texas agents set up periodic auction sales in Brenham, Navasota, and La Grange, then came down to auction off the animals. People thought Ray Lum was an honest man—for a mule dealer—but farmers at his auctions had better listen close. Lum "telegraphed" the hidden defects of the stock he sold, but listeners needed to know the code: "one lamp burning" meant blind in one eye, "hitting on three" meant a bad leg, "giraffe" meant a too-tall, too-lanky horse, "snide skin" implied an

FIGURE II   Round Top area farmer plowing with a team of oxen,
ca. 1890. (The Institute of Texan Cultures, San Antonio, courtesy
Mr. and Mrs. E. W. Ahlrich)

unspecified, hidden defect, and "stumpsucker" meant a nervous addiction to chewing on wood.[117]

Young Ed Lathan was a mule man, but on cold mornings he could hear "old man Washington Reese" go into action with his ox Old Tom as the big animal began to plow. Mule and horse handlers used reins and hard work bits (sometimes wound with barbed wire) and silent mind control, but "bull punchers" operated entirely differently. Punchers looped one rope casually around the horn of the control ox but chiefly directed their animals by voice commands. Ox handlers almost constantly sang, shouted, and hollered at the yoked oxen and could be heard for long distances.

Ox teams were anachronisms by 1926, but some farmers still swore by them. Henry Jaeger's grandfather came over from Germany as an ox man, and—like many first generation European immigrants—only belatedly converted to the use of horses and mules.[118] Harriet Smith, Edna Ebner, Johnnie Loud, and Earnest Hancock all grew up using

oxen and liked them well enough.[119] Oxen were slow, placid of disposition, enormously strong, and to a degree unpredictable. Johnnie Loud's
family transported winter cordwood with oxen, and they could pull
heavily loaded wagons through mud so deep "the axles be on the
ground, grazing the ground, no mules could pull that." Sometimes the
Louds' yoke of oxen pulled a cord and a half of "green cord wood" at
once—a huge load. "They's one of em, he was run as a bull a long time
before they castrated him, finally made a work ox out of him. We load
him up so, and you couldn't stall him. He'd get on his knees, and when
he got on his knees something was coming!"[120]

Several-yoke ox teams had been used to transport cotton in the early
days, and Henry Fuchs's father had seen big wagons on the roads in
Fort Bend County. Bull punchers rode on horses beside these five-yoke
teams pulling huge wagons of cotton or cottonseed. They constantly
popped the whips and shouted, but rarely hit the oxen, who labored on
their way under verbal control. The teamsters rode beside the wagon
on a kind of bull-puncher pony-path that ran alongside the road. On
one occasion, a young man replaced the regular driver on one of the big
seed wagons, "and the second load of cottonseed they never could get
up to that railroad car with those oxen, because he didn't know how to
maneuver em. And I never did figure that out, how in the world they
maneuver any kind of oxen."[121]

Plowing a field with a single yoke of oxen was an easier task, but all
agreed with Earnest Hancock that you had to keep the animals' water
needs in mind. "They'll work well until about 11:30, but now when they
want some water, you better take em and let em go get some. Cause,
you don't, they gonna carry you and the plow and all and go get it. You
can't hold em when they get thirsty. You got to always keep that in your
mind."[122] In truth, oxen could be discipline problems. Once, Howard
Matthies's grandfather was hauling stove wood in the hot summer
when his ox team suddenly "turned off the road and went down to the
waterhole with that wagon." Grandfather Matthies's oxen were named
"Old Red" and "Old Blue," and "when they wouldn't control, he'd go up
there and cut a piece of their ear off with a pocketknife."[123]

Drastic measures sometimes were resorted to by horse and mule
men, as well, but most farms had both animals, and many farmers
expressed a strong preference for mules as plow stock. Big Clydesdale-
style draft horses had been in vogue for a decade or so around the turn

of the century, but these tended to overheat in the hot Texas summers, and many farmers came to agree with Howard Matthies's father that "they stomped more dirt tight than they plowed loose."[124] Two big draft horses could pull a heavy double-mouldboard bedder plow, a job usually requiring four mules, but such animals had feet the size of dinner plates and could be destructive. As Johnnie Loud told, "Them big old foots! They step on somethin, it's gone! If they step on a plant, it's gone, cause it twist all to pieces and crumble it up, them big old wide feet."[125] Conversely, some people farming the heaviest, stickiest blackland soils still favored work horses with a good bit of draft horse in them, since the "big old foots" did not sink into the mud so far.

Mules were different—and better, most farmers thought. They had small, neat feet and picked them up carefully as they turned around at the end of a row. Mules were more intelligent than horses, much easier to train, and possessed "hybrid vigor." They lived perhaps ten years longer than a horse, stood the heat better, ate less (and more carefully), and less frequently got sick. Furthermore, as Howard Davis explained, "Lots of people can't work a horse. They'll balk with you, they're tender, a whole lot of em don't like to be worked."[126] Horses that would work often rushed at a task and wore themselves out, mules conserved energy and stayed the course. A hot mule took its time turning around at the end of the rows, the better to cool off; an overheated horse might keep on at full speed until it dropped dead of heatstroke. Mules did not injure themselves as horses would: if the load seemed too heavy, they refused to pull it; they did not fight each other as often as horses; and if they ran away they avoided hurting themselves. One man had a team of mules hitched up with a saddle mare that ran away a mile and hung up on a fence. The man found his mare frantic, kicking, and trying to get loose but his mules standing "still as a cat stood."[127]

Many people agreed with Robert Wilhelmsen, who noted: "With plowing, I'd rather plow mules. They have a good transmission, they have one speed. That mule would just plow right along." After Wilhelmsen made about three rounds of the field with the cultivator, his father's "Spanish mules" went on automatic. "You'd make about three rounds, then you could tie the lines around em and just talk to em."[128] The Wilhelmsens also had several horses, but farmers such as John Skrabanek so favored mules that they refused to keep horses on their places. In Robert Skrabanek's growing-up years, his father owned only one horse, a mare taken in trade from a local Anglo-American, and he kept her just long enough to use her for the only purpose he thought she was good for, breeding to a jack to make a mule.[129]

Skrabanek kept three teams of mules, Emma and Marry, a matched team of off-white mules that were his favorites, a second team of smaller, grayish mules named Tobe and Mabel, and a third, more-troublesome team named Kate and Jack. Emma and Marry were Skrabanek's show-off, go-to-town mules—handsome, well-cared-for animals with special decorative harnesses that the other teams did not have. Kate, one of the troublesome team opposed John Skrabanek from time to time by disobeying, balking, plowing a crooked furrow, or otherwise exercising her contrary nature, and the contest of wills between man and beast went on as long as Kate lived. Robert Skrabanek often heard his father cursing Kate in the field in pungent Czech, a language well suited for this purpose, and from time to time he observed some discreet mule beating. Robert's mother criticized her husband after these episodes, and John expressed regret but noted "that damn mule makes me so mad I want to kill her, I'm going to break her of her meanness if it kills me."[130]

Sometimes farmers won out in confrontations with recalcitrant work stock, and sometimes they didn't. Robert Wilhelmsen's father kept a length of heavy railroad rail around for disciplining an animal by forcing it to pull the heavy object around the field for an hour or so to "get his attention," and Howard Davis's father sometimes did this in a more drastic way. When one of the family's big cotton mules refused to pull a heavy wagon, Davis "knocked him down with a club, then he pulled."[131] Eddie Wegner had a neighbor whose mule balked in the field, and the usual remedies—putting sand in his mouth, beating him with a stick, lighting a broom weed fire under his belly—did not work. The mule avoided the fire by walking a few feet forward, then balked again. Furious, the neighbor "went to the house and got a good-sized fence post and a drop auger, dug a hole right beside the mule, put the post in, and tied the mule to that post—left that old balking mule stand there in the field all day." At sundown, the man unhitched the mule, hooked him back up, and made him plow a few rounds of the field to show him who was boss.[132]

Howard Davis, however, never won out over one black workhorse he owned. Harold recalled:

> I was gonna make him pull [a wagon] when I first got him. I said, "I'll make you pull or I'll kill you, one." I didn't have five hundred pounds of hay in that wagon, and he just stopped. I beat him with a pole over in the field there until I nearly killed him, but I didn't—I never did make him pull. He broke my lines and singletree, too, just tore up everything. I had to take him to the house and turn him loose and go to town and buy a pair of lines that cooter done tore up. I was gonna make him pull, but I didn't. I didn't make that horse do nothing, ever."

Thereafter, this stubborn black horse never pulled a wagon, and to get him to plow in a team Davis had to give him special consideration every time he used him.

> I had to kiss his butt. If he balked, you'd say, "Whoa," get off your plow and go around there and shake the collar around, move the bridle around on him and take your plow out of line a little bit and clean it off where it'd be a little easier pulled. Then, put it back round but don't put it back in too deep to start off. You had do it right or you didn't plow no more that day.

This black horse was Howard Davis's strongest work animal, so he had to use him, but some days he got so mad that he nearly "took that horse out of that plow, take him over to that river, and I'd have got him right close to that high bluff, and I'd of cut his throat with my pocket knife, and I'd have rolled him in that river!"[133]

From time to time, John Skrabanek also grew furious at his stubborn mule Kate, but the day she was found dead in the field his eyes "watered up a bit" and he avowed in a hoarse voice that she "was a real strong mule, even if she was stubborn, and there was not any load she couldn't pull if she put her mind to it."[134] Though they might fight battles to the death with them, Skrabanek, Davis, and most other farmers of their generation were like Ed Lathan; they "loved stock." By this winter of 1926, Texas mules approached their all-time high of just over one million animals.[135]

As farmers went about their work, they watched the skies for rain, monitored the dryness of the various soils on their farms, and readied work stock and harness for bedding up—"putting the land on rows," the first act of the next crop season. Ideally, this would be accomplished before Christmas so that barnyard manure and corn and cotton stalks turned under in the fields had plenty of time to rot before spring plowing and planting time arrived. Many believed the best crop years came after this bedding up had been accomplished early and there had been plenty of time to get "winter on the land."[136] Already, however, the play of weather determined timing of activities, especially for the blackland farmers. Farmers on firm and well-drained sandy lands usually could get into their fields to plow no matter how much rain fell; farmers on the blacklands needed their soils to be just right—not too dry, not too wet—conditions that farmers joked sometimes occurred only during their dinner hours. Slow to drain "black waxy" soils in rainy periods often became hopelessly waterlogged, perhaps even shaking like jelly when teams or tractors passed over them. Nineteenth-century farmers on the blacklands sometimes had run rows up and down the hillsides to promote faster drying of their sticky soils, despite the erosional damage this did to the land. By 1926 a lot of blackland soils clogged the creeks, and most had repented of this destructive practice. ("You know, I ruint a lot of good land," Albert Wilhelmsen's uncle often remarked in his old age.)[137]

Stalk cutting came first, then manuring, then bedding up. Most farmers used one-or two-row stalk cutters to shred last year's corn and cotton stalks. Pulled rapidly across the field by paired work stock, stalk cutters looked like heavy-duty, riding versions of the old-style "push mowers" used to cut lawns, and agricultural historian Samuel Evans has well described their use.

> The cutting apparatus consisted of a revolving drum, or frame, to the outside, to which were affixed several sharp blades, or knives, detachable for sharpening. The frame could be raised or lowered by a lever arrangement. In operation the machine was driven astraddle the cotton row, the frame was lowered so that the weight of the implement and the operator pressed the knives into the earth, and their revolutions cut and broke the standing stalk into small pieces.[138]

However, in stalk cutting as in everything else, older techniques per-sisted beside newer ones in the old counties along the Brazos and Colorado, as farmers adjusted their farming practices to soils, field con-tours, and the depth of their pocketbooks. While state-of-the-art, two-row, riding stalk cutters swiftly progressed across some fields, farmers a few miles away "knocked stalks" with clubs by hand in medieval fash-ion or pulled heavy limbs down their old rows to flatten the stalks. Robert Wilhelmsen's father cut stalks on his family's hill farm with a special rotating stalk cutter of his own design, weighted down by rail-road iron. Riding implements did not work well on the family's up-and-down fields, but this heavy walking stalk cutter did the job. Some miles away on the fertile bottomlands along the Brazos, no rotating cutter worked, and stalk cutting required more improvisation. Cotton plants sometimes grew eight-feet high in the Brazos bottom, with basal stalks "thick as a man's arm." Special steel-tipped, "two-row slides" cut Brazos valley cotton stalks, and "you had to keep them things real sharp." As Skeeter Stolz told, after the stalks had been cut with the slides, farm-ers raked them into rows with two-mule rakes, allowed them to dry, then burned them at night: "Used to see that all over them places, just fire everywhere at night."[139]

After stalk cutting came manuring of the fields, and most farmers of Fayette and Washington counties manured their fields as zealously and precisely as they did everything else. Few area families depended on commercial fertilizer. Most people penned work stock and milk cows each night in barns, stables, and "lots" not for protection, but to con-centrate their manure, then spread that manure on the fields with mule-pulled manure spreaders or wagons and shovels. Robert Wilhelmsen's mules often pulled a wagon full of manure across the field, taking voice commands from Robert as they went while he stood knee-deep in dung in the back of the wagon shoveling it out. Wilhelmsen well knew the spots in the field that needed manure the most, and others had a similarly precise knowledge of their soils. Henry Jaeger's family put manure on their blacklands and the ashes from twenty-five cords of wood used in fall syrup making on their sandy lands, which, in their judgment, needed potash and not dung. A meticulousness and precision typified these operations, as so many others. Kermit Fox noted of his parents, "They would strive that crops be hoed clean, that rows be plowed straight, that fences be strung taut, that turnrows be free of weeds, that floors be scrubbed pale-clean; and this list could go on and on."[140]

After stalk chopping and manuring came putting the land into rows—plowing the fields for bedding up—and here as elsewhere Texas farmers' practices varied with soils, equipages, available work stock, and family traditions. Writing in 1898, cotton expert C. P. Brooks had noted the variety of agricultural practices among Southern cotton farmers, variations caused by cotton farming's 1,300-mile range of operations, soil differences, the different lengths of growing seasons, and the "many systems of farming born of dissimilar training and traditions of the farmer."[141] Nevertheless, and despite at least one important variation on the general pattern, by 1926 most area farmers broke the land to make beds in early winter with the big lister-buster plow, or bedder.

Farmers monitored the sky and soil, and on a given day in late November rose early to harness four mules or horses to the bedder and move to the edge of last year's field. Normally, the former cornfield— this season's cotton field—had gotten "in the weeds" the most and needed attention first. As winter light grew across the land, the farmer made his last fine adjustments to the harness and the four singletrees, two doubletrees, and the "evener" linking the four animals to the massive metal-shanked plow stock, with its symmetrical double-curved blade. The farmer carefully wrapped the plowlines from each pair of animals around his left and right arms, firmly grasped the wooden plow handles, and told the waiting team to "Get up." Muscles bunching, the four big animals moved forward in unison, the sharp plowshare knifed into the ground and began to make the almost indescribable sound of sharp metal powerfully slicing through earth, and two waves of soil rolled sideways in opposite directions from the moving plow. The team walked four old "middles," water furrows from last year's field, while plow and plowman cleft the first of last year's old rows like Moses parting the Red Sea. Running ten inches to a foot deep, the heavy lister plowshare coursed powerfully through the center of the old row, throwing half of it one way and half the other, and leaving behind the first middle (water furrow) of this season's field.

The strain of pulling the large, deep-running, double-mouldboard plowshare immediately registered on the animals; their muscles bunched and flexed, and their breathing labored. As Grover Williams recalled of his family's mules: "You really had to talk to them—you didn't whip them—we knew how to talk to them. They'd do what you wanted them to do, they'd bust a gut for you. When they were pulling, you could see those muscles in their legs, and the back-band was standing off the back. They was gonna bring you out or tear something up."[142]

Behind the team, the plowman concentrated on keeping his first "streak" across the field exactly straight and on taking on the thick, buried stumps of the old plants head on with the point of the plow. As he did, he felt the soil change across the field: here, a lighter sandy place where the plow picked up speed; there, a sticky, dense area where it slowed down and the animals strained. Running a bedder did not take a large amount of strength—if everything had been adjusted correctly, the plow animals worked well together, and the plowman knew exactly what he was doing. Otherwise, it could wear you out. Henry Fuchs described the process when it was working well: "When your point is sharp, in ordinary soil . . . you see, you got your four mules and your big evener, doubletree, and then two little doubletrees on that, it's heavy, and that beam is made for it, and it goes right on through. Your point had to be sharp, though; you can plow up cotton stalks and you can hear it pop at every stalk—'pop, pop, pop, pop, pop.'"[143] So tough were some of the cotton stalks, however, that the plowman felt his sharp plow point, powered by four work animals weighing a thousand pounds each, deflect slightly as it cut through the stalks. As Howard Matthies noted, "When it was rough and the cotton stalks tough and green, you had to spit in your hands, sometimes, to hold that thing."[144] But the real test of the plowman's skill came at the end of the row, as he maneuvered four animals with four sets of plow lines in a tight 180-degree turn to line up to bust the next last-year's row. Running a light one-mule plow up crop middles to cultivate was one thing; this was quite another. Lined up once again, the four animals entered the four old middles and the lister buster headed back in the direction it had come, again taking on an old row and throwing half of it one way and half the other. This time, the pass across the field "finished off" the first new bed of this year's field on one side, as it threw half of the next new bed to the "landside," as before.

Throughout this long day and the ones after it, with occasional rests for the work animals, bedding of the fields went on. Albert Wilhelmsen observed, "You worked from when the sun come up till the sun went down, you didn't look at your watch."[145] In the silence of these long, lonely days in the field, plowmen sometimes sang, prayed, talked to themselves, or "shouted"—uttered loud, melodious, wordless work cries that could be heard for long distances. Blackland farmers in particular always plowed with a certain urgency, since the job had to be done, winter days were short, and they did not know when the next rain would come to again lock them out of the fields. As the bedder went back and forth dividing last year's rows, this year's rows formed up exactly where last year's water furrows had been, moving precisely one half row to the right or left. In the simplest practice, followed by many, farmers bedded up their fields in the way described above in the late winter, left buried stalks and manure to rot for two or three months, "rebedded" the field in exactly the same fashion in the spring, then immediately planted cotton and corn in the top of the new beds. Beds were needed to keep seed from rotting in wet periods, to give at least ten inches of loose soil under the new cotton and corn plants so their roots could go down easily, and to provide the young plants maximum exposure to the warming rays of the sun.

Not all farmers possessed the animal resources to run a lister buster, however, and a second method of bedding up, "two furrowing," was almost as common. It required three passes across the field to accomplish what the lister buster did in one pass but only half as much animal power. For two furrowing, two work stock pulled a "turning plow," a steel-shanked mouldboard plow that looked like a lister buster split in half. The turning plow cut deeply but threw soil only one way, usually to the right. To bed up with a turning plow, the plowman cut through the old row just to the right of the line of old stalks throwing half of the soil to the right, then he came back down the same row on the other side of the stalks doing the same thing. That left a "balk" up the center of the old row down the line of corn or cotton stalks, which then was taken out with a smaller version of the bedder called a "middle buster." Pulled by two animals, the middle buster plowshare threw soil both ways, lowering the middle to its final depth and completing the new rows on each side. As with the bedder, double furrowing moved the new rows one half row to the right or left.

Beyond the relative simplicities of bedding up by lister busting or double furrowing lay much individual variation in plowing practices. Farmers had their own ideas about how to farm—their individual family traditions, different equipment, and particular work stock. Some people plowed the old middles with sweep stocks, shallow-running plowshares that moved some dirt to either side but mostly just loosened the soil, then bedded up with lister busters or turning plows in the usual way. This resulted in the new beds being formed over the old, deeply loosened middles—"soft bedding," farmers called it, believing that it particularly helped out the young corn. Many farmers "flat broke" their fields with turning plows or disk plows in the fall, then lister busted or double furrowed it into rows in the usual way in the spring. A plowman flat broke a field by working in from its perimeter in a rectangular pattern, always moving in toward the unbroken landside in the center. This could be done with a turning plow or the newer double- or triple-disk plow to create a level, broken-up surface ready for bedding up at planting time. Farmers flat broke their field in late winter because they believed this did a better job of burying stalks and manure, because they had a weed problem and thought this suppressed weeds better, and for assorted other reasons. There were manuals for how to farm in 1926, but few read them, and "book farmer" was a term of contempt. Eccentricities abounded, as in the case of the man Howard Davis knew who always planted his corn in the water furrows, and no farmer hazarded to tell another how to go about his business.

In bedding up, as in stalk cutting and other stages of the crop cycle, old ways and new ways long coexisted. One man near Round Top listerbusted his land into beds with a new Fordson Tractor in 1919, while his black renter a field away whooped and shouted at a single ox pulling an obsolete, wooden-shafted, Dixie Boy plow. The one-animal wooden-beam plows required up to eight trips across the field to accomplish what a lister buster plow—animal- or tractor-powered—accomplished in one. In fact, bedding up was so much trouble for one-mule farmers that they often just bolted small turning plowshares on their light wooden plow stocks, ran up each side of the old row a couple of times throwing dirt to the row, then let it go at that. The old rows remained in the same place year after year. Farther east, in East Texas and the Deep South, many farmers still plowed like this in 1926, although such practices had been criticized as inefficient for half a century.

A few families did not bother to bed up in the winter at all, waiting until just before planting time to get their rows ready, although most area farmers regarded this practice as contemptibly slothful. More common were individuals who, like Otto Fuchs and John Skrabanek, went to the other extreme in diligent land preparations for next year. When scattered "winter weeds"—harmless things, most believed—sprouted in Skrabanek's immaculately bedded fields in deep winter, he could not stand it and sent the family work force out to chop them down.

The necessities of late cotton picking, various winter chores, and bedding up often kept children out of the rural schools until sometime between Thanksgiving and Christmas. Plowboys, and the occasional plowgirl, began early. Albert Wilhelmsen recalled: "I never was tall. Neighbors'd say, they couldn't see us behind the plow, but they would hear us. Wasn't but kids, you know."[146] Older sons might inherit the farm in the end, but in the meantime they paid the price, often starting school latest in the fall and dropping out earliest in the spring. A deep prejudice existed against female plow hands, since their presence behind the mules revealed to neighbors a family that did not possess adequate manhood even to break its own land. However, sometimes families were so deficient in boys that girls had to "be made the boy." In East Texas, this happened to Evarilla Harrell and Susie Davidson, who both soon discovered that they rather liked to plow and do other heavy fieldwork.[147] Lydia Domasch, who grew up near Warda in Fayette County, not only became her family's designated boy but had to do women's work, as well. She experienced the loss of education that many older sons reported:

> I didn't get much schooling. More than half the time I had to work with my father at the river bottom because there were not enough men. My brother got more schooling than I did. I was fourteen years old when I started plowing with four mules at the river bottom with a disk. Also, I had to fix lunch and bake bread the night before. In the morning we had a mile and a half to walk to the field. When I came home from the field, I had to pick up the eggs in the dark.[148]

Many former students of rural schools told similar stories. These schools scheduled opening and closing dates not just for the average cotton cycle, but for the particular season's cotton cycle. In the bad drought year of 1925, schools started several weeks early; in the following good year, with a lot of cotton to pick, they started two or three weeks late. Despite these adjustments, many parents often felt they needed to keep their children out of school to help with the farming; family economic survival took precedence over education. Georgia Lee Wade explained:

> We would go enroll [in September] and get those books. And then we couldn't go back to school no more till that cotton is picked. When you finished picking cotton, long about maybe the middle of November, then we would go to school every day until about March. And when March come, well, you started to planting corn and cotton and we'd be in and out of school. We would have to go to the field and plant that cotton and corn, and then go back to school until it got up, for time to be chopped."[149]

Ed Lathan's Mount Fall School was just down the road from his house, but he had the same problem. "Dry days, I didn't have a chance to go to school, I had to be in the field working with my folks. It rain, [they'd say], 'Get ready for school, boys, we can't work in the field.' I went in the school, but right in the main pinch of time, I might have to stay out of school two, three days every week."[150]

African-Americans, Germans, and Czechs—nearly all rural scholars faced the same difficulties. Oldest son Herbert Wegner's school career concluded much earlier than his younger brothers', who later went on to college.[151] Mance Lipscomb's school days ended at age eleven as "a third grade scholar" when his oldest brother Charlie turned eighteen and left home. This sharecropper family had to have a male plowman, as Mance explained: "Papa had done run off, and I had to answer for a man's place. That's why mother put me out in the field. How I'm gonna go to school when I be out there plowing and chopping cotton, picking cotton, hoeing weeds and things? I was doing a man's job when I was eleven years old."[152]

Most struggled to get all the education they could. James Wade recalled that many children persisted in attending school, despite frequent absences and slow progress due to the demands of cotton farming. "I know when I started to school, it was plenty boys and girls going to school eighteen and nineteen and twenty years old. Be still going to school."[153]

After the fields lay neatly in rows in this early winter of 1926, thousands of other rural students in Washington and Fayette counties

FIGURE 12 Teacher and pupils at the one-room Hill School west of Round Top, Fayette County. Schools like this were once common in rural areas, serving as focal points for dispersed farming communities. (Mrs. Lorenz Kiel, Warrenton)

began to walk footpaths and rural roads to one-, two-, and three-room rural schools. Roads might be preferred, but beeline trails across the countryside often provided the shortest routes to school, and distance traveled was critical, especially for those children whose farms lay on the peripheries of their common school districts. Kermit Fox recalled that "It was common to see rag-wrapped barbed wire sections here and there where students regularly crawled over the fence." In rain and mudtime, these almost recreational treks across the countryside turned unpleasant, and children regularly showed up at school "soaked to knee level," or worse.[154] However, according to Grover Williams, the short-cuts were still taken, even in the dark: "During that time, we knew every trail. Day or night, you could come home. At night when you couldn't see, you had to follow the trail with your feet, old cow trails and stuff, cutting through those woods. We took shortcuts, and we walked it every morning and walked back in the evening."[155] Roy Schmidt's parents processed his horny, callused, field-hardened feet each fall for shoe-wearing and school-trail-walking by soaking them in hot water and scraping them with a knife "like you scraping a hog."[156] Lawrence Schmidt had such a long trek to his Greenvine School that all the jelly in his standard jelly sandwich usually percolated through his mother's porous bread down to the bottom of the lard-can lunch bucket and had to be "sopped up" at noontime.[157]

To facilitate student pedestrians, a maze of rural common school districts, each usually with its "white" and "colored" school, were scattered across the Fayette and Washington County countrysides—one of the most basic elements of the infrastructure of this rural world. Elected, three-person school boards administered each district, and county school superintendents supervised them—after a fashion— from distant Brenham and La Grange. Because of the large number of schools and the condition of the roads, many a country school never saw its county superintendent from one year to the next. Washington County had 46 common school districts containing 116 school buildings, and larger Fayette County had 82 districts with 157 buildings.[158] Although a fortunate few rode ponies or plow horses to their rural schools, most students walked, and parents generally believed that five miles out and five miles back each day was about the maximum. Wherever the school building was placed in its district, the location favored some children and disadvantaged others, and the question of "moving the school" periodically resurfaced as the most volatile political issue in district school board elections.[159]

When students arrived at their rural schools each morning, they found unprepossessing wooden buildings. Leola Tiedt tersely described the many rural schools she attended and taught in: "They all looked like the same—built about like a barn, with a few windows on each side, house windows. And when it got dark, you couldn't see; there wasn't any way of reading or anything."[160] Likewise, Kermit Fox's description of his one-room La Bahia School typified many. Sporting a fading coat of white paint (a grace note many did not have), La Bahia School was a long rectangular building with no vestibule, cloakroom, or hallway. Inside, there were shelves on the walls and hooks and nails for students' coats and hats, but only one cabinet. Large windows let in light on each side. Desks were arranged in six rows, girls on one side of the room, boys on the other, little kids sat up front in the small desks, big kids sat to the rear.[161]

A large, jacketed wood stove, focus of all things in winter, stood in the middle aisle. Teachers often started a big pot of soup or stew cooking on the stove in early morning, to which students added contributions of sausage chunks or vegetables—this for a hot communal dish at noon lunchtime. On cold and wet days, according to Kermit Fox, the stoves provided both comfort and discomfort: "We were permitted to remove our muddy shoes and hover about the wood stove. Even sitting barefooted for a while to let the socks dry was a welcome relief. On the coldest days nothing could be done about those seated near the reddened stove almost scorching while those seated along the outer walls shivered."[162]

La Bahia School was fortunate in its teacher, the experienced H. C. Henninger, a veteran of several other rural schools. Henninger had the daily instruction of seven grades in several subjects down to a science, carefully timed by his pocket watch. At any one moment, two or three grades were up front at the "recitation bench" or the blackboard receiving direct instruction from Henninger, while the rest did seat work and prepared to go to the front.[163]

Those caught up with their seatwork and interested in some advanced instruction going on at the front of the room watched, listened, and learned. Older students in the upper grades often helped younger students in lower ones—the common peer instruction, which went on everywhere, and which nearly all teachers encouraged. Rural schools offered excellent basic instruction in English and math, many believed, and in the old counties along the Brazos and Colorado they effectively turned German- and Czech-speaking children into reasonably fluent English speakers by the end of the first year. If children could attend them with sufficient frequency (rather a large "if" in this agricultural world), rural schools often worked very well. Three years before this winter of 1926–1927, the massive Texas School Survey of 1924 firmly had established this fact—much to the dismay of consolidationist administrators sponsoring the study at the Texas State Board of Education.[164]

Discipline problems seldom troubled H. C. Henninger or most rural school teachers, although Kermit Fox recalled one occasion "when the mark of [Henninger's] temper was left near the north pole of our world globe, the crater in the paper mache matching our teacher's fist."[165] Rural schools were small, close-knit, family-like settings in which teachers were respected, older students helped keep younger ones under control, and "a whipping at school meant a whipping at home." Leola Tiedt perhaps had been a discipline problem for some of her teachers, but after she became a teacher herself, few dared to challenge her. Possessing a naturally authoritarian manner, Tiedt presided over her Fayette County classes in 1927 with near effortless control. An ordinary rule violator might receive what students called "the Tiedt torture," a sharp upward pull on the sideburns after a stealthy approach from behind, and occasionally more serious punishments might be arranged. Two boys, who persisted in spitting on each other, finally were marched into the cloakroom by Tiedt and forced to spit on the wall, periodically remoistening their mouths from a water bucket, for one full hour, then to clean the mess up.[166] Grover Williams's teacher, "Professor" Daniel Thomas, had similar excellent control, though he sometimes administered punishments with a switch. At the dreaded command, "go out and cut me some thorns," a student went outside the school and selected a sturdy switch from a nearby thorn bush, brought it to Thomas, and then watched as the teacher methodically trimmed off thorns—hopefully, all of them—with his pocket knife. Then, "He'd trim them and line you up there. And he'd give you about six lashes, and if you had any dust or anything on your clothes when he got through it was out. Then when you got home you got another one."[167]

An occasional disciplinary problem of rural school teachers involved the boy trapper, who laid a line of traps down his route to the school and ran them every day. Unfortunately for the school, skunks were the most important furbearer in this farming countryside, and many recalled that wet, skunk-impregnated clothing of the student trappers stank horribly in the radiant heat from school wood stoves. Howard Matthies remembered one boy who regularly ran a line of traps down Indian Creek on his way to school and who caught more skunks than anything else. "Henry Edward 'Punk' Whitener, he'd stink all over, and the teacher would say, 'Ah, Henry Edward, I'll have to excuse you.' That's what he wanted, then he could set more traps."[168]

The weeks from completion of bedding up to the end of the Christmas season often were the closest approximation to a real agricultural downtime in the old counties along the Brazos and Colorado. Men and boys in particular trapped and went hunting, and boys and girls alike studied Sears and Roebuck catalogues in fond hopes of what they might receive for Christmas. Christmas celebrations at home, schools, and churches ended this favored period of the yearly round. After Christmas, winter rains usually set in with increased frequency, roads worsened and became impassable, and the period of mud, cold, isolation, and sickness that some called "mudtime" arrived for area farm families.

Trapping and hunting were winter sports. Wild turkeys, white-tailed deer, black bears, buffalo, and limb-shattering flocks of wild pigeons once had frequented Fayette and Washington counties, but trappers and hunters of 1927 had only lesser game to seek. Boys often set Victor steel traps under baited stakes or in den mouths for striped and spotted skunks, possums, coons, or the occasional mink. Then, the young trappers skinned out what they caught, dried the pelts on homemade frames, and mailed the pelts to Sears and Roebuck or the Funsten Company of St. Louis. The few dollars they received for their efforts nevertheless were appreciated as the Christmas season approached. Along the Colorado, Howard Davis found trapping distasteful, though his brothers and uncles did a lot of it, often catching possums worth fifty cents to a dollar and a few excellent minks worth five to seven dollars.[169]

Some, like Otto Fuchs and his family, hunted mostly for sport, but others hunted for meat. Lydia Domasch recalled, "We went hunting on Sunday afternoon for squirrels and rabbits. We would eat anything just so we had meat."[170] Rabbits and possums graced the tables of many during this winter of 1927, and various no-gun methods sufficed to take both species. Cottontail rabbits often were pursued with dogs until they took refuge in a hollow tree or log, then were "twisted out" with a flexible stick and captured. Another method was to walk carefully through a brushy area studying the ground in front of you until you spotted a rabbit in its "bed." At this point, you might shoot it with a .22, as the Fuchs boys often did, hit it with a club, or, as Ed Lathan recalled, "you could go to whoopin and hollerin and excite him to death and pick him up— wouldn't get up out of his bed, just reach down and pick him up."[171]

African-Americans specialized in similar no-gun methods and consumed more rabbits, possums, and small birds than did the Germans and Czechs. Grover Williams often hunted rabbits and blackbirds with a "rubber shooter" slingshot using heavy-duty ammunition of "steelie" fragments made from old cook-stove lids. African-Americans consumed "blackbird pie" with some frequency, and blacks along the Washington County Bluffs used the Southeastern Indian technique of "bird blinding" to take robins at night. Mance Lipscomb explained: "Back in them woods and hills and things, over on the Bluffs, you'd see lights lit up round in there miles and miles when the robins was plentiful in there. They killed sacks of robins. Didn't have no gun, just carry a plank or a stick and knock em out of the bushes with that." Bird blinding went on in deep winter, "just according to the year and how cold it was. You get a bunch of them birds and pick em and cook em, they just as fat as they can be."[172] Grover Williams and his brothers knew the haunts of local possums and could go out and find one pretty much whenever they wanted to. They treed him, climbed the tree, shook him out (not an easy task), took him away from the dogs, and carried him home. Some preferred to skin the possum, some to bake it with the skin on, and possum fanciers of both preferences sometimes liked to hang the carcass up to "taint" for a day or so before roasting it. The Williams brothers used ashes to take the hair off the possum, gutted it, then turned it over to "the ladies to high season him and put him in the oven and bake him."[173]

The most elite of winter blood sports was the practice of coursing rabbits with greyhounds, another no-gun method. The well-off Otto Fuchs family did this, as did African-Americans James Wade, Mance Lipscomb, and many others. There were even organized meets, such as the one held by the Austin Coursing Association in 1925.[174] The ordinary hunting party simply went out into an area frequented by cottontails, swamp rabbits, or jackrabbits, jumped a rabbit with the dogs, then watched the swift hounds attempt to run the rabbit down. With more hunters in the party, each with his own dog, the chase became a competition between men to see whose dog, if any, caught the rabbit.

Some rabbits, especially the swift jackrabbits, got away, often by zigzagging back and forth down a fence line. The rabbit passed easily under the bottom strand of the barbed-wire fence, the greyhounds did not. Mance Lipscomb sometimes said of himself that "anybody likes dogs better'n me, they have to start eatin em." Mance owned several greyhounds, including one three-legged gift dog that did surprisingly well pursuing rabbits but tended to crash on hard turns.[175] James Wade often hunted with Mance, frequently besting his dogs, or so he said. He and other competitive greyhound men would go out on cold days and walk for many miles to see who's dog caught the most rabbits, and their money bets might be substantial. Wade had a champion pair of "straight-back, cold-blooded" dogs, one of several kinds, and he thought they were the best around. "Everybody that kept em had a bad rabbit they couldn't catch. Well, they're so good I done hoorahed the guy. Ever time they find one they couldn't catch I just tell em to tell me where he was. Say, 'Take me to that, I'll get him.'" On one occasion Wade went to a man's house who had one of these resident "bad rabbits" often flagrantly visible in a field nearby. Taking the lead by turns, Wade's two dogs ran the rabbit a mile out and a mile back, but they caught him.[176]

As Christmas approached, young trappers and hunters neglected their steel traps and hunting dogs and thought more about what they might receive for Christmas. Howard Matthies and his brother and sisters had done this until many of the pages fell out of the Sears Roebuck Catalogue, though the youngsters probably suspected that this year's gifts would run heavily to the usual nuts, fruits, and candies. The Matthies family did not have quite enough cotton land, and Christmas money usually was scarce. On Christmas eve the family got ready to attend the Lutheran church service at nearby Greenvine. Two adults and six children would ride in the two-seated buggy, and Howard's father prepared them for the cold:

> There was no windshield on those buggies, and it took you at least a good hour driving in that old surrey. So, Daddy put two big rocks on the heater early in the morning, and they stayed there all day. Just before we left, he wrapped them in an old quilt, piece of wagon sheet, or a cotton pick sack, and that's where we held our feet to stay warm on our way to Greenvine church to have our Christmas program.[177]

A big Christmas tree lighted with candles graced the church, and Matthies recalled, "I can still see that old gentleman, that was his job every year, he had to watch wherever there was some cedar burning from the candles and 'outen' them with a wet rag on a stick."[178] The special church service lasted all of three hours, with virtually every boy and girl of the seventy or so children in Sunday School taking part. Then, between eleven and midnight, church ended, families remounted the cold surreys, buggies, and wagons, and every child became galvanized by thoughts of what he or she would find when they got home. Santa Claus always came to the closed-off room with the unglimpsed Christmas tree during church service on Christmas eve. After a dark ride that seemed endless, the Matthieses arrived home, rushed into the Christmas tree room, noted their few wonderful toys (once, three boys shared one BB gun), and feasted on the walnuts, pecans, apples, and oranges that they found under the tree. The next day brought a trip to Grandfather Matthies's home for Christmas dinner and more feasting—always the Christmas goose and *Schwatzhauer*, the traditional goose-blood and prunes pudding appropriate for this festive season.[179]

Christmas dances at the German and Czech dance halls attracted many, including upon occasion the Otto Fuchs family. The high point of Christmas dances at the La Bahia Turn Verein Hall, the Cedar Creek Schuetzen Verein Hall of Carmine, or the Round Top Rifle Association Hall came with the raffling of gifts hanging upon, or resting beneath, the massive native cedar tree in the middle of the dance hall. Prizes were raffled off, then the men stripped the big tree of its swinging apples and dangling sticks of peppermint candy and distributed them to the children crowding all around. "Then the tree came down and was dragged out through the front double doors as a bevy of youngsters still searched the branches for an overlooked morsel. Then the dance resumed." After a while, a sweeping crew of strong young men formed up with brooms along the back of the hall, then in unison began to sweep the hall. "To me the sweepers looked victorious when squeezing against each other they thrust the rolls of dust through the double front doors into the stillness of the night air." Then the dancing began once more.[180]

Others stepped to slightly different drummers at Christmas time. Among the Wends of Serbin, costumed youths wearing women's cast-off clothing, white red-striped tunics, homemade masks, and cow-tail beards went from house to house asking children if they had been good during the year and what they wanted for Christmas. Sometimes they requested the children to recite prayers and rewarded them with candy when they accomplished this; sometimes they spanked the hands of wicked children with a ruler. The leader of these *Rumplich* carried a long staff symbolic of his high office among the elves. By 1926, however, this older form of Christmas elf was on the decline, being increasingly replaced by Santa Claus with his bag of toys.[181]

The African-American Christmas along the Brazos sometimes began with the sound of bugles and guitars. On Christmas morning men dressed up "like a Sandy Claw" roamed from house to house, beginning at first light. "Hollerin 'Christmas cheer!,'" Hunt from "Mr. Moore's bottom" often came by the Lathans with his guitar,

> picking it and singing, and my daddy would give him a big drink of whisky. My mother would cook maybe seven, eight cakes, pies and things—give him all he wanted to eat. Ain't long since we'd killed hogs, had them good old home cured sausage, bacon, spare ribs, give him a bit of that. He stay there and play his guitar, we call it "serenading" in them days. Then he'd leave our house and go to somebody else's house, get him another drink of whisky. This country was thick-settled with people, I mean black people, and it more sociable, more friendly, than it is now. In them times, weather didn't stop em. The men, as I foresaid, they called it serenading— going from house to house, picking the guitar, blowing bugles. And ever house you went to had something to offer you.[182]

However, on the Bluffs, as at the Matthies's farm on La Bahia Prairie, presents under the family's tree depended on that year's cotton season. Lathan's father more often than not had to explain, "Sandy Claws po', he didn't have many toys."

After Christmas and the New Year, cold, rain, and occasional freezing rain and sleet came down with increasing frequency, as the old counties along the Brazos and Colorado entered the yearly period of mud and isolation—mudtime. Farmers watched their bedded fields and were pleased to see "winter on the land" in the forms of ice and crusted sleet, harbingers of good crops, many believed. Meanwhile, however, roads turned impassable, creeks rose, and sometimes only the telephone got through to town. La Grange town folk on the railroad enjoyed "firemen's masked balls" and weekly touring road company presentations in the Casino Opera House, such as "Wilhelm Tell" and "Ingomar, the Barbarian," but few persons from the countryside attended these. In blackland areas the mud sometimes grew so deep that families could not even get off their farms, let alone navigate miles of terrible roads into town.

From Christmas on, rural students traveling cross-country school trails sometimes had trouble getting through mud and creek bottoms, and sometimes they reached their schools only to be trapped on the wrong side of a flooded creek. Stream crossings were a problem at the best of times. Sometimes students took off their shoes and waded, sometimes they walked trees felled as footlogs. Edna Ebner and her brothers and sisters crossed a large creek on the way to Bell Settlement School by way of a high-wire act. The children slid their feet along the bottom strand of the barbed wire fence spanning the deep creek while they went hand-over-hand along the top strand. Edna loved attending her rural school, but she feared heights and deep running water and sometimes cried before she forced herself to make the perilous crossing.[183]

Almuth Matthies attended Boundary School and recalled a recurrent problem with the two creeks the family had to cross.

> Those days we had to cross a creek down below the school, and a lot of times the bigger boys held on to the little ones. They pulled off their shoes and even if it was cold, they walked across it. When we waded through a creek, everybody had a school satchel that was waterproof. We'd put our books in there and a dry pair of socks, so when we got to school we'd sit at the stove a while and dry our shoes and put on dry socks.[184]

Other families attending school had even more formidable creeks to cross. The Matthieses often housed stranded scholars from other neighborhoods on occasions when heavy rains fell during the school day and creeks rose and became impassable. Rural school teachers kept a weather eye out at all times and, in attempts to make sure the children got home safely, often dismissed class when serious rains began.

Lucky children had plow horses to ride to school, as did Leola Tiedt and her brothers and sisters, but after heavy rains the Tiedts had to change their route to school. Almuth Matthies later taught eight years at the Boundary School he earlier had attended, and one year the mud got so bad his little pony repeatedly went belly deep and finally could not go. One day his father told him, "Son, you better ride that blue horse. You already wore that one out."[185]

On one occasion, the mud froze into rutted concrete and Matthies's horse slipped and slid on the rutted surface on the way to school. "When I got to the school house, there was nobody there. I got off the horse and my feet were so cold I had no circulation. I couldn't stand up for a while. I finally got going and built a fire. That was the general rule when you went to a country school, the first one there on a cold morning built the fires."[186] Most rural teachers felt they had to get to their rural schools, no matter what the weather. Attendance fell off drastically during periods of rain, mud, and cold, but teachers always had to assume that some children still would show up at their schools—wet, half frozen, and much in need of a warm room. Once a Washington County teacher arrived to find only one little girl in attendance at her Armstrong School, and she held her on her lap by the wood stove and taught her English all one long cold day.[187]

In the course of one winter walk into Gay Hill School, teacher Inez McCauley encountered a man in tears on an icy bridge. His horse had fallen down and could not get up. With McCauley's help, neighbors came to the horse's aid and with the assistance of a tarpaulin finally got the horse on its feet. Presumably, the rider then dried his eyes and rode on his way. In truth, however, mudtime and the winter roads of 1926–1927 were "enough to make a grown man cry."[188]

Buggies and cars literally used wagon tracks in mudtime. As vehicles ran the roads, they made cow-track-like ruts that grew deeper and deeper as time went on. Since bar ditches usually were nonexistent and roads ungraded, rain water naturally followed the ruts downhill. This led to deeper and deeper ruts, water standing in ruts, and formidable mudholes at low places and stream crossings. The traveler gazed at these mudholes with suspicion, wondering what unseen horrors lay in their murky depths—ruts so deep a vehicle would "bottom out," or terrible potholes gouged out by the death throes of other bogged vehicles.[189] Cross-country road travel always was an adventure. Kermit Fox recalled:

> At times the roads on our Prairie were bogs of mud. At times
> it rained so that we shielded ourselves with an oilskin lap
> cover and then again a heavy hairy lap-robe was needed to
> deflect the chilling drafts. I can still hear the rumble as
> the steel-tired wheels bumped across the hollow-sounding
> wooden culverts and rickety bridges and how now and

then you had to duck or ward-off the many rattling sienna beans closely hugging the sides of the narrow roadway.[190]

As roads worsened, farmers who had to travel tried to find solutions to the problems of mudtime. The Whiteners, who had to get corn to the nearest grist mill to grind their daily bread, hitched four mules to the wagon to make it into Burton. Later, "We'd have to take the bed off of the wagon and just put some planks on the running gear and stack that corn up, so the mules could pull the wagons through the mud."[191] A little later, not even this worked: four-mule teams bogged in the mud or broke their leather traces straining to pull the hills, and people finally stopped trying.[192] No wheeled vehicles ran the roads, and only riders or foot travelers made it into town for supplies or medicine—if the creek did not rise too high.[193]

Long before this stage was reached, most automobiles stood unused in farmer's barns and garages, since mud outmatched motorcars on the wagon-track roads of Washington and Fayette counties' mudtime. Many farmers at first had viewed automobiles as toys for townsmen and a danger to be avoided on rural roads. Stock panicked at the sight and sound of them, and farmers needing to make cross-country trips with spooky animals sometimes studied county road maps trying to calculate how best to avoid the hated cars. The affordable Model T Ford, the "mechanical cockroach," somewhat reconciled farmers to motorcars, and by this late winter of 1927 many of them owned one. The high-centered, narrow-wheeled, buggy-like Model T's worked well in mud, although they were underpowered, and, as one woman told, "You'd get stuck from the first turn of the wheel if you didn't know what rut to take."[194] Sharecropper Mance Lipscomb had a Model T and, like many other owners, touted its abilities to "jump" mudholes. The usual technique was to stop the car, put it in first gear, then: "give it speed, say 'Wwrdrdr drdrdr!. Man, it'd split that water wide open! Couldn't stall that thing, man. But you had to be in a hurry."[195] However, there were limits to the automobile's power to navigate the mud. Howard Matthies attended the eighth grade in Burton, and his family lived only about a mile from where the paved road began, but "half the time that mile from the pavement to the house was impass-able." By mudtime in early 1927, the Matthies's vehicle stood on blocks, the better to preserve its fragile tires.[196]

Deeper in the countryside, the isolation of mudtime could be life threatening. Illnesses were abroad, colds turned most easily into dreaded pneumonia, mud blocked emergency travel, and some people told cautionary tales of family members suddenly stricken ill and doctors who could not, or would not, cross intervening flooded creeks or became so delayed they did not arrive in time. Many farmhouses had telephones by 1927, but these did little good if the roads were impassable or the doctor already out on a call. Families on the Carmine and Burton systems listened for the tell-tale emergency rings summoning all to the phone for the message that someone had died.[197] On the Burton telephone network five long rings signaled trouble, on the Carmine system, one long continuous ring.

Doctors served as a last resort for many farm families, who usually tried to cure their own ills with patent medicines or home remedies and turned to medical science only when all else failed. Various herbal remedies often were used—fig-leaf juice for ringworms, peach- or sassafras-leaf poultices for headaches, dogfennel or slippery elm or "cam-eye" tea for fevers, persimmon-bark tea for sore throat, balmonia tea as a purgative (one of many), red-oak-bark tea for diarrhea, and many others. Many older persons among local Germans, Czechs, and African-Americans favored such traditional remedies. Mance Lipscomb's part-Choctaw mother knew many medicinal plants, and if any of her eleven children had a problem: "Mamma'd go out there in them woods—she never wore a coat—and down next to that water, in what you call them branches, give her a minute, she'd come right back out there with some kind of old weed, piece of bark, or some old somethin. And first thing you know, whatever it was we had, well, we didn't have it no more." [198]

Other families favored remedies recycled from various common substances in use around the farm, including kerosene, turpentine, whisky, bluing, vinegar, and lard. Kerosene cured head lice and warts. Turpentine worked well on red-bug bites, cuts, scratches, punctures, and scorpion stings, and served as an ingredient for sore-throat gargles, many of which also included whisky. Bluing followed mud applications for bee and wasp stings. Lard joined turpentine on chest poultices for colds and "croup" and became an ingredient in other salves and poultice applications. Active ingredients in these remedies using kerosene, turpentine, or whisky, in particular, often were interchangeable and depended on family traditions. In general, rural households along the rivers divided into two main camps on the matter of recycled reme-dies—those favoring cure-alls based around turpentine and those favoring cure-alls utilizing kerosene.

Patent medicines formed virtually a third camp of home medical practice. Newspapers abounded in ads for them, including one or two that claimed to raise the dead. Nearly everyone had some Grove's Tasteless Chill Tonic around for the chills and fever of malaria. Running for many decades, the standard Grove's ad was a marvel of brevity, noting: "Has stood the test 25 years. No cure, no pay, 50 cents."[199] Watkins Salve, Raleigh Salve, and Hunt's Lightning Oil all made the common man-or-beast claim, and someone named S. Harrison testified for the latter: "I would rather think of running my farm without implements as without Hunt's Lightning Oil. Of all the linaments I have ever used, both for man and beast, it is the quickest in action and richest in results."[200] "Wine of Cardui, Woman's Relief," claimed to cure women's "dragging down pains, profuse periods, weak-ening drains, dreadful backache, headache, nervousness, dizziness, irri-tability, tired feeling, inability to walk, loss of appetite, color, and beauty."[201] And for a half century the ad for Dr. Pierce's Golden Medical Discovery to "make the sour and foul stomach sweet" began with the same lead essay, "The Stomach Is Like a Churn."[202] Topping the claims of all other products, however, were those for the life-restor-ing "Elixir" of Hungarian scientist Thaddeaus Tietz. Tietz, who said that he periodically tested his product on himself, stated that "mere removal of the blood from the body until respiration stops, suffocation, drowning, and the like means of ending life have no terrors for him."[203]

In truth, life ended all too soon and too easily in the winter coun-tryside, and people often went beyond these common remedies in hope of a cure. "Magnetic healers" offered obscure electric therapies, and Wends (and perhaps some Germans) relied on the *Lebenswezker*, or "life awakener," to cure various serious conditions, often traveling many miles with a sick family member to seek one out. The life awakener was a hollow tube about ten inches long with a small disk on the end con-taining several small needles set close together. When the needles were placed against the afflicted part of a patient, a spring drove them lightly into the skin, barely puncturing it. A special imported oil then was rubbed into this irritation.[204] Another curative object, specialized for hydrophobia, was the "madstone," still in use even though the Pasteur Institute in Austin now offered effective (but painful) cures for area mad-dog-bite victims. In the Burton area, Ernest Bayer and Frieda Mae Guelker practiced yet another type of common cure, healing by Biblical practice and Christian faith.[205]

Wends and African-Americans both harbored beliefs that deadly illnesses might be caused by the malevolence of others, and magical diseases needed magical remedies. A "witch" in the Wendish community of Serbin reputedly lived in a house full of frogs, sometimes kept her neighbors' cream from turning to butter, and perhaps did more serious things. Some among the Wends possessed the *Seventh Book of Moses*, an infamous manual of both white and black magic.[206] James Wade, Georgia Lee Wade, Mance Lipscomb, and Bubba Bowser believed that some people had "voodoo power" to harm others. Bubba Bowser was convinced that, in his youth, he had been attacked by one of these practitioners. Angry at Bowser for his relations with her daughter, this woman enticed him to eat a piece of "Christmas cake" that had secret ingredients of salamanders and scorpions. He explained, "She cooked that stuff and put it in that cake, and when you cook anything poison and crumble it up on anything, if it can get on your flesh, it'll go right on to your blood vessel and come alive. And I ate it, and in about three weeks it just like a horse got the grubs. They go to biting and I have fits."[207] Fighting voodoo with voodoo, Bowser employed the services of a counter-sorcerer, who soon cured him with the aid of a special carved stick the man called "Old Tom."

When all of the cures failed, death had to be accepted and dealt with. Normally, the sick died at home and were laid out there, and neighbors, friends, and family came over to stay up all night during the "wake" and "watch the corpse." As Kermit Fox noted, "Dying in a place other than in one's own home, with family members close by, was then almost unheard of."[208] Corpses rarely were embalmed, although in warmer seasons the mercantile store furnishing the coffin normally surrounded it at the laying out with preservative jars of ice. Funeral services might be held in the home or the nearby church, and after that a wagon bore the coffin to the graveyard, where family and friends had gathered to dig the grave and pay tribute to the deceased. After a brief service, pallbearers lowered the coffin into the grave with two heavy canvas straps. Then several men among the mourners seized shovels and filled the grave, while all stood by to show their respect. Fox noted: "A light wooden frame covered only with cloth was then lowered to cover the coffin. This must have been a psychological shield for those in attendance. The thudding of shovels full of earth and rock falling onto the deep-lying coffin made a sound I still find to be unwelcome today."[209]

Sometimes the isolations of mudtime impacted even funerals. Olefa Matthies's mother died in the depth of winter, and her body ended up staying overnight in the Burton mercantile store that furnished the coffin. Roads were too bad to get the body home for a proper lying in state with family members paying their respects by watching over the corpse. Olefa Matthies told, "They always said she laid there in state with the rats." Also because of the muddy roads, many people failed to attend the graveside service the next day, and: "She was buried there in water, I'll never forget that. The grave filled up with water. They dipped all day, but she was just laid into water."[210]

Despite threats of illness and death, certain individuals still traveled Fayette and Washington County roads during this mudtime of early 1927, as the season imperceptibly shifted toward spring. German singing, shooting, dancing, and athletic clubs still met from time to time, no matter the weather or the road conditions. An old German saying held, "Where people meet, there you may abide in peace, for bad people have no songs," and members of the Piney Concordia Gesang-Verein felt so strongly about song practice nights that members sometimes swam the winter Brazos to attend.[211]

Carrying on a thirty-year tradition, rural mailmen also ran the muddy roads. The mailman at La Bahia rode a horse most of the time and led a sure-footed mule, which he mounted when conditions got especially nasty. The Carmine-area mailman used a closed, covered buggy with the reins coming out through a little slot—this to protect him from the cold.[212] Interviewed in 1974 at age eighty-six, retired mailman Jonnie Bauer recalled little of his early life, but the years spent driving a "star route" between Warrenton and Ledbetter had left one indelible memory: "It was so cold, sometimes, so cold!" he said.[213]

Texas's first rural mail route had been launched from La Grange in 1899—a twenty-seven-mile circuit by pioneer carrier Henry Kreamer—and other routes later were added at about the rate of one a year until most rural farms received mail by 1927. Much appreciated by isolated farm families, rural mailmen soon attained celebrity status, with local papers reporting on their comings and goings as they did those of other important community leaders.

When virtually no one else dared, the mailmen ran the roads. Pioneer carrier Charles Albrecht remembered muddy lanes, flooded creeks, slippery clay hills, hailstorms, and freezing rain and recalled, "It was nothing to have the top of your gig blown off by a storm or trees blown across your path." Once, Albrecht borrowed a rowboat to get a sick man's medicine to him across a flooded bottom. Another time: "We were caught between two flooded creeks, unbridged. I threw my mail pouch over my shoulder and sent Billie, my horse, with a gig across the creek, and I crossed on the top of a barbed wire fence."[214] Sometimes a mailman got stranded while on his route and called in "to start his substitute on the next day, while he continued the rest of his trip." In 1912, parcel post began on a trial basis and became immediately successful, much to the dismay of local merchants, who loathed Sears and Roebuck. After a time, sizes and weights for parcels increased to seventy pounds and one hundred inches "girth and length combined."[215]

Kermit Blume of Ledbetter was a latter-day inheritor of this proud tradition, running his route in a Model A Ford with mud-grip tires, a real "mudclobber," local Germans said. Blume's zeal to "make it through" was legendary. He recalled: "One fellow on the mail route told me, 'Mr. Blume, it rained and it washed out a gully through there, you can't get through.' I said, 'Oh, I'm gonna go down there and look.' I had a grubbing hoe in the back. I chopped around a little bit on it and went right on through and never looked back."[216]

A few others went out and abroad in mudtime. Grover Williams's grandparents were zealous churchgoers, so the family took off their shoes and walked to church through the mud every Sunday, no matter what. The church in sight, they put their shoes back on. Sometimes, if things dried up a little, the well-off Matson family of Williams's Flat Prairie community "broke ruts" into Burton in their powerful V-8 Fords, then were followed by less affluent neighbors in four-cylinder Model T's.[217] Courting males sometimes braved the deepest mud, and Howard Matthies was one of those who did. On the way to his girl friend's house for her birthday in his Model A Ford, he discovered that the roads were far worse than he had thought. Over and over again, his wheels accumulated black mud until: "they rolled out on the outside, and you got out there and took your hands—had on a white shirt—and cleaned all that mud off. Then you could back up again, get a running start, and make it bout here from the barn. Again, you had that same thing to do. I cleaned wheels seven times."[218] Eddie Wegner also courted in a Model A, a certified "mudclobber," and his attitude toward the mud was, "When we had to go, we had to go." Returning a date's forgotten shoes one time, he drove into her family's pristine driveway "lustily, cutting a big deep ugly rut all the way down to the house to deliver those shoes." Her father looked out the window and remarked, "'Wonder who is that *Schweinhund* that's messing up the road?' That's a 'hog-dog,' translated, and that's a pretty low creature, you know," Wegner explained.[219]

Very often, however, in the dark and cold of this late winter landscape, only the wizard electronics of telephone and radio connected remote farmsteads to the outside world. Carmine served as center for one typical telephone system, a cooperative association of shareholder families who built and maintained their own lines and contributed one or two day's labor a year to system upkeep. During the 1920s, families paid about three dollars a year "connection fee" and annual dues of around nine dollars. Each crank telephone had a battery maintained by the householder. These usually were dated to remind owners when they needed replacing, but people still neglected them, to the detriment of all. Several weak batteries on the circuit reduced its efficiency, making it difficult for everybody to hear what people said. The Carmine system had several "party lines," with up to twenty-five families on each loop. To call someone on the same line, you simply picked up the separate ear and mouth pieces, looked at the posted "ring code" on the wall, and rang this family's unique sequence of "shorts" and "longs." For other lines on the system, you rang the Carmine operator (or a substation) and asked for your connection. Every call placed within a line rang all of the phones on the line, so during the day a family's phone rang almost continuously, and family members had to listen carefully for their particular coded ring. On a full line of twenty-five families, the family ring code might have as many as six different rings in a unique pattern of longs and shorts, so a person had to pay attention. Like a gambler monitoring the sequence of symbols registering one by one on a slot machine, the listener ceased paying attention after the first wrongful ring came in.

The central operator, or substation operator, made connections between the several lines and occasionally communicated emergency messages to everyone on the system after signaling them to their phones with one, long continuous ring.

The Fuchs family's big farmhouse served as voluntary substation for part of the Carmine system. Eight telephone lines, instead of the usual one, entered the house. As Kermit Fox told: "It was our duty to make connections for the lines requested as parties called in. This, of course, gave us the chance to listen in on any conversations involving the entire neighborhood," and in the case of "poor connections, it often became our chore to repeat the message from one person to another."[220]

Many people "listened in" to other people's calls during this long, dark (and boring) winter of 1927. No chance of being detected existed, since you listened in only with the earpiece and could not possibly give yourself away. Every call placed within your line rang your phone, so "keeping up with the neighbors" proved easy to accomplish. Sometimes so many people picked up their phones at the same time that the signal grew noticeable weaker. "You couldn't talk too much business on those party lines," Ora Nell Fuchs told, and Mrs. Herman Schoenemann affirmed: "You had to watch what come out of your mouth! You could hear a lot of good old gossip, those days."[221] People listened in not just to amuse themselves, but with a degree of neighborly concern. "Taking care of the neighbors" was important to all, and in time of need people wanted to help. Just as during the nineteenth century, farmers had heard someone signaling the call for help with three long blows on a steer horn, the horn signal that meant, "Emergency, come to me!" now they might pick up their phones after a long, continuous ring to hear (as Carmine system users did on December 29, 1924), "This is the Fuchs farm, our barn is on fire!"

Early telephone systems were recreational, as well as functional. Several neighbors on a line sometimes got on the phone together for "conference call" discussions about impending social affairs, crops, and a hundred other things. In one northeastern Texas community, system users knew that they could pick up their phones at a given time and listen to a spirited, thirty-minute, harmonica concert emitting from a certain remote farmstead. The musician got off the line every ten minutes or so, waited to see if anyone wanted to use it, then came back on with his trademark rendition of "Pretty Red Wing."

Other mysterious music came through the cold, still air on winter evenings. Crystal radio receivers took advantage of the "night effect of ground wave" to pick up distant stations of the first radio era: WSM, Nashville; WGN Chicago; WOAI, San Antonio; XERA, Viacuña, Mexico; and a few others. Crystal sets were unimposing collections of small wires and gadgets: a ten-inch, one-inch-in-diameter copper-wound "tuning coil"; a quartz crystal about the size of a quarter that miraculously powered the whole thing; a "whisker" or wire-line "tickler" that the operator moved about the surface of the crystal until the end made contact with a "live spot" on the crystal; a metal sleeve that the operator moved along the copper tuning coil until a radio station was heard; a set of head phones; and a jury-rigged antenna stretched to a tree outside the house, more often than not recycled from the wire of a Model T's junked generator coil.[222]

These small, trivial things drew incredible music from the dark air, but only for the listener on the earphones. Faint and far came the sounds of the Light Crust Doughboys, the Chuck Wagon Gang, and Bob Wills and the Texas Playboys. Every evening in the late winter of 1927, the Skrabanek family sat in their front parlor under the bright gasoline lamp and, as Mr. Skrabanek, insisted, "did something useful." John Skrabanek mended equipment, his wife patched clothing and darned socks, the girls knitted and sewed, and the boys did something constructive, even if it was only oiling a baseball glove. One by one, as the Skrabaneks did this, they donned the earphones of their crystal radio to listen to the wonderful "Czech Music Hour" emitting from distant Temple. As he worked and listened to the music, John Skrabanek thought about spring planting time and his carefully selected cotton and corn seeds in the dark barn, and he saw in his mind's eye the twin waves of shining blackland soil rolling left and right from the prow of his advancing bedder.[223]

CHAPTER 5

In the Fields

As the first of February came and went, John Skrabanek read farm magazines, consulted the *Farmers' Almanac* and the *Husbandman* (the latter in Czech), and studied local signs ranging from the budding of redbuds and other trees to the actions of animals and insects. Meanwhile, other local farmers covertly watched the Skrabanek family's fields for the first signs of planting. John Skrabanek had a local reputation to uphold of "being the first, or among the first, to plant" and of not making mistakes. He knew others would follow his lead, and if he planted too early or too late, others would follow him into error.[1] Planting early had become a primary survival technique for Texas farmers. Early planting of corn guaranteed some kind of crop even if summer drought arrived prematurely; early planting of cotton tried to beat the boll weevil, whose numbers and destructive effects increased in geometric ratio with every twenty-seven-day weevil generation during the growing season.

Miles to the southeast, on the edge of the Brazos bottoms, Bubba Bowser's father had a similar reputation for choosing exactly the right time to plant, though—unlike John Skrabanek—Bowser always put his seeds in the ground much later than most. The elder Bowser, in making his decision about when to plant, took into account the weather signs of this new year, the stages of the moon, and the complicated predictions of certain almanacs combining moon stages with the signs of the zodiac. Timing was critical, and the timing of planting was the only thing the farmer had entirely within his control during the dice-roll of season. As Bubba Bowser observed, the season was up to God.

> Cotton breeds with the earth, and peas and things, just like a woman breeds with a man. And if you catch that earth and it ain't right, it ain't gonna receive nothing, and you can't make nothing. It just like a woman, the earth and your plant mate together. If you plant it on the wrong time, they ain't gonna mate up. You can't do nothing bout the season, but you can not put your stuff in the ground on the wrong time. But, now, God got to send the season.[2]

Skrabanek planted early, Bowser late, and both usually succeeded. Bubba Bowser said that his father would "get the first bale of cotton ever year, and those people be chopping when we be just planting. And that cotton came up just clean and don't never stop growing. He had a time. He wasn't gonna do nothing till his time come."[3]

Nothing so preoccupied farmers as their cotton planting times, but they had many other crops to worry about. Beginning with the transplanting of the little cabbage plants soon after February 1, a succession of garden crops went in, then the potatoes, then the field corn, then the subsistence field crops of peas, melons, molasses and feed canes, then finally the cotton, the crop that must not fail. Frank Janish usually removed his hardy cabbage plants from the cold frame and set them out precisely on February 2, but his cotton-planting date depended on the signs of the year. Cabbages would be processed into crock after crock of sauerkraut by early summer and served as one of the staffs of life, but cotton brought in the family money. Without the cash crop of cotton, as Janish told, "Boy, you was entirely blowed up!"[4]

Beginning around the first of January, various signs in the heavens and on the earth predicted long-term weather for the new year. Farmers differed in how much attention they paid to weather signs (and in how much they admitted they paid attention to them), but few entirely disregarded such portents during this time before official forecasts. Signs of an unusually long winter (and late planting time) were

hogs carrying sticks, thick fur and hair on domestic stock and wild animals, squirrels building large nests, and a variety of other things—
some accepted by many, others the idiosyncratic beliefs of individual
farmers. People always were coming up with new weather predictors.
A neighbor told Howard Matthies's father during a dry spell, "Ernst,
you know what, the moon is shaped like a canoe, and that means it's
getting ready to rain."[5]

Howard Matthies's grandfather and many others paid special attention to daily weather during the last six days of the old year and the first
six days of the new, believing these days predicted general climate for the
forthcoming twelve months of the year. Grandfather Matthies began
keeping a daily journal soon after arriving in Texas in 1870, and a preoccupation with weather dominated his entries. He wrote, "Jack Frost this
morning," or "Another Jack Frost, in three days we gonna have rain," or
"Jack Frost and ice means that in 36 hours or so we'll have another
norther." For Matthies, the number of stars within the ring around the
moon foretold the number of days until rain, and the first passage of
wild geese in the spring told him his seed corn should be in the ground.[6]
Many farmers watched and listened for spring "firsts" of animals and
plants to catch the rhythm of the coming season—the first geese overhead, the first redbud tree in bloom, the first sound of a cicada. Some
watched certain local farmers in almost the same way—for example,
John Skrabanek's first trip across his corn field on his riding planter.

Doubters sometimes poked fun at believers in these timing signs by
making up apocryphal ones to set beside them. For example, one such
person told that a farmer should plant corn when the Sears Catalogue
in the privy had been used down to the harness section and plant cotton when he woke up and his sleeping wife had kicked her gown up
over her head.[7]

Farmers who believed in weather signs but felt deficient in detecting
and interpreting them sometimes sought the advice of neighbors who
had reputations as weather prophets. People around Burton often consulted an old bachelor farmer most knew only as "June Bug" for detailed
weather predictions, as others did Mance Lipscomb's mother farther
east. Lipscomb said: "My mother was a seance on when to plant, never
missed it in her life. People come to be schooled by her on the farms
where she was working on. She was known aware, see; she had sense
enough to not plant and sense when to do it."[8]

Lipscomb's mother "planted by the moon," although she was "known aware," with abilities transcending simple formulas. During this era of flickering coal-oil lamps, moon and constellations glowed as brightly above the dark countryside as in medieval times, and medieval beliefs about celestial effects persisted. Many persons still timed planting of their gardens, potato patches, and corn and cotton fields according to moon stages in 1927, and many others paid attention to the twenty-eight-day cycle of dominant constellations—the "signs of the zodiac." Biblical support for this was easily found, since Ecclesiastes 3:1–2 told, "To everything there is a season, and a time to every purpose under the heavens: a time to be born, and a time to die, a time to plant, and a time to pluck up that which is planted."

Perhaps more people believed in the power of the moon than in any other celestial influence. Following the basic principle of sympathetic magic, "like begets like," people planted crops bearing below ground in the waning or dark of the moon and crops bearing above ground in the waxing of the moon. Just as the moon flourished and increased, so would the corn and cotton. Irish potatoes foolishly planted on the increase of the moon ran to leaves and vines with little below ground, many thought, and cotton planted on the waning moon failed to mature bolls, blew off on the ground, and otherwise came to disaster. Fayette county agent W. H. DuPuy already traveled the countryside giving lectures and demonstrations of scientific farming during this spring of 1927, but most people still paid more attention to the moon in the night sky. The Winchester correspondent to the La Grange Journal noted, "Farmers hereabouts are busy planting cotton; some of them are waiting until the full moon materializes."[9] It was not just a matter of belief and of old traditions passed down from the forefathers; Mr. and Mrs. Gus Keiler of the Round Top vicinity, as did many other people, felt that they had seen clear demonstrations of lunar power. Gus had been planting corn back in 1917 when his wife called him in to the house for a cup of coffee. Gus took only twenty minutes off before returning to his mule and walking planter left standing in the field, but "the moon changed in between times" to a waxing stage; consequently, the corn planted before his coffee break failed, and the corn planted afterward made "big corn."[10]

Many people believed that the signs of the zodiac and the stages of the moon influenced other aspects of human life besides the growth of the crops. An increasing moon favored animal fertility; so, a farmer might wait until the waxing moon to take his mare to visit the "Aggie jack" or even to get married himself. According to one source, the preferred time for Washington County weddings during the nineteenth century was during the increasing moon.[11] The moon even affected household meat processings, though here, as elsewhere, people disagreed about the lunar orb's effects. It depended upon whether one's priority was pork in the smokehouse or pork in the pan. Some, like Eddie Wegner's parents, favored hog butchering during the decrease of the moon, since this ensured better meat preservation. Conversely, Henry Jaeger's parents believed that, "if you kill at the decrease of the moon, that meat, if you'd fry it, it'd shrivel together, and you didn't have nothing left but a little bitty old hard knot." According to this view, sausage wrongfully processed on the waning moon "fried down to nothing." As the moon declined in the sky, so did meat in the pan.[12]

During this early spring of 1927, it was a rare family that did not possess one of the many almanacs which cross-indexed the signs of the zodiac with the stages of the moon to give precise direction to human activities. In ancient times, astronomers had divided a central belt of the night sky into twelve, thirty-degree arcs, called "signs," each dominated by a bright constellation of stars. Since all the constellations except one were named for animals, the belt became known as the zodiac, or "zone of animals." In time, each sign of the zodiac became associated with a particular body part, planet, and element. The sign Scorpio, the scorpion, for example, became associated with the loins (body part), Mars (planet), and water (element). Every day of the month was dominated by one of the twelve signs of the zodiac. Each of the twelve appeared at least once a month for a period of either two or three days. All good planting calendars labeled each day with the sign that ruled over it (depending on which constellation was foremost in the sky at the time), the part of the body and the planet associated with the sign, and the element to which it was most closely akin.

No two farmers' almanacs offered exactly the same advice for a given day (something that gave pause even to the most zealous of true believers), but all offered recurrent "best" days for any activity, calculated from the conjunction of the two cycles, the cycle of the signs and the cycle of the moon. For example, a farmer customarily planting corn sometime during the first week of March might consult his almanac to pick out a day dominated by Cancer (a "water sign") with an increasing moon. Other signs and moon phases favored the death of plants (often also in the farmer's interest), and sometimes became very specific about other activities. T. E. Black's widely used calendar and guide, *God's Way*, observed:

> Best time to break habits is on the new moon or in the sign Pisces in the Feet. Best time for canning all vegetables, cooking preserves and jelly, and making pickles the signs I give in my Guide are from the last quarter of the moon to the new year. Kill meat when the signs are in the knees and or feet, or from the last quarter of the moon until the new moon. Advertise when the signs are in Libra or Scorpio. Ask for jobs or deal with creditors when the signs are in Leo, Libra, or Scorpio. Cut hair to stimulate growth of it in Cancer, Scorpio, or Pisces.[13]

For every true believer in the signs, however, there was someone who scoffed at them. Almanacs advised farmers to plant potatoes under the sign Taurus in the waning of the moon, but Howard Matthies's father sometimes retorted, "I don't plant in the moon, I plant in the ground." Almanacs recommended the neutering of farm animals in Capricorn on the declining moon (this to minimize blood loss), but the doubting Matthies rebutted, "The sign for castration is when your knife is sharp."[14]

Still, a large number of Fayette and Washington County farmers consulted their almanacs as planting time for corn and cotton approached during this spring of 1927. Most farmers customarily planted their corn and cotton "around" certain dates, which varied from family to family, so, why take a chance? Why not plant on a date during this traditional planting period that one's almanac said was a good day? The plantings of major field crops were fateful acts fraught with peril, so it seemed only prudent to align one's best efforts with the stars and moon.

Henry Jaeger and his father were two of many believers. Around 1910, the elder Jaeger had tested the relative efficiency of *MacDonald's Almanac* and *The Old Farmers' Almanac* on his crops and determined to his satisfaction that the former produced better cotton and corn; thereafter, the family stuck with *MacDonald's*—even though it was published in distant New York state. One year, Henry Jaeger planted some of his cotton "on the right sign," then was locked out of the field by a rainy spell and had to plant the rest after it got dry enough "on any old sign, just so I could get the cotton in the ground." Planted under false stars, the latter cotton struggled while the earlier cotton flourished—"you could see it on the row," a huge difference. At this point Jaeger really became a true believer.[15] As did Jaeger, Frank Janish thought that applications of the signs could prove truly powerful—if one knew precisely how to use them. A black man of Janish's acquaintance, for example, claimed he could choose just the right day and hour and give a big tree a single cut with an ax, "and that tree gonna die."[16]

Sometimes, however, beliefs deteriorated under the impact of other hard evidence. Eddie Wegner's father believed in the signs, and in the beginning Eddie did also, at least to some extent, but one year rain kept Eddie out of his blackland fields until desperately late. Then he planted at the absolutely worst time according to the signs and still made excellent cotton. Thereafter, Wegner disregarded the signs except for one activity: only the most powerful of "death signs" in conjunction with the dark of the moon seemed appropriate for grubbing up the scourge of Johnson grass.[17]

Weeds were on farmers' minds as planting time for corn approached in the last week of February and the first week of March. First, farmers rebedded their fields to suppress weeds sprung up since the bedding up of late fall in 1926; then, they flattened the tops of the rows by dragging a harrow over them and planted corn down the flattened centers of the rows with walking or riding planters.

The way farmers rebedded depended in part upon how much rain had fallen and how flattened and washed out their rows had become, and in part upon the severity of their weed problems. Washed out rows required drastic rebedding, and farmers in weed-plagued alluvial bottoms (where every "overflow" seeded fields with new crops of weeds washed in from upstream), and those on sandy uplands (where every weed seed seemed to germinate) needed to rebed to destroy weeds. Many farmers hitched four mules or four horses to their big bedders and formed old rows into new ones exactly as in the late fall, while others double-furrowed with their turning plows to accomplish the same thing. As in the late fall, the new rows were thus reformed a half a row to the right or left of the old ones. A few lucky farmers with high, unflattened beds and scattered weeds simply ran up the middles (water furrows) with sweeps or small middle buster plows that threw dirt to top off the rows on either side, and let it go at that; the rows of late fall remained in place, ready for harrowing and planting.

Although planted about a month apart, corn and cotton fields were rebedded, harrowed, planted, hoed, and cultivated in much the same way. Some families used new John Deere spring-toothed harrows to flatten the beds and pulverize the soil before planting, but most used home-made harrows of one sort or another—long 2-by-6-inch boards with railroad spikes driven through them, 4-by-4-inch boards with bois d'arc limbs nailed on the back, and a variety of other rigs. Harrowing went quickly, and when it ended the farmer studied the sky, assessed the weather signs, looked at his almanac, and made a decision about which day to plant. Family planting traditions, soil conditions, weather signs, almanac predictions, and fears of late frost or early drought all jostled for attention in the farmer's mind, as he determined the date to commit his seed to the ground.

In nineteenth-century times, farmers had grooved the top of the flattened rows with a light plow, then planted by hand in the seed furrows. By spring of 1927, however, virtually all area farmers used mechanical planters of the walking or riding varieties to accomplish this task. Often pulled by a single mule or horse, the walking planter looked like a small, simple, wooden wheelbarrow with a hole in the bottom, though it actually was rather more complicated than that. One variety, the Dowlow, included a small plow that went before to open the seed furrow, a narrow-edged wooden wheel that ran down the opened furrow, a reciprocating lever from the wheel to the seed box that opened and closed the seed orifice to drop seeds at preset intervals, and a pair of little plowshares on the back to cover them up.

Walking planters worked fine and lasted a long time, and some in operation in 1927 dated from the last century. However, many farmers chose to dispense with the inefficient furrow-opening part of the rig in favor of a second horse and plow. In field after field across the old farming counties along the Brazos and Colorado, the passer-by saw a two-stage planting process. First, a few yards ahead down the row, came one plowman using a light sweep to open the planting furrow in the top of the row, then came a second plowman with the walking planter.

Riding planters effectively replaced the two-stage planting with a single pass down the row, and many area farmers had one by 1927. If the walking planter looked like a small wooden wheelbarrow, the riding planter resembled a fragile, two-wheeled cart with a big metal seed can perched on the back. Pulled by two work stock, which walked in the middles on either side of the row being planted, the riding planter opened the seed furrow, dropped the seed at intervals determined by the operator's adjustments, and covered them up with small following plowshares all in one operation.

Compared to bedding up, hoeing, and picking, running the riding planter was light, pleasant fieldwork. Robert Skrabanek, however—with his father's critical eye on him at all times—found the task nerve-wracking. The level of seed in the seed bin had to be constantly monitored, since there could be no "skips" in the row, places where seed had not come up. In addition, planter settings were delicate; the "depths of the plowshares making the planting and covering furrows had to be just right, not too deep and not too shallow, and had to be watched closely at all times." Finally, John Skrabanek "demanded that the rows be planted absolutely straight."[18]

Like most other farmers, John Skrabanek immediately followed planting with swift passage over the field by a homemade, two-row log roller pulled by a single mule—this to pack the soil over the seeds. Thereafter, Skrabanek fidgeted over his field as he waited for the corn or cotton to come up. He visited it every day, dug into the beds to sample seed germination, and waited and watched like a nervous husband outside a delivery room. John Skrabanek, Otto Fuchs, and many others termed themselves "dirt farmers," but with professional pride. Robert Skrabanek recalled: "He showed me how to get down on my knees and inspect the planted seed to see if it was coming up. We removed the dirt over and around the seed very carefully so as not to disturb it in any way and then put it back and patted it gently. This was done with tenderness, since every potential plant was important."[19]

Farmers such as John Skrabanek were careful about their seeds, but nearly all the corn and most of the cotton were hand-selected from the best of last year's crop, not "pedigreed seed" bought in the store. Among the field corn, some sort of "yellow dent" variety predominated, though farmers selected the best ears for seed year after year and after a while simply thought of it as "their corn." Numerous varieties existed, though of dubious distinctiveness, since corn freely cross-pollinated in the fields with the corn of neighbors. The hybrid corns, which eventually would increase yields from fifty bushels an acre to one hundred bushels an acre, grew only in the fields of agricultural experiment stations in 1927.

Farmers more commonly planted store-bought cottonseed than corn, though during the 1920s two-thirds of all families used their own seed or got it from friends and neighbors.[20] Cotton cross-pollinated in the fields even more readily than corn, and as a result tended to deteriorate—to "run out"—over time, periodically requiring "fresh seed," which might be purchased in the store but more often was obtained from a neighbor. Farmers fought this little-understood tendency by selecting only the best of each year's crop as seed cotton for next year, and by often trying different seed stocks obtained from neighbors. The search was not just for the cotton variety that did best on a particular farm, but for the varieties that did best on each *field* of the farm.[21]

Possibilities abounded. Far more than with corn, seed men had focused on developing new strains of cotton, and a wide variety existed. Each had (or claimed to have) certain advantages over all the rest. Northern small-bolled varieties grew fast to beat the weevil; Celebrated Texas Storm Proof resisted blowing to the ground in thunderstorms of early autumn; Lone Star (developed from one stalk of Jackson cotton found in a field near Smithville, Bastrop County, in 1905) supposedly combined large bolls with weevil-beating rapid development; Half and Half, all the rage around 1914, claimed to produce lint-to-seed weight ratios of one-to-one, rather than the usual one-to-two. Unfortunately, Half and Half also contained many abnormally short fibers, and some buyers would not even accept it by 1927. Many Texas farmers, to the extent that they actually knew what kind of cotton grew in their fields, favored the Mebane, Rowden, Lone Star, Cook, Burnet, Quallah, and Kasoh cotton varieties. These were real cotton strains, but many others were only "trade names." Well aware of farmers' concern with their cotton running out over time, seed men constantly renamed their products. The "King" variety of cotton, for example, also was marketed as King's Early, King's Improved, Early King, Improved King, Re-improved Early King, and a half dozen other names. In 1923 the 38th Texas Legislature passed the Cotton Seed Registration and Certification Act in an attempt to eliminate these dubious practices.[22]

In any case, whatever pedigreed cotton a farmer planted in his field began a swift transformation into something else. One turn-of-the-century cotton expert noted: "Cotton is a plant which sports easily, which responds quickly to any differences in environment, soil, climate, treatment, and fertilizers, and which can be greatly modified in form and habit in a few successive crops. The flowers are large and open, so cross fertilization is not only common, but usual."[23]

Corn went into the ground around March 1st and cotton around April 1st in the old counties along the rivers, and no sooner did the seed germinate in the soil than the unpredictable events of season began to impact the crops. Farmers normally saved back seed for at least one, and often two, additional replantings, should disaster strike, and they often had to use them. The shape of these disasters varied with soils and local microclimates, whose tendencies farmers knew very well. Corn or cotton on Herman Schoenemann's sandy-land farm might fail to penetrate the ground surface because of a hard "packing rain" at the very worst time, or have soil eroded from around its roots after emergence, or be "froze off" from one of the late cold snaps that plagued this low-lying, creek-bottom farm.[24]

Often, these early crop disasters divided along blackland and sandy-land lines. Heavy, packing rains sealed off seeds from the surface on sandy lands, but not on blacklands. Conversely, long, cold rainy periods often rotted seeds in blacklands, necessitating replanting, but not in well-drained sandy lands, where seeds survived and germinated. Sandy-land soils were colder, many thought, more vulnerable to frost damage than blacklands, which absorbed solar radiation better and warmed up faster. Sandy lands sprouted more weeds, most agreed, but they did not keep one from getting into the field to chop and plow them down for long periods of time, as muddy blacklands could. One could "lose a crop" to cold, since even temperatures above freezing weakened young cotton plants to the point that they had to be replanted, or one could lose a crop to weeds—and especially in the blacklands. Sandy-land farmer Edwin Ebner once helped a neighbor in desperate weed chopping on a "real blackland farm" close to his place and well recalled how bad it could get. Prolonged rain had kept this farmer out of his fields until, "They had cotton in there, and we chopped in there, but you didn't get but one row chopped maybe in half a day." The neighbor's cotton field was a jungle of struggling cotton, "bloom weed, cockleburs, Johnson grass, and all kind of stuff." Mules cultivating in the field emerged from the rows with tails nine inches in diameter from the massed cockleburs.[25] On the fertile blackland fields of 1927, everything grew big and tall—cotton, corn, and, if rain fell and the worst happened, "careless weeds," cockleburs, and Johnson grass.

As the two main field crops, corn and cotton, emerged in turn from the soils during this spring of 1927, so did quick-growing weeds, and an army of family choppers and cultivators swung into action. "Cotton was a product of large families," one contemporary observed, and at no times during the crop cycle was this so true as during spring chopping and fall picking. Asked when he began farming, Teddy Keiler replied, "as soon as I was able to catch hold of a hoe," and Howard Davis began chopping so early he could not even remember beginning. Chopping time often brought every family member—man, woman, and child— into the field, and sometimes the work force was impressive. Howard Davis, his father, and his mother all chopped left-handed, while his sister and five brothers chopped right-handed. In Fayette County, when the young cotton got up three inches high and attained its four-leaf stage, Otto Treybig's entire family—his father, mother, eight brothers, and four sisters—took up their hoes and moved into the cotton field.[26] The yearly war on weeds and race with the weevil had begun.

Chopping and cultivation was a linked process. Verlie Wegner explained: "The whole family would hoe. We would thin it and get the grass in between and next to the cotton stalks. Then it would be plowed again, because you chopped the dirt away from the cotton, and if a rain or something would come up, it would make them fall over or collapse them. So, as quickly as they could, they would cultivate dirt up against these stalks, because they were tender because they grew in clumps, to hold it up."[27]

Choppers and cultivators began first in the cornfields, then—sometime about the second week in April, on the average—moved into the cotton, and farmers treated their corn and cotton much the same. They set their planters to plant both seeds about twice as thick as needed, this to make sure they had a "perfect stand." The old saying for corn held that you planted "one for the cut-worm, one for the crow, one for the blackbird, and one to grow." As soon as corn and cotton were up, "skips" where seeds had failed to germinate (or crows had been especially busy) were filled in by hand reseedings. During the first chopping, hoe hands moved slowly along the rows, carefully thinning the corn to single plants twelve to twenty-four inches apart and the cotton to "hills" of one to three plants about seven inches apart, the width of a cotton hoe, while at the same time removing emergent weeds. Chopping also removed soil from the row by the action of hoeing weeds and excess corn and cotton plants toward the middles, so farmers immediately followed it with cultivation—a light plowing of the middles to throw dirt back toward the rows and little plants, kill weeds, loosen the soil, and deepen the water furrows. In both corn and cotton, repeated cycles of chopping and cultivating followed until "laid by" time, when corn and cotton had grown so tall and spread so wide that they shaded out weeds and no further trips up the rows could be made.

An average of three choppings and three cultivations brought area crops to this laid-by stage, but the number of cycles depended on soils, weed problems, weevil problems, rainfall, and the farmer's diligence. Frequent cultivation maintained soil moisture, accelerated crop growth, and matured cotton bolls before boll weevils could destroy them. The more weeds, the more farmers had to chop and cultivate, and during periods of heavy rain, when weeds flourished and work stock and plows could not go in the fields, hoe hands had to fall to with a vengeance; losing one's crop to the weeds was a real possibility. In especially rainy and weedy periods, choppers often chopped from row to row and from field to field and then turned around and started chopping again at the beginning, without a break. The number of chopping and cultivating cycles also depended on how much the head taskmaster hated weeds in his fields, and John Skrabanek hated them more than most. In an average year, one with no unusual weed problems, the hardworking Skrabaneks chopped their cotton five times and cultivated it seven.[28] Calculated on the basis of an average peak-to-peak row interval of three feet, this totaled to 33.36 miles traveled per acre during chopping and cultivating.

Many craftsman-like subtleties entered into the chopping-cultivating cycle. Fathers often made special cut-down cotton hoes for their children, started them out on a row, and kept them under close surveillance for a while before letting them go off on their own. A sharp cotton hoe could easily sever a young toe, but the farmer also worried about his crops. Eddie Wegner's parents taught him to chop weeds out by the roots and not just "peck" at them, cutting off their tops, and the best way to ensure this was to pull the weed into the furrow with the hoe. Wegner explained: "Then you're assured that they're not hanging on by one little root. Like, a lot of those weeds, that's all they need, is one little root left on them and they go right back to growing. I've seen a lot of my hands just chop right over the top of that weed and leave a pretty good stump, and that'd green back out, you know. The quality of workmanship is a big thing in that."[29]

Skill and care with the hoe, "the quality of workmanship," proved especially important during the first thinning and weeding chop of the corn and cotton, when the hoe hand moved fast but dropped the heavy hoe with great delicacy to sever excess corn and cotton plants from others a scant quarter of an inch away. Roots were shallow and vulnerable at this point, so the hoe wielder had to thin and weed carefully. "You got to be pretty artistic with that thing," Robert Dement recalled.[30] Wielding the instrument of doom, the skilled chopper did not just remove crop plants mechanically, every few inches, but made swift judgments about their viability based upon leaf coloration and growth pattern. A good many cotton choppers, for example, spared short, sturdy, dark-green cotton plants and executed tall, spindly, yellowish ones, and they made similar decisions about the corn.

Choppers varied in speed, skill, and diligence. Grover Williams's brother "Snook" chopped so carelessly that "later, you could see it on the row"; high weeds soon flourished on the rows where Snook had gone.[31] Conversely, Mance Lipscomb's mother hitched up her skirt around her hips and chopped so skillfully and speedily down the rows that no man could match her. Mrs. Lipscomb sometimes went into a state of religious excitement when she chopped. "She didn't never stop moving in her legs and foots, and never stop singing when she want to. She had the Spirit in her, gospel could hit her anytime. When she get her heart full, everything was under pressure in her, and it could just boil over."[32]

Skilled hoeing required a sharp hoe, and the hoe hands often crouched down on their knees in the field to resharpen hoe blades with files, the hoe handles sticking out behind them "like tails."[33] Sandy soils quickly dulled hoe blades and plow points, forcing frequent resharpening. In the course of a chopping season, sandy-land hoes wore down inch-by-inch with constant use and grew "shiny as a new dollar."[34]

Cultivation also required delicate control, especially the first time through the field. Before the turn of the century, farmers had often cultivated with light, one-mule wooden plows with sweep plowshares, and some still used these in 1927 for one last trip up the middles before laid-by time, when nothing else could get through. A sweep was an arrow-head-shaped plowshare that cut shallowly into the soil, loosening it up and throwing some soil to either side, but dropping most of it back in the same place. Double plowshares on the same sort of light plow stocks—double-sweeps or double-shovels—gradually replaced the single sweeps, but these still required two trips up and down the row to clean it of grass and throw soil to the plant roots.

Such primitive cultivators had become obsolete by 1927, however, and most farmers used either four-sweep or six-sweep walking or riding cultivators to straddle the row and cultivate both sides of it at the same time. Mechanically complicated, both riding and walking cultivators required various delicate adjustments so the arrays of little plowshares on each side cut at the right distance from the plant roots and at the correct angles, and operators had to watch what they did. Mance Lipscomb recalled: "We had to strain on little bitty cotton, cause, be careful or we gonna cover up that cotton. We knowed how close to get to it. Everybody couldn't use that cultivator. And when it got up knee high, we could get away from it a little further. It wouldn't be worrying us so high that way."[35] Wallie Schmidt explained: "How much you plowed depended on how thick your crop was. If your cotton or corn was real small, you had to go slow, you had to hold your team back and make em walk slow. You couldn't do more than four or five acres. And when it was big so you couldn't cover it, I covered as much as ten, twelve acres a day."[36]

Different soils required different cultivator adjustments. Robert Wilhelmsen found it extremely difficult to set the family walking cultivator exactly right for their main cotton field, since soil in the field changed four times, from fine sandy loam to heavy blackland, in the course of a single row.[37] Robert Skrabanek began chopping at age six and running the walking cultivator at age nine. Prideful of his promotion to the cultivator, Robert found that he liked the task—liked the near silence, with only a jingling of traces, the sound of the passing breeze, and the "pleasant, soft soil sound" the six little plowshares made as they coursed through the soil. Skrabanek noted that as the quitting times at noon and dusk approached, the mules' innate sense of time clicked in. Most of the day, they moved at uniform speed, but as the

two feeding times approached, they quickened their pace on rows running toward house and barn, then slowed down on rows leading away.[38]

Walking cultivator operators, such as Skrabanek and Lipscomb,
guided the sweep assemblies with their hands; riding cultivator plowmen guided them with their feet. As Kermit Fox described, guiding
with the feet required skill: "With a horse-drawn implement this could
be tricky. As the rider, one had to watch the course of the team especially at the ends of the rows. At the same time, one had to properly
guide the sweep assembly with the feet. It took caution to let the inner
pair of sweeps slide along within six inches of the stalks, yet not make
a miscue that would plow a gap into the planted row."[39] Like other farm
families, the Fuchs used their cultivators all they could, tricky though
they were. As one farmer explained, "The more you can cultivate, the
better you're off—you save on hoeing."[40] Depending on weeds and
stage of the crop, a skilled chopper covered one-half to one-and-a-half
acres a day, a cultivator ten or more acres.[41]

With the entire family in the fields for chopping and cultivating,
provision had to be made for child care, and parents put their young
children in or under wagons, placed them in the shade of field-side
trees, tied them to a bush, staked them out, or penned them in homemade shelters and playhouses of various degrees of elaborateness. A
mother might worry about spiders, snakes, scorpions, and "polecats,"
but she had to be in the field and so did her children—all of them.
Chopping season was one of the two "all hands on deck" times for the
farm family, when weeds threatened and economic survival hung in the
balance. In Elvera Schmidt's family, as in many others, the rule was,
"nobody stays home."[42]

A good many area families, usually the landowning ones, built little
playhouses for the small children and skidded them back and forth to
the fields with mules. Eddie Wegner recalled that his father pulled their
child shelter out and back every day, usually stationing it on the turnrow.
Like the little field house Ora Nell Fuchs recalled, the Wegner's shelter
had been constructed water-tight, with a rived board roof and wooden
floor and was provisioned for the day with water, cookies, and a few
toys. Eddie Wegner recalled, "The sides and the back were hinged at the
top and could be hung at a 45-degree angle and hooked with a piece of
well chain, which made the six-by-eight building about twice as big as it
would have been with the sides down." Wegner and his sister played in

FIGURE 13 Young Robert Wilhelmsen of the Salem community, Washington County, carrying two syrup buckets filled with a noon meal for his father working in the cotton fields. Visible in the background are examples of the center-pole haystacks preferred by many area farmers. (Robert Wilhelmsen, Washington County)

and around this little building while their father, mother, brothers, and sisters worked in the field. One of Eddie's earliest memories was sitting in this field house and watching his mother chop away from him down the row and calling after her, "Mama! Mama! Mama! Mama!," as she gradually went out of sight across the hill field. Eddie's older sister made fun of this "squalling brat" behavior, but Eddie felt relief only when his mother chopped back into sight, coming the other way.[43]

Landowners and sharecroppers, most families had the same child-care problems in the field. Mance Lipscomb's mother had no elaborate playhouse and had to leave her children under a field-side tree, but the young Lipscombs had a faithful guard. Lipscomb explained: "It's three of us raised up under one dog. That dog wouldn't let you come up to that tree to save your life. Lay that baby out under a tree, put him in an old blanket and something there where he wouldn't get in the sun, and that dog was laying right down at that tree. A lot of snakes is on that river, and they'd come up there under that shade, cause that baby's in the shade. That dog see snakes come a-crawling up there, great big old moccasins and pilots, and that dog done killed em—shook em and had the guts out of em."[44]

Considering the problems of child care, young children began accompanying their parents in the field almost as soon as they could walk. At first, they just toddled alongside their working parents or rode on the pick sacks. Then, fathers made little, cut-down child hoes and mothers devised little pick sacks made from pillowcases or feed "croker sacks." As Herman Schoenemann explained, his two little boys left their field pen even before this time: "Then, you'd have like a walking cultivator. We'd put a box up there on that top, and they'd set in there, and they'd ride, ride along with you."[45]

As in Howard Matthies's and Eddie Wegner's families, for a time this child fieldwork was permissive. Wegner told: "My people were very compassionate people. We were indoctrinated to do field work in our early years. However, when we complained of being tired or hot, they weren't hard and said, 'You've got to do this.' They let us go, you know. But we learned how to chop cotton when we were five, six years old."[46] At some point, however, field discipline came down harder. Howard Matthies recalled, "The next year, you were man enough to carry a row yourself. And sometimes they'd say, 'Oh, you gonna have to do better, you left too much grass or you cut away too much cotton.'"[47] Finally, field discipline became strongly enforced, perhaps even with imposed quotas for rows to be chopped or poundage of cotton to be picked. Parental demands for child fieldwork often depended on the family work force. Mance Lipscomb began cultivating at age eleven, after his oldest brother left home. Ora Nell Fuchs's parents had a fine blackland farm out from Carmine, but only two little girls to help work it. Consequently, Fuchs's mother did fieldwork all the time, even some plowing, and Ora Nell and her sister came under strict field discipline very early. As she tersely summed it up: "Home from school, put on different clothes, hit the cotton patch."[48]

One of the problems with child field labor was that children were children and had to be kept under surveillance or they would sometimes "play off," no matter how much the weeds threatened the cotton. George Lester Vaughn's father enforced strict field discipline for his sons, perhaps to the point of child abuse, but even he could not keep them from occasional rock throwing at woodpeckers and dirt-clod wars in the field.[49] Susie Davidson and her sister and brothers, when their father had plowed out of sight, would drop their cotton hoes and play impromptu baseball using hapless king snakes as balls.[50] Another infant cotton chopper received a spanking for leaving excessively large skips between plants, "thinking in her child's mind that the less cotton that grew, the less she would have to pick the next fall."[51] Some people recalled their childhood field labor almost as a kind of slavery. An old story from Antebellum times told to Oliver Whitener by his father had as its point the necessity for surveillance and harsh field discipline for the hard labors of cotton chopping and picking. Needing additional laborers in his fields, a farmer contracted with a monkey raiser for use of his band of monkeys. Asked later if the monkeys had done the job, the farmer replies, "Yes, they did, but it took a man to every monkey."[52]

Many farmers would have liked to hire additional hoe hands during cotton-chopping season, but not all had the chance. Virtually every family member on area farms frantically wielded hoes down his or her family's rows of cotton and corn. Finally caught up on their own work, Emil Albers and his brothers occasionally chopped cotton for Fayette County neighbors for fifty or seventy-five cents a day, can see to can't.[53] Mance Lipscomb's brother and sister, Willie and Lily, began fieldwork as a two-person child chopping team paid one adult wage. They worked side-by-side down each row, receiving a joint seventy cents a day.[54]

Lured to John Skrabanek's farm by below-average fifty-cents-a-day wages and wonderful, generous noon meals, various blacks, Mexicans, and Anglo-Americans chopped cotton for the Skrabanek family every year. The Skrabaneks chopped also, trying to demonstrate the speedy, efficient, and untiring labor expected of all their hired hands. While they worked, family members also monitored worker behavior and exchanged private messages about them in Czech. "So-and-so is chopping like a half-dead man," that sort of thing.[55]

Desperate to get the weeds out of the cotton and corn, many area farmers exercised strong discipline over their children and hired hands during chopping season, but these stern German and Czech fathers were nothing compared to their "overseer" counterparts at the big cotton farms along the rivers. Recruited from Austin under false pretenses, and horrified to find himself under virtual penal servitude at a big Brazos valley farm west of Hearne, Willis Sorrels described one such intimidating bossman: "He rode a great big old black horse—bald-faced black horse. And ever time you seen him, he's in a gallop, you see. Ever time you seen him coming he's riding at a gallop, great big white-handled six-shooter on his side and great big old whip like a quirt but twice as long as a quirt." Overseers like this man in the Brazos bottoms "don't treat colored people like they're people at all, they treat you like you're some kind of animal," Sorrel said.[56]

A local boy instead of a displaced townsman, Mance Lipscomb spent most of his life working on large bottomland farms, and he more or less concurred with Sorrels's description of the "overlords" or "pushers" who directed the daily activities of the hired-hand or sharecropper work gangs, called "letts."

> You know what bossman is? Telling you what to do and what not to do, a pusher and a shover. Well, we called em overseer. What he say, why, it went. And we was scared to do something he didn't want us to do. Is two things gonna happen, you either got to get whipped or leave the place if you didn't do like the bossman said. One man riding his horse, he could corral a hundred people, one word spoke a hundred times! He say, "I want you boys to get this cut of land done today," or tomorrow. Whatever the time he estimated for to get it finished, a hundred people agreed to it. No word back, say

"I can't do that." It wasn't no can't. And if you couldn't do it, he'd fuss, cuss you, whup you, kill you, or run you off.[57]

Lipscomb did not exaggerate. As a teenager he had been chopping cotton in a work gang near the fence line of another farm, while that farm's work gang chopped just beyond the boundary fence. Customarily, overseers released women from the field a half hour before the men at noon so they could return home and prepare the noon meals. One man had forgotten to split wood for his wife's cook stove and now needed to do this so she could prepare dinner. After trying to explain why he needed to leave the field early to the elderly, somewhat-deaf overseer without much success, the man tried to walk away from the field, only to be blocked by the overseer's horse. Three times this happened, and the third time, fearful of being stepped on by the horse, the man reached up for the reins. At that point the overseer drew a .38 pistol from his boot and shot the man twice, once standing and once on the ground. Lipscomb recalled:

> "Boom! Boom!" We heard it and we looked up, and he was falling then, and he wasn't no further from us than from here to that road. I said, "Whoa! They shot him down." And his wife commenced to screaming and hollerin, and the women, some of em, they run, and some of em went back to get over him, you know, cause he was dying. He just laid there, and he had a hoe file in his hand, and he fell with his arm out this-away. Man, they just went there and looked at it. Another arm was under his back, and he was dead. His tongue was sticking out and his eyes was open.[58]

Later, following standard practice in such matters, someone "found" a knife in the vicinity of the shooting, supporting the overseer's claim that the man had come at him with one, and the overseer went unpunished.

As Willis Sorrels avowed, for a black person "that Brazos bottom is trouble."[59] Born a slave, Laura Smalley sharecropped sixteen years on one bottomland farm, "where there were sure fine white folk for you to work at." Her eccentric (and hard-drinking) landlord had only one quirk, and in the bottoms white landlords and overseers often got to indulge their quirks; this man liked to fight his field hands in the field.

Smalley explained, "He wouldn't try to hurt none of em, but he'd jump down off his horse to fight em—he'd jump right down by the plow where his half-hands working and commenced knocking em, you know. And they had to fight him, and they'd fight him, too. He sure was a good old white man, though." At the end of the day the "good old white man" often said, "Let's go to town, boys, and drink it off!" Just as this man's "half-hands" had no option but to fistfight him in the field, now they had no option but to go drink with him.[60]

Disadvantaged, impoverished, and exploited though they were, sharecropper families along the Brazos lived simpler and perhaps less laborious lives than the families of many small upland landowners. There, a diverse farm economy of corn and cotton, subsistence field crops, feed crops, potato patches, gardens, and a menagerie of domestic livestock made relentless demands on farm families for twelve hours a day, twelve months of the year. When families rose before dawn to attend to farmstead animals, for example, they ministered to cows, calves, mules, horses, hogs, guineas, turkeys, chickens, geese, ducks, dogs, cats, honey bees, and perhaps a few other creatures. Especially during the crop year, demands of fieldwork, cooking and house cleaning, gardening and food preservation, and diverse household "chores" fell heavily on everyone, but particularly the women, who often did double duty. As a consequence of all the work, large farm families had to be organized almost with military discipline and precision, and many wore virtually a "uniform," as well. Males in Howard Matthies's family, for example, invariably were issued straw hats, feed-sack shirts, overalls, and (in the winter) jacket-like "jumpers" made of old cotton sacks. Howard's mother and sisters wore feed-sack dresses, multipurpose cotton aprons, and "slat bonnets" to protect them from the sun. He remembered: "When Grandpa Matthies didn't have anything else to do, he would cut cedars, you know, and they'd put cedar in there to make [the bonnets] stiff. A lot of em used pasteboard, but you get out in the field and you were caught with a shower of rain, then your pasteboard was gone."[61] Nor was rain falling on the Matthies women during fieldwork all that uncommon.

The assignment of chores and work roles in farm families depended on family demographics—the number of children, the ratio of boys to girls, and the various ages of brothers and sisters. Small families and boy-deficient families were in trouble. Ora Nell Fuchs and her sister

FIGURE 14 The Christian Matthies family poses in front of the board-and-batten home on La Bahia Prairie near Burton, ca. 1910. The Matthieses, like many small landowners of the time, enlarged their home as the family grew; evidence of a structural addition can be seen in the different materials of the roof. (Howard Matthies, Burton)

could not afford to specialize, since each of them had to do nearly everything.[62] In their family, as in others also deficient in males, older girls had to be "made the boy" to help out with such heavy labor as plowing, wood cutting, and clearing new ground.

This happened to Lydia Domasch, Susie Davidson, Evarilla Harrell, Fannie Chism, Blundina Berkmann, and many others, and some liked their masculine labors and some did not. Lydia Domasch resented being kept out of school to plow spring fields and still having to perform the usual feminine chores around the house—baking bread before daylight and picking up eggs by coal-oil lantern in the hen house after dark, following a long, hard day behind the mules.[63] Susie Davidson, on the other hand, recalled: "My favorite chore wasn't cooking, for sure. Outside work: plowing, hoeing, hauling logs, sawing wood. See, 'Knot' [her brother] left home when he was 13 years old, and the next spring I went between the plow handles. I was papa's plowboy, wood hauler, and everything else till I was 17."[64] Born in 1884 to a family that did not see its first male child until 1890, Evarilla Harrell told the same story: "I didn't let nobody beat me picking cotton, cause I had to make the boy. I helped my daddy do everything. I was the next to the oldest in the group, and my oldest sister tended to the children, but I didn't want to tend to the children, noway. I helped daddy, I made a hand with him. I sawed rail timber, I just did whatever there was to be done."[65] Born in a sharecropper's family in 1898, African-American Fannie Chism enjoyed working like a man so much she stopped only at age seventy-three, on doctor's orders. The doctor, she said, "told me I'd better put that plow down. I hated to give it up because I like to farm better than anything I've ever done. Shoot, there ain't any place around here that you can look at that I ain't plowed. I plowed all over, I cleared new ground, I've done all kind of work in the fields—splitting rails, fixing fence, clearing new ground, cutting wood with a crosscut saw. I ain't seen a knot that I couldn't split. I can split them now if you want me to."[66]

Many men appreciated such capable women, especially if they married them. Howard Davis's wife had come from a family with no boys, and: "her daddy had learnt her to plow before I married her. She drove one of them cultivators—she could hook up a pair of horses, put that in the ground, just good as I could. She could do anything any man can do, I don't care what it was."[67] Blundina Berkmann of Fayette County took wifely independence even further. She drove the buggy when the family went into town, her big husband seated alongside, led the way into the store, then did all the family buying. Blundina even wagoned family cotton to the gin and arranged for its sale by herself, something almost unheard of for a woman.[68]

Howard Matthies and Kermit Fox both came from families with nine children—about the average number in the old counties along the rivers—and the complicated division of labor in their families typified most. Matthies had four brothers and four sisters. Few demands were made on one sister, who was mildly retarded, but everyone else had assigned duties, both before and after school, with Howard's father in charge of the boys and Howard's mother in charge of the girls. Two boys milked cows each morning, one fed cows and horses, one fed hogs, and one—Howard—churned the daily milk for butter. Typical of many, the oldest boy often stayed home from school to do fieldwork or to help his father. After school, his younger brothers helped with whatever fieldwork needed to be done. In crop season, older males tended to be assigned skilled tasks, such as running the cultivators, and younger males (and females) to be ordered to wield the hoes. At picking time, everybody picked. Howard's mother assigned daily work for the four girls, who rotated bed making, dishwashing, sweeping, and other household tasks, then helped with fieldwork—especially chopping and picking—as needed. Howard's mother rarely did fieldwork, though she sometimes helped in emergency circumstances with chopping and picking, especially if there were rumors of a Gulf storm on the way, but she did virtually all the cooking and all the sewing for this family of eleven. As time went on, certain family members gravitated naturally to certain tasks they were especially good at (or perhaps nobody else wanted to do). One of Howard's sisters, a poor hand at fieldwork, ironed for the whole family—a difficult task that often took her two full days to accomplish.[69]

Kermit Fox and Robert Skrabanek grew up in similar families and both had a youngest child's perspective on large-family interdynamics. Since there might be almost a generation between them, older brothers and sisters often served virtually as surrogate parents for their youngest siblings. This could be both good and bad. At age four, Kermit Fox had a special relationship with his grown-up sister Lydia, age nineteen, and thought of her as his "second mother."[70] Conversely, Albert Banik often chafed under the command of his older brother August. One day, for whatever reason, Albert repeatedly refused to open a gate for his brother and was severely punished with a rope. He recalled: "August again took hold of my arm and this time he really let me have it. This time I decided to open the gate. This experience taught me to always obey authority if it is reasonable."[71]

Other younger children in large families experienced problems derived from the pecking order. For example, the Skrabanek children bathed in turn in a Number 3 washtub, first the two girls, then the three boys, of whom Robert was youngest and last. As each bather added water to the tub, the water got deeper and deeper but also dirtier and dirtier, and sometimes Robert did not finish his bath feeling very clean.[72]

Periodically, discord rocked the domestic serenity of the best of farm families, even the ones that closed ranks and went into action with military precision at chopping and picking times. All one year, the several Matthies brothers scuffled over taking turns with their one BB gun, but much deeper rivalries also occurred. Boys and girls competed for scarce parental attentions with their nearest siblings or resented the authority of an older brother or sister. Sometimes father and mother seemed aloof, remote, and somewhat unapproachable—almost old enough to be one's grandparents. The oldest children had rights of authority and seniority, but they missed more school and had to work harder than the others—or so they often thought. Youngest children often bathed last, served themselves last at the table, and brought up the rear in a lot of things, and sometimes that rankled. Many times, children formed alliances with the nearest siblings of the same sex, but occasionally these near relationships turned acrimonious. One woman revealed to her sister during an argument fifty years later that she had always urinated in the washtub just before she got out and the sister got in. All this explains why one farm wife occasionally pulled her apron over her head to meditate, pray, and shut out the sights and sounds of her quarrelsome household. Husband and children knew to leave "mother" strictly alone at the times when she took refuge under her apron.[73]

Farm families needed all the teamwork and solidarity they could muster, however, since the threats of season—weather, weeds, and insects—menaced corn, cotton, and other crops from the moment their seeds went in the ground. "Las Vegas is a piker compared to the farmer," Eddie Wegner said without exaggeration.[74] The first threat was weather: a late cold spell that turned thriving young cotton plants to "possum-eared cotton"—weakened plants the farmer had to plow up and replant—or too much rain, or too little. Likewise, as Mrs. Otis Dean observed, "if corn came up during rainy cold weather, it would get only knee high and yellow as a ducks's foot—replant."[75] Estimating the coming temperatures and rainfall, farmers usually planted their corn about four inches deep and their cotton about two inches deep, but sometimes they regretted their decisions. Asked how deep he planted, the acerbic Teddy Keiler replied, "sometimes too deep, sometimes not deep enough."[76] How well the crops prospered depended on the weather of that year, something unpredictable. Sometimes the cycle of early weather favored crops on the blacklands, sometimes it favored crops on the sandy lands, and sometimes all was a disaster. Henry Jaeger affirmed, "Farming is the biggest gamble you can go into."[77]

Long after the first chance of cold had passed, farm families watched approaching thunderstorms with mixed emotions. Crops often needed rain, but every passing cloud hung a Damoclesian sword of hail over the cotton and corn; after five minutes of destructive icefall, it could be planting time again. Every spring from 1900 to 1927, the La Grange *Journal* and Brenham *Daily Banner-Press* recorded the passing hail storms, now decimating crops around Oldenburg, now crops around Sand Town, now somewhere else. The 1909 lament of the Carmine correspondent to the La Grange paper had been echoed many times before this spring of 1927: "Since Friday's rain and hailstorm everything looks broken and finished. This year, our section is only a shadow of her former self, a condition due to the storm."[78] In time, each farm family's luck tended to run out, as it did for the Wilhelmsens of the Salem community of Washington County. Crops were up and doing well when a big hailstorm marched across the land in a storm swath three miles wide and twenty miles long and pounded their young corn and cotton into the ground.[79] The threat of hail hung in the sky and in farmers' bad dreams throughout the spring and early summer of 1927.

Area farmers could do nothing about the weather, but weeds, a constant enemy of the crops, were another matter, and the farm family waged relentless war against them with sharp hoes and mule-powered cultivators. Weeds were swift-emerging plants that loved disturbed ground, deeply loosened soil, and barnyard manure—in short, the farmer's fields. Farmers knew weeds intimately and had names for every kind: goose grass, nut grass, hurrah grass, Johnson grass, persimmon sprouts, white thistle, cocklebur, Mexican bur, burdock, morning glory, coffee bean, careless weed, bull nettle, burn nettle, stinking gourd, tie vine, and others. Some weeds seemed to come and go—bad some years, virtually absent from the fields in others. The plant Eddie Wegner called "Mexican bur" (a short, spiny bush producing a yellow flower) was one of these. In certain seasons every furrow you plowed called forth "a solid stand of Mexican bur—it'll come up fast like hair on a dog, so, the seed must last for a long, long time."[80] Tie vines were another sometimes problem and could be especially troublesome in late-season corn. Johnnie Loud recalled: "You'd have a lot of trouble with that corn, cause, see it'd be all up around your ears. And wasps and stinging scorpions sure did like that—man, you'd get stung so much, so much." Like other weeds, under the right conditions tie vine also could come up "thick as hair on a dog."[81]

Any weed could be a problem in a particular year, but a few were terrible problems every year and in an especially wet spring could threaten to "just take that cotton away from you." At the top of this list were cockleburs and Johnson grass, the plant that Texas farming historian Samuel Evans accurately described as "the one unconquerable weed."[82]

Not that cockleburs were not bad enough. Robert Dement explained that if you could not get in the field to cultivate the rows or plow the middles because the field was too wet, the cockleburs might virtually take over, since they grew as fast as the cotton. "I've seen it just as thick around cotton as the cotton was. You had to get down there and pull it away from it. I've seen fields, and ours too, sometimes, where they just take the cotton away from you. I mean, folks just had to give up because it rained so much, and they couldn't get in there and plow it."[83] Herman Schoenemann hated cockleburs, which gave him fits on his sandy-land farm, where "you get a heavy dew overnight and seed will come up." He said that "them cockleburs will come up thick as hair on a dog's back, and I don't care what time of year a cocklebur'll come up, if he don't get but two inches tall, he gonna make a seed."[84] As well as growing thick as the dog's hair, cockleburs also stuck to the dog, and in bad cocklebur years living things on the farm became festooned with seeds, which stubbornly clung to fur, hair, and cotton cloth. The Matthies family's fields on La Bahia Prairie had few weeds, and when Howard Matthies's father found a single cocklebur, he gave it special attention. "In the corn field, if Papa saw a stalk of cockleburs, we'd pull it up or cut it off, put it on a wagon. That would go under the washpot."[85] Landowners sometimes believed that renters and weeds often went together, due to slovenly hoe discipline, and once a tenant family left the Wegner farm in midseason and the cockleburs took their field. Eddie and his father labored mightily, cutting and burning cockleburs, but even some of the ones they burned still came up. An old saying asserted that a cocklebur would come up seven years from a single seed.[86]

To Eddie Wegner and to most other farmers, Johnson grass was far worse, and, as Wegner did, many people "fought it tooth and nail" for many years and failed to win the battle. On one occasion Wegner rode by an elderly neighbor's place and found him pulling Johnson grass from his field. Watching for a time, Wegner said, "Don't you know there's hardly any end to that?" The man replied, "I well realize that." Wegner asked, "How long have you been fighting it?" and the old man said, "All my life."[87]

As Wegner correctly noted, "once Johnson grass gets a hold on land, it's like the plague." The curse of Texas cotton fields, this weed loved blackland soils and "the best cotton lands in the state." Each mature stalk produced hundreds of seeds, all very viable, and tiny enough to be dispersed by floods, heavy runoff, wind, and the droppings of birds and work animals. Johnson grass grew three to six feet high and had a tangle of underground roots, or rhisomes, that sometimes penetrated four feet deep. Even if one laboriously grubbed it up, the least root fragment left behind produced a new plant. "Frighteningly persistent," this "one unconquerable weed" did best on rich, cultivated land and was the blackland cotton farmer's worst nightmare.[88] Landowners sometimes threw renters off their places because of a lack of diligence in Johnson grass suppression, as Laura Smalley's "good old white man" did her in the Brazos bottoms. Johnson grass even became a political issue in rural school districts, where farmers suspected passing scholars' horses of spreading the terrible weed in their dung.[89]

Farmers unfortunately had not always been of this opinion about Johnson grass and had seeded it far and wide. Around 1830, Johnson grass was first imported from its home in the Mediterranean areas of Europe, Africa, and Asia by no less than the governor of South Carolina. The new arrival was touted as a wonderful pasture grass, the South's answer to northerners' timothy hay. Fifty years after its arrival, in 1884, seed dealers still sold Johnson grass seed to Texans for five dollars a bushel at the same time that anti-Johnson grass forces expressed vitriolic opposition. One man wrote in *Farm and Ranch* in 1888, after quoting several enemies of the devil weed, "He who in the face of such testimony as the foregoing, sows one seed of this grass to propagate it, may justly be looked upon as an enemy to the race."[90] The latter opinion won out, and in 1895 and 1901 the Texas Legislature passed acts making it illegal for anyone to "sow, scatter, or place on land not his own, the seed or roots of Johnson grass" and prohibiting railroads from allowing Johnson grass to make seed on their right-of-ways. However, the statutes proved unenforceable, and Johnson grass seeds spread widely by water, wind, birds, and—in hay shipments—by railroad. Ironically, the only thing that kept this failed pasture grass in partial check was heavy grazing—a fact that did area cotton farmers little good. Around 1900 inventors and hucksters had marketed different solutions to the Johnson grass problem (as they also did for the boll weevil), but none worked. One partly successful "secret" method required the farmer to plow, harrow, and cultivate his land seventeen times and hoe it several times more, so that the cost of cultivation for a given season almost equaled the value of the land.[91]

By this spring of 1927, some Fayette and Washington County farms had a great deal of Johnson grass, and some had only a little. The farmers that had it chopped and cultivated incessantly and made the best crops they could with the grass in the field, and the ones that did not patrolled unceasingly to keep it out. Fritz Meinen, who otherwise placed no credence in the signs, diligently attacked his Johnson grass on the three days before and the day after the August full moon, believing that only on these four days would the "old roots all die."[92] The Wegners carefully scythed down the grass they had in one small corner patch on their farm before it could make seed, thus keeping it at bay, and not until World War II would lazy renters allow it to engulf their farm. Albert Wilhelmsen's father insisted that his sons pluck up any wisp of Johnson grass from the family's fields whenever they encountered it, put it in their pockets, take it back to the house, and burn it— this without fail and taking priority over all other activities. Fifteen years later, Albert would land in New Guinea as part of the U.S. invasion force only to find "that damn stuff" there before him.[93]

Other threats hung over the cotton fields in 1927—old enemies that waxed and waned in severity depending on the particular crop season—insect pests like army worms, cotton bollworms, pink bollworms, and Mexican boll weevils, and the deadly fungus pest of cotton root rot, which spread plant to plant under the ground. By 1927, farm families had a fighting chance with all of these but the incurable root rot, for which there was no remedy. Early and late, thriving cotton plants suddenly might wilt, "keel over," turn brown, and die. This occurred in patches in the cotton field and was particularly severe on the heavier blacklands in the wetter years. Sandy-land farmers rarely were troubled with root rot, also known as "poison soil," "dead soil," and "root blight," and blackland farmers simply regarded it as a cross to be borne. They had little choice, since no effective fungicide existed and the only cure was a conversion to pastureland or clover for several crop years, an option few families could afford. If root rot killed a patch in the field, the farmer often left it unplanted for the following year and hoped for the best thereafter. Like the deep, clinging mud, root rot was a price one paid for farming on the fertile, drought-resistant blacklands. One year, Gus Draeger's blackland farm had root rot so bad he made two bales on twelve acres.[94]

The boll weevil, a "small, black, clumsy, long-snouted, hump-back comical appearing insect," also had become a fact of the farming life by 1927, and cotton farming by that year might well be described as a process of "living with the weevil." Farmers farmed to keep the weevil in check, occasionally applied arsenic-based pesticides, and hoped for cold winters, moderate rainfall, and other acts of God to keep the weevils down. Mild winters allowed larger numbers of weevils to survive the cold, starting them off with higher than average populations in the spring. Survivors emerged from leaf debris in fields and nearby woodlands in early spring, searched out the little cotton plants, crawled about for a time feeding on leaf buds, then bored into the little "squares," which later became the blossoms, to lay their eggs. Later generations attacked the developing bolls. A weevil generation took only 27 days, thus allowing five generations during the approximately 150-day growing season of the cotton plant, and Samuel Evans well stated the extent of the farmer's problem.

> Later in the season, when the number of the weevils became multitudinous, their habit of feeding upon and laying eggs within the cotton or buds or squares, or in the absence, inside tiny bolls, caused tremendous destruction. Each square or boll punctured, died, and fell from the plant. An egg hatched in two or three days into a tiny footless grub, the larva, which fed upon the contents of the square, and, after fourteen to seventeen days, was transformed into a pupa which resided for approximately ten days, before emerging as an adult to begin the life cycle

of another generation. Under ideal conditions for reproduc-
tion, which fortunately seldom existed, the progeny of a
single pair emerging in the early spring could reach something like one hundred and thirty-four million before the
coming of frost.[95]

Farmers destroyed weevil-carrying crop debris from the previous season
by burning or thoroughly burying it, then planted as early as possible
and cultivated as frequently as possible to hurry the crop to fruition as
early in the fall as they could—this to escape the worst of the weevil's
geometric population increases. When weevil populations soared,
farmers resorted to hated pesticides, which by 1927 had attained some
effectiveness.

In slightly earlier times all had used "Paris Green" or "London
Purple," arsenic pesticide dusts applied by hand. Gus Draeger told,
"Those old two-handed dusters, God Almighty! I walked a many a
time with then dusters, swallowed some of that poison, too."[96] The
farmer mixed the pesticide with flour, put the mixture in two porous
sacks, tied the sacks on either end of a stick, went out in the field on
foot or on horseback when the dew was still on the cotton leaves, and
moved up and down the middles shaking the sacks over the rows.
Harold Davis recalled watching his father do this, trotting his horse
along the cotton rows in a cloud of purple dust. "They got on that horse
and made them sacks hit that saddlehorn and shuck that poison out,
trot that horse down the field, that dust would shake out."[97] Only the
color of the dust was different—Paris Green instead of London
Purple—at Grover Williams's grandparent's farm in 1927, a time when
the Otto Fuchs family already used a state-of-the-art, five-row, water
sprayer to vanquish their weevils.[98] Williams described his grandfather's method of application.

> We used Paris Green, I think they called it. It's something
> like arsenic. See, the old man, he must have been immune
> to all of that, snake bites and arsenic and poison. He didn't
> have the equipment like the affluent farmers had—you
> know, sprayers and stuff, whatever. He had to get him a long
> stick, just as wide as the row. The only protection he had on,
> he had on maybe an old handkerchief across his mouth. And

he had a little dust bag on each end of that pole he had to walk. He'd let it touch the cotton [on either side.] He would just shake it over, just walk around and shake it, hoping he'd get enough on there to stop the boll weevil from piercing that boll. Anytime a weevil would pierce one of those bolls, that lock of cotton would be damaged when it opened up. It wasn't like a plane coming over with a great big old mist; it was just enough where it didn't do any good. We still had a lot of boll weevils and worms and stuff like that.[99]

The image of his grandfather walking the furrow, pole across his shoulders, partly obscured by a green cloud of arsenic dust, remained vivid in Williams's mind. The method had been recommended as the best available practice as late as 1909 by Texas A&M crop scientists, but it did not work very well.[100] The poison went on unevenly, it killed only the weevils abroad on the plant at the time and not those in the bolls, and soon additional weevils hatched out. Herman Schoenemann told of a neighbor's discouraging test of the pesticide's effectiveness: "This one fellow, he caught four or five boll weevils and put em in a jar and filled the jar full of dust. The next morning, boll weevils was up there under the top trying to get out."[101]

Around the turn of the century, when the weevil first arrived, "book farmers" had advised cotton growers to pick up infected cotton squares from the ground in the fields and even to pick off weevils by hand. Teddy Keiler vividly recalled his father picking up cotton squares, day after day, then exposing them to the sun to kill the weevils. However, this proved equivalent to throwing Brer Rabbit in the briar patch. Keiler explained: "They put em in all the sacks they could find and threw em out in the sun. Next day, somebody came over, a neighbor, he said, 'Yeah, that didn't do no good—getting the squares, either. I emptied mine, wanted to burn em, and the weevils already had hatched, and they all flew out over the cotton patch.'"[102]

In 1927, even with early planting and improved pesticide sprayers, weevil infestation remained a hit-and-miss thing; here, as elsewhere, blind chance stalked the farmer. Weevils varied in general severity from year to year, but beyond that it was all luck. As Howard Davis told, one farm might get a little rain to cool off things for the weevils at just the right time, and a large bunch might hatch out and destroy the cotton.

FIGURE 15 A farmer uses a makeshift, mule-drawn spraying system to put insecticide on his cotton plants. (Special Collections, Manuscript and Archives, Sterling C. Evans Library, Texas A&M University)

Down the road a mile, that little rain did not fall and weevils were not so bad. One year the Davis farm was "all eat up" while a man nearby made thirty-five bales. Success and failure were a mile apart, and it was all luck, just part of the "crap shoot."[103]

Season after season, the boll weevil drastically altered the fortunes of area cotton families. On one occasion Gus Draeger joked to his father in the early spring that they might make a hamburger out of the cotton on one field, but not much more, and to his consternation the joke came true: "I'll be derned if we picked enough to buy us a hamburger—boll weevil got everything."[104] Texas had produced a huge crop in the previous year of 1926—18,618,000 bales, but production averaged only 186 pounds of cotton per acre, just over one-third of a bale.[105] Samuel Evans observed: "The figures for cotton production in Texas by decades show a downward trend of yields from 1900. We may justly surmise that the boll weevil was a major cause of the seemingly steady drop in per acre yields over a period of thirty years."[106]

Weevils, army worms, and root rot were demons each farm family usually fought by itself, but when hail destroyed the crops, or a key family member fell sick in crop season, or the river flooded the corn field, neighbors often sprang to the rescue. They did this in the spirit of neighborliness and Christian brotherhood and sisterhood, but also in full recognition that the next time disaster might fall on them. The face-to-face rural community provided the only safety net anyone had, and "taking care of the neighbors" also meant maintaining the network of reciprocities that sustained one's own family. After hail fell on farmers' fields around Salem in Washington County, neighbors outside of the deadly hail swath pitched in to help the Wilhelmsens and other families replant before it became too late to do so.[107] After the Brazos rose to flood the Stolz family's corn, neighbors came to the rescue. "Neighbors all come help us," Skeeter Stolz remembered. "We didn't have nothing but wagons and mules. We'd haul it out on a Sunday, and the water'd be running in the beds of the wagons. We saved all the corn and lost all the cotton."[108] Howard Matthies's mother sometimes walked over to a neighbors' place to cook and clean for a family whose mother had fallen ill, and far upriver along the Colorado, at remote Turner Farm, neighbors often came over to sit up at night with Nona Mae Tatum's brother Jake, dying of heart disease at twenty-eight. "I can remember," Nona said, "everybody came and set up with him at night and day, whatever. And mother would make teacakes; she always made teacakes for everybody that came to set up with brother Jake."[109]

Death in the family summoned neighbors to a family's assistance, even in cases where the bereaved were black and the neighbors white, although there might be a difference in the quality of the neighborly response. A few German families, including one family that had a telephone, lived in the mostly African-American Flat Prairie community. In dire emergencies, blacks could approach this man to request a message to be relayed over his telephone, and—after a while—he usually did this. Grover Williams explained: "Say, if somebody died at nine o'clock and you went up there at nine-thirty and told him, if he was busy it would be three o'clock before he would call, you know.

FIGURE 16 Examining a cotton square for signs of boll weevil infestation. (Special Collections, Manuscripts and Archives, Sterling C. Evans Library, Texas A&M University)

Everybody's sitting down and stuff like that. When I was coming up, everything I did was done under adverse conditions."[110]

Emergency assistance functioned most strongly within ethnic communities, with blacks helping blacks, Czechs helping Czechs, and Germans helping Germans. Individuals were linked by many ties of kinship and friendship within these face-to-face geographic groupings, which functioned almost as extended families—"kinship communities," historian Kyle Wilkison aptly termed them.[111] Many persons have echoed Nona Mae Tatum's explanation: "We stuck together. Everybody loved everybody and associated with each other. You'd help them or they'd help us—that was your living, to help each other."[112] Children visiting at neighbors often were punished as swiftly as the neighbors' own children. One man recalled, "If some old folks caught me doing something wrong, they'd whup the devil out of me, then send me home and write Mamma a note and she'd whup us again."[113]

When key family members became disabled during the fierce weed battles of spring, neighbors commonly helped. Bubba Bowser told of assistance in an African-American community: "I tell you, it was nice doing around here, then. Mama say, 'Go help so-and-so,' and we'd go help chop his crop out and wouldn't charge him a nickel. Now, people rather do wrong on credit than do right on cash."[114] And Ed Lathan affirmed of this same community: "People was more neighborly. If a man taken sick, or something of that nature, and his crop needed work-ing, maybe my daddy would take his kids and his team and go over there and work his crop for him."[115] Claude Goode's story of neighborly weed armies echoed those of many. Goode's father almost died of a burst appendix and lay in the hospital for seventeen days while the weeds took his crops. Goode had no money to hire choppers—he could not even pay his doctor bills—but one morning a hundred neigh-bors turned up at first light, and each person selected a row in the field and chopped it to the end. In the afternoon, other neighbors arrived with cultivators and began to cultivate behind the choppers, complet-ing the job by two o'clock. "We had the cleanest fields in the commu-nity," Goode recalled.[116]

"Taking care of the neighbors" in the rural kinship communities also involved various other customs of mutual aid, including work swaps, barterings, food exchanges, "free range" rights on other people's land, and a variety of community work events that were also social occasions.[117]

Usafruct rights on other people's land—rights of trespass—were a form of borrowing, and this type of borrowing was evident in the turkeys that still freely crossed fence lines; school children, trappers, hunters, and pecan gatherers who ventured on neighbors' lands; and farmers on their way to store or gin who felt free to take "near cuts" across other's properties, though careful to obey the countryside's iron dictum of "close the gates." The custom of borrowing also extended to more movable types of property. Neighbors freely approached neigh-bors for the loan of hand tools, planters, cultivators, and other farm equipment, and people found it difficult (or unwise) to refuse these requests; next week they might need to borrow something themselves. Being thought "un-neighborly" was no minor thing; in the remote countryside, isolated by terrible mud for weeks or months of the year, it was something a family could not afford to let happen. Foodstuffs often were borrowed, as well. "When a farmer ran out of corn," one man explained, "he could borrow a load from a neighbor till gathering time, and it was quite common to borrow a side of meat till hog killing time."

Such a food borrowing often began with a polite offer to pay, which, as the borrower expected, immediately was refused. A family whose cow had died or gone dry sometimes borrowed a neighbor's cow "for her feed" until she could be replaced.[118] Work stock or even the neighbor's children might be borrowed upon occasion to help with some field task, as when one young woman's uncle borrowed her services to run his walking planter.[119]

Excess food of all kinds—garden vegetables, watermelons, fish caught on fishing trips, and many other items—often was given away to neighbors, setting up reciprocities for the future. Unlike pork, beef could not be preserved by smoking, so when Southerners killed a steer they commonly took cuts of it around to the neighbors, then expected the neighbors to soon do the same. In Fayette and Washington counties, however, this informal beef exchange had evolved into formalized "beef clubs," to which virtually every landowner family—German, Czech, black, and Anglo—belonged. Beef clubs had detailed bylaws, elected officers, and often a "clubhouse," where every Saturday the yearling of the week was divided among members. Twenty-four families belonged to a club, corresponding to the twenty-four cuts of meat. Each family contributed a yearling to the club in an order determined by lot, and each week they received a different cut of meat until at the end of the cycle they had gotten a whole yearling back, though assembled of body parts from twenty-four different animals. On a given Saturday, someone from each family went down to the clubhouse to find the family's allotted portion hanging from the family meat hook. Then he or she took it home for Saturday dinner.

An obvious problem for the beef club might be the member family that contributed a poor-quality, underweight animal as their part of the meat exchange. However, Robert Skrabanek recalled that, far from shirking or skimping, members of their club "normally fattened and butchered their best steers and vied for compliments about the quality of the beef they produced."[120] Just in case, however, all clubs had rules to deal with the chinchy contributor. Kermit Fox explained, "Records were kept throughout the year so that at the end of the club-year, monetary adjustment was made using a predetermined price per pound."[121] People who had contributed underweight steers paid money in, those who had contributed overweight steers took money out. Weight was not the only issue, however. Working from an antique German-language chart of the parts of beef, Lawrence Schmidt served as "cutter" for a Greenvine-area beef club for several decades, and he recalled that if a family contributed a bad or scrawny steer with "blue meat" the matter was noted, socially disapproved of, and hurt the family's reputation. The word got around, and next year this family might be refused entry to a beef club, and in 1927 no beef club meant very little beef to eat.[122]

Another reciprocity among neighbors in the rural kinship communities was the "swapping" of things—foodstuffs, commodities, and even work. Living on La Bahia Prairie, Bat Dement had plenty of pastureland but no trees, so every year he swapped hay for firewood with a neighbor in the post oaks.[123] Howard Matthies's blackland farm grew wonderful Irish potatoes but no sweet potatoes, so every year his family exchanged a wagonload of its potatoes for a wagonload of sweet potatoes from "Daddy's aunt that lived over there at Round Top in that deep sand."[124] Families also swapped work in much the same way. A farmer might contribute so many days labor by himself or his sons in a neighbor's field in exchange for so many days labor from the neighbor or his sons later on. By 1927, many of these neighborly work swappings had become cash transactions of a kind, though with much the same expectancies about reciprocity. One farmer might hire a neighbor's son or daughter to chop at fifty cents a day wages, then—on a later occasion—that man would hire his son or daughter.

By this late spring of 1927, the long nineteenth-century list of occasions when neighbors joined together to both work and socialize had shortened. Barn raisings, house raisings, log rollings, corn shuckings, rail splittings, pea thrashings, and spinning bees mostly had become things of the past, though old timers recalled these from their youth. Quiltings, hog killings, and goose pluckings still were practiced, but the quiltings and goose pluckings were usually limited to participation by women. Eddie Wegner described the goose-plucking gatherings at his home.

> The best way I can explain it, it was kind of like a quilting party, if you know what a quilting party was. All the neighbor ladies would take turns picking the geese at the different neighbors' houses. I can still see all the neighbor ladies when they were at our place. They would herd the geese all in the smokehouse. This was during the summer months, of course, and we didn't have any meat in the smokehouse. They would

FIGURE 17 Pioneer home-demonstration agents often introduced new technologies and practices in social events similar to traditional communal work occasions. Here, Washington County housewives learn to make comforters at an occasion much like a traditional "quilting." (Special Collections, Manuscripts and Archives, Sterling C. Evans Library, Texas A&M University)

sit on their stools, their chairs, at the entrance to the smoke-house, and whenever one needed a goose, well, she'd catch one more goose and tuck its head under her arm and com-mence to picking it. And they had a great time a-gossiping, goose picking, or whatever.[125]

Although the list of cooperative gatherings was diminishing, one new work occasion had been added. The old method of gathering hay involved only the family work force, but the new mule-powered "mechanical baler" often required cooperation among several families. By 1927, haying had mechanized on many area farms, becoming a work occasion involving several neighbor families and often lasting more than a week. Nearly every farm had its patch of native bluestem grass, often surviving intact from the original prairie ecosystem, and sometime in early July the neighborhood hay crew began to move from farm to farm, getting in the hay. The Fuchs family had purchased a full compliment of equipment necessary for mechanical baling—bar mower, dump rake, bull rake, and "power press," or baler—but many families could not afford that, purchasing only part of the rig and combining their equipment with that of the neighbors. John Skrabanek's family owned the mower, and summer haying began when they cut their meadow, left the grass to dry in the field, then passed the mower along to the neighbors. After two or three days, all the hay had been mown and dried, and the hay crew maneuvered the ponderous, mule-powered baler owned by a neighbor to the Skrabanek's hay field. There, the crew of seven or eight began raking the hay into windrows with the one-mule dump rake and scooping them up for the baler with the two-mule bull rake.

Balers were horse- or mule-powered; the animal went around in a circle, stepping over part of the works at one point, powering a long, heavy wooden plunger that moved and compressed the hay. At the baler a crew of "feeder" and "binder" stuffed the hay into the machine, compressed it into a bale, and tied it off. Feeder and binder worked as a team during this somewhat dangerous task. As one former hay hand recalled, the binder "rhythmically maneuvered the hay on the table into a somewhat twisted mass and usually with the help of a straight-pronged feeding fork plunged this wad of hay into the depth of the open box the moment the plunger flew open." The feeder needed to remember to extract foot or fork from the closing jaws of the baler as the plunger moved forward again to compress, or the result would be unpleasant. Meanwhile, reaching into the ponderous apparatus, the binder ran baling wire back and forth to bind each compressed segment of hay into a bale.[126] Hay baling might require a crew of eight people to rake the hay, press it, bale it, and haul it to the barn, but still only processed 100 to 125 bales in a long afternoon's work.

After the first family's hay meadow had been baled, workers put the wheels back on the baler and mules pulled it to the next farm, where the process was repeated. Robert Skrabanek recalled the socializing that accompanied this cooperative work task: "The three Czech families spent a lot of time together when we made hay. The women cooked big dinners for everybody and alternated houses where we ate dinner every day. After the haying was done, each family made a freezer of different-flavored ice cream, and we all got together to celebrate the occasion."[127]

Hay making took place after "laid by" time, when hoe hands and plowmen could no longer get up the corn and cotton rows, and farmers said their crops now were "up to the Fellow up yonder."[128] African-Americans and Anglo-Americans often used the term "laid by" for this stage of the crop cycle; Czechs and Germans used it less frequently, although the latter might say in German, "I am through plowing now the cotton."[129]

Non-Czechs much too readily deserted their fields and went off on foolishness like fishing trips and visits, John Skrabanek thought. The Skrabaneks chopped and cultivated their corn and cotton right into July—until they could no longer force their way up the rows—then, like many other families, they shifted to the sweaty midsummer labors of haying, gathering corn top fodder, and preserving garden produce. Some Anglo families nearby were quick to declare their crops laid by, though bowing to public opinion to the extent that they gave one more chopping to the weeds in the part of their fields nearest the county road. This was not good enough for John Skrabanek, however. After a mild questioning of patriarchal authority on the matter at the evening meal, Mr. Skrabanek closed the argument with his standard credo, "We're Czechs, they're Americans," and committed his whole family to the task of chopping their entire field "clean" one last time the next day.[130]

Nevertheless, at some point even John Skrabanek left his corn and cotton fields to God and went about other business. The ears of corn were fully formed, requiring only curing in the field, and the cotton plants had spread out until their leaves were big enough "to shade the ground and keep the ground clean."[131] Ed Lathan told of making the decision to quit chopping: "A certain time, you watch the crop, a good farmer, he know when to start, he know when to quit. After it go to maturing bolls, and after it all blossom up a certain time, we called it 'lain by.' We wouldn't do nothing but walk out in the field, it a bright morning, and just look at it, say, 'Well, my cotton is doing fine,' make mirations over it. We didn't just keep chopping it till it opened."[132]

The Fourth of July signaled laid-by time for many farmers in the old counties along the rivers, the day when family haying crews or corn-top-gathering crews swung into action. A good many families, like those of Grover Williams and Robert Wilhelmsen, did not own or have

FIGURE 18 Rosie Rek of Fayette County astride an iron-wheeled, horse drawn mowing machine. (Fayette Area Heritage Museum, courtesy of Louis J. "Buddy" Polansky)

access to the new mechanical hay balers, so they processed their wild bluestem hay in medieval fashion, cutting it in the field, hauling it loose in wagons, and stacking it in conical haystacks outside their barns. Many craftsman-like skills entered into this process, as they did into so many other aspects of the farming life.

The Wilhelmsens first cut the grass with a horse-powered "bar mower," then gathered it into a cotton wagon with tall sapling poles stuck into the side slits. One man on the ground forked the grass up to another man on the wagon, who carefully placed it into layers and did not allow it to become tangled up. This facilitated removal and careful stacking at the haystack pole. Hay hands exercised great care to pile the hay high on the wagon and still keep it layered and secure from sliding off. Finally, they transported the high-mounded hay to the twenty-foot-high center pole of the haystack near their barn. There, one person forked it off and another—the most skilled hand—stacked it carefully around the pole. One needed to get it tight around the pole so that rain could not get in between hay and pole, and slightly slanted toward the outside to shed water, but not so slanted that the hay would slip off. The hay stacker sought to "layer it in" to "kind of tie the hay together." Finally, a thick pad of hay (or a piece of tin, if one was available) was pushed down over the pole at the top, then some sort of circular weight—a woven wire ring with rocks attached, an old wagon wheel rim, a rubber tire—was placed over the pole on top of that. This weighted down the hay, helped to stabilize it around the pole, and slid down the pole as hay was withdrawn from the stack near the bottom. When the Wilhelmsens needed hay for feeding, they drew it from the four-foot level of the stack with a homemade, iron "hay hook" or "hay puller," which was three-feet long and pointed like a harpoon, with a hand-hold on the other end. The stock feeder thrust the hay puller deeply into the stack, then withdrew it with a big loop of fresh hay from the inside.[133]

Farmers sometimes harvested and stacked grain sorghums in much the same way, though often they stored these in their barn lofts or fed them green. Howard Matthies's family grew a few rows of sweet sorghum, each day cutting some with a butcher knife and "carrying it out in the pasture for the horses and cows to eat, that was every night you did that."[134] Corn-top fodder was more important to the Matthies's, however, as it was for most farmers. Everybody grew corn, and as soon as July arrived and cotton had been laid by, families cut the tops of their corn plants just above the now-matured ears, dried these tops in the field, bundled them up, then stacked them around tall poles exactly as they did loose hay. Strangely, the tying of corn tops into bundles normally took place at night. As Frank Janish told, "we cut four rows and laid them on one, then, at night we had to go tie it—dark, like in a sack—and I was afraid."[135]

Frugality and practicality dictated this nocturnal corn-top bundling. Only during humid night could corn tops be tied with other corn tops, eliminating the need for hemp cord. In the early morning, each family member went down a middle between two rows of corn, cutting tops from the two rows and laying them in small bunches in the middle to his or her right. Meanwhile, someone else approached from the other direction doing the same. Thus, four rows of corn tops accumulated along one middle, lay in the field to dry for one or two "dinner suns," then were bundled up by night workers moving down the dark "tie rows." Wallie Schmidt explained:

> I used a knife to cut it off and throw it on bundle piles, usually two piles to a bundle. And then, if there was a little moisture in the air, and the tops had laid on the ground there for two days, you could go over there into the field after sundown and tie em up in bundles. If it too dry, you had to wait till past midnight, and then start tying it. Sometimes I'd tie from twelve midnight till sunup. It's not so easy done, but you had to do it. You can't carry a light and tie tops; you knew how to do it without light.[136]

Farmers tied nine- or ten-inch bundles of corn tops with other corn tops, a process requiring flexible stalks, slightly wet with dew. Kermit Fox described the method:

> We accomplished this tying by gathering several free-lying clumps of tops, then taking one selected stalk that wasn't either too thin nor too thick, wrapping it around the bundle, as we somewhat compressed it, kinking the butt end of the tying stalk around its thinner tassel end, bending the butt 180 degrees and tucking it under itself. If you knew how to do it, had learned the rhythm and managed well the thumb-thrust, it would be an easy-appearing, deft maneuver. Breaking stalks that were too dry could be most frustrating.[137]

After tops were tied into bundles in the field, as Wallie Schmidt explained, "You had to stand em up on the corn stalks, and then another night when the weather was clear and the moon was pretty bright you'd go down there and follow that row and pick em up and put em on your back and carry em to a pile—six, seven, rows on a pile, there. And in the morning you'd take a pair of mules and a wagon and drive by them piles, and load em up, and haul em off."[138] Kermit Fox's family preferred to carry bundles from their field in daylight, and he recalled: "It was a bit of a competitive game to see who could carry the most bundles at one time. Some could manage as many as fifteen or twenty, and, as they would wind through the cut field of corn, they looked like some pre-historic creature waddling about. The human was totally hidden by the mass of bundles balanced on his head."[139]

Not everybody liked this bundling of corn tops in the dark field. The bundler had to work by feel as much as by sight and soon became wet with chilly dew, and many people's thoughts turned to what might lie under the half-seen corn tops. Elvera Schmidt said, "I always kicked them before I picked them up, I always had that snake in my mind."[140] For Johnnie Loud, the worst finally happened.

> I tied em for many years, I did all of the tying of my fodder at night. But one night, moonshiney night, when it got little past dusk dark, I went down there. I first felt it, I said, "Yeah, you dry enough, ready to tie." And so I reached down and picked me up a pile, as much as I think would make a bundle, and I put it up against me, and I felt something wiggling, and I thumped it down, I looked, and I guess it was four or five spreading adders under that first pile! That broke me. I never did tie no more at night.[141]

Loud and others piled bundles of corn tops in concentric patterns in teepee-like, conical "shocks" on the edges of their fields, let them "sweat and cure" for a week or so, then carried them to the barn and carefully stacked them around tall cedar poles exactly as the Wilhelmsens stacked their hay. Stock feeders pulled corn-top bundles from the bottoms of stacks with harpoon-like hooks, while the special shape of the stacks kept them from toppling or collapsing as the stacks gradually slid down their poles. Hook wielders remained alert as they withdrew bundles for feed, since over time corn-top stacks accumulated wasp nests, snakes, and the occasional skunk den; in field or barnyard, surprises often lurked in the corn tops.[142]

Cutting of corn tops was only one of the subsistence frugalities of midsummer. The hundred-acre landowners of Fayette and Washington counties somehow built new farmhouses and sent sons and daughters to college with "five-cent cotton" and five-hundred-dollar cotton crops, but the way they accomplished this was a relentless quest for self-sufficiency in everything else but cotton. Families tried to raise every-thing they needed on their farms, and laid-by time at midsummer witnessed massive efforts at food preservation. Farm wives and their daughters took the lead in summer food preservations, but families usually worked as teams; as Otto Treybig told, the family garden was "everybody's job."[143] The Janish farm strove for self-sufficiency and with good reason; the Janish family had fifteen children. Echoing every other landowner family, whether Czech, German, black, or Anglo, Frank Janish told, "Our living was made at home. We didn't need much more to buy then but the sugar, coffee, and stuff like that. The rest of it we raised all on the farm, year in and year out."[144] Besides their corn and cotton, the Janishes butchered three yearlings and nine hogs each year, raised a huge garden, and cultivated peas, peanuts, watermelons, cantaloupes, cashew melons, Irish potatoes, and sweet potatoes as subsistence field crops.[145] Given enough corn in the crib, pork in the smokehouse, potatoes in the potato bank, and dried field peas in the field, no Janish would starve, no matter what happened to the gambler's crop of cotton.

Laying hens and milk cows held a special place in the food economies of families such as the Janishes; not only did they provide fresh protein foods for the daily diet, but excess eggs, cream, and butter could be bartered or sold at a nearby store for coffee, flour, sugar, kerosene, and the few other items families did not produce on their farms. Often, not even sugar needed to be purchased, since families kept bees, and farm wives expertly substituted honey for sugar in their recipes. Families commonly sold excess hen eggs, less commonly their cream and butter. Milk cows relentlessly produced raw milk every morning and evening, and families consumed this largesse in every form imaginable. They drank it as whole milk, skimmed milk, buttermilk, and clabbered milk, and ate it as butter, cottage cheese, or "cook cheese." The residues of "whey" (left over from cottage-cheese making) and skimmed milk became components of chicken feed and hog slop.

The Otto Fuchs family milked ten cows twice a day, separated the cream with a centrifugal cream separator, then took the cream to the Carmine creamery.[146] The John Skrabanek family consumed most of their butterfat as butter or cream—much of the latter as a major ingredient of the daily staple of mashed potatoes. As the milk soured after its cream was skimmed off, the soured milk was not discarded, but was set aside to "clabber," then was bagged and hung on a line outside the house to consolidate into raw material for the tasty filling of the daily kolache pastries. Even the whey dripping from the bags was saved for hog slop. Only when excess cream kept around the Skrabanek kitchen began to go bad did they sell it to the store in Snook. Robert Skrabanek sometimes took a can of this rejected cream to the store and recalled that the family cream usually smelled better than the cream in the storeowner's reservoir. Country stores followed the same rigorous "waste-not, want-not" dictum as the farm families they served; asked when cream got too bad to purchase, the storeowner replied, "when it's got maggots in it."[147] Stores sometimes purchased less-than-fresh eggs, as well, and store clerks might be greeted on Monday mornings by the assertive "peep, peep, peep" of newly hatched chicks.

From time to time during the midsummer of 1927, house-wives cleared work areas in their kitchens and masterminded food-preservation labors sometimes lasting for days. By the late 1920s, most landowners' homes had water-bath canners to process a wide array of garden vegetables into Ball glass jars in quart, half gallon, and gallon sizes. As the garden season moved toward fall, the accumulated food jars filled the shelves in the smokehouse and expanded into the house, sometimes ringing bedroom walls two or three jars deep. Grover Williams's grandmother, for example, located Ball jars of preserved vegetables and fruits around the walls, under the beds, and everywhere she could find space to put them.[148]

Some families still followed much older practices of preserving food by drying, and peaches, figs, green beans, pumpkin-slices, English peas, lima beans, pinto beans, and field peas soon hung in flour sacks on the walls of kitchens and smokehouses. Area corn and cotton fields often contained other crops as well, and sometimes when landlords did not want them to—peas and pumpkins in the corn and watermelons and popcorn in the cotton. Field peas occupied a special niche among Southern subsistence crops; many kinds existed, including blackeyed peas, zipper peas, crowder peas, whippoorwill peas, and others. Area farmers often planted them in "skip rows" in the corn, seeding every third or fifth row in peas, or planted them in the middles after the last passage through the fields before laid by. Copious quantities matured even in drought-plagued crop years, and the field-dried peas were con-sumed by hogs, chickens, turkeys, cows, and people and the residuum turned under to provide nitrogen for the soil. The poorer the family, the more likely it was to gather and consume large quantities of field

FIGURE 19   Beehives in the side yard of the Squire Reeves farmstead, Fayette County. (Percy Faison album, Fayette Heritage
Museum and Archives, La Grange)

peas. Grover Williams and his brothers picked cotton pick sacks full of peas in the late summer, shattered peas from dry shells by repeatedly jumping on the pick sacks from the back of a cotton wagon, then—on a day of high wind—winnowed peas from shell debris by slowly pouring the contents of the sacks from wagon bed to ground cloth. Weevils threatened dried field peas as they did dried corn, and Grover Williams's grandmother placed a portion of snuff and a metal spoon in every container of stored peas to keep them out.[149]

Potatoes—Irish and sweet—were another survival food, producing large quantities from small patches of ground and preservable without processing. Germans and Czechs grew both kinds in the old counties along the rivers, but by 1927 the white, or Irish, potato predominated.[150] Families grew many bushels of these each year in both spring and fall gardens and preserved them in the crawl spaces under their houses or in special "potato houses" or "potato banks." At the farmhouse where Mrs. Gus Keiler grew up, the family preserved large quantities of potatoes in a twelve-by-eight-foot potato house, a "real building" with thick board-and-batten walls filled with sand and a small door at one end. The family stored Irish potatoes on one side, sweet potatoes on the other.[151] Following an older (and possibly Native American) practice, Grover Williams's and Ed Lathan's families preserved each year's potato crop in a temporary "potato bank," built anew every year. Lathan said, "I would dig a little hole somewhere in the garden or yard, and maybe I'd fence off the place, put a lot of hay in there. And take my wagon, go in the field, and pull my corn and get a bunch of them corn stalks. Put them potatoes in that next, throw a little hay over them, then put them corn stalks on top of that hay like a teepee, and then throw dirt on top of it." Lathan left a small space at the top of the potato bank "so it'd catch a little air" and a small hole at ground level so he could reach in and get the potatoes out.[152]

Families grew so many potatoes that they often planted them in special "potato lands" apart from their main gardens, and cabbages sometimes occupied separate "cabbage patches" for the same reason. Despite an increased use of water-bath canning techniques, families still preserved cabbages in brine crocks in the age-old way, and sauerkraut joined potatoes, field peas, and corn as one of the four main vegetable food crops. Germans, Czechs, blacks, and Anglos all made sauerkraut, although the first two doubtless made more and often consumed it at nearly every main meal.

Preserving cabbage was a simple process (sometimes also used for green beans and kohlrabi), but the scale of the operation galvanized every family member into action. At Eddie Wegner's farm, Robert Skrabanek's farm, and many others, cabbage-processing day required harvesters, slicers, shredders, crock-packers, and cabbage-stompers, all "working like a well-oiled machine." Skrabanek men cut over two-hundred heads of cabbage with butcher knives and carried them in big washtubs to the farmhouse kitchen, where Skrabanek women sliced each in half, cut out the pithy portions and tougher outside leaves, and consigned the rejected parts to the hog-slop pile. Then, all hands took turns using the "kraut cutter," a sliding board with adjustable blades, to shred tub after tub of cabbage. Shredders placed successive four-inch layers of shredded cabbage in a fifty-gallon barrel, topped each layer with salt and a little dill, then signaled bare-footed young Robert Skrabanek to tread these down into the larger mass of cabbage as a Sicilian treaded grapes. After that had been accomplished, shredders placed the next layer of cabbage in the barrel, Robert treaded it down again, and so on until the barrel had been filled. Not surprisingly, Robert's feet became badly wrinkled from the briny solution before the day was done. After the layering and mixing process had filled the fifty-gallon barrel, the Skrabaneks left the kraut to ferment for a while, then squeezed most of the salt water out, transferred the kraut to ten-gallon barrels and pottery crocks, and covered it with water. Tight-fitting wooden lids fit snugly on each of these, preserving the sauerkraut, one of this family's dietary staffs of life.[153]

Some thirds-and-fourths renter families preserved almost as much midsummer food as the Skrabaneks and Wegners, whose smokehouses, crawl spaces, potato houses, and kitchens gradually filled to overflowing with stored foodstuffs by late summer of 1927, but such renter families were much the exception. Renters normally had smaller gardens and fewer milk cows and hogs than did landowners, and sometimes the renters had none of these things at all.[154] One 1920 government study found that 39 percent of Texas farm families owned not a single milk cow and 32 percent had no gardens.[155] At Allenfarm on the Brazos, the Terrells allowed each sharecropper family to keep a small garden, and William Terrell's father directed the farm's day hands in the cultivation of a three-acre garden behind the commissary store from which both the Terrells and some black employees got fresh vegetables. Few vegetables were preserved, however. Cropper families got most of their food from the commissary on "cash terms" or "crop terms." To buy on cash terms was to buy with cash, paying the lower cash prices; to buy on crop terms meant to buy on credit until the fall cotton crop came in, paying the cash price plus ten percent. By late spring or mid-summer, most croppers bought on credit, drawing the usual weekly rations of the "three M's," meat (salt pork), corn meal, and molasses.[156]

By this time on some cropper farms, commissary provisions had deteriorated to their lowest point of the year—the meat had maggots, the meal had weevils, and the molasses barrels had reached the rat level, as Willie Lipscomb recalled: "You go down and get syrup, different things like that. Syrup and salt pork, rats done run all over it. You get down to the bottom of the syrup barrel, it half full of rats! They forget to put the bung in, and the rat go there and fall in the barrel and drown. They sell you that syrup right on."[157]

Wild foods gathered from the creek and river bottoms, or from along grown-up fence lines, supplemented the diets of both landowner and renter families during this late summer of 1927, though such things had more value to the renters, who usually had no orchards, vineyards, bee hives, or berry bushes. The bottoms were still to some extent a no-man's land, the last remnant of the wooded commons, and families went there to gather dewberries, blackberries, red and black haws, plums, persimmons, mustang grapes, wild honey, and pecans, each in its respective season. Pecans differed from the wild fruits in that they were worth money at the store, and some landlords now objected to pecan gatherers in their bottoms. Bubba Bowser told of one landowner's attitude: "Steve Moore used to tell us, 'Y'all pick up one of my pecans and crack it, give me half.' His pecans! Them's God's pecans. A man ain't got nothing in this world but his soul. That's all you got is your soul."[158]

Ignoring their landlord, Howard Davis's family often gathered God's dewberries along the Colorado for his mother to make jelly and also to "eat the fire out of them dewberry pies." As did many others, the Davises also gathered "washtubs full" of wild mustang grapes for Mrs. Davis to make jelly, although many families preferred to process these into wine.[159] Most German and Czech families made gallons and gallons of mustang-grape wine every midsummer, a task enjoyed by nearly everyone. Howard Matthies's father tried to put up around thirty or thirty-five gallons every year—a large but not uncommon amount. Families often served the sweet wine from mustang grapes to Sunday visitors or mixed it with lemonade or well water as a kind of wine punch for workers in the field.[160] The Skrabanek family gathered mustang grapes in their post-oak "pasture," where "picking mustang grapes was the men's job since they grew on vines high in trees, and we had to use ladders to get to them."[161] As did the Skrabaneks, after the Wegners gathered their grapes, they put them in a large barrel, "stomped them with a big long-handled stomper," fermented the juice with large quantities of sugar in big crocks, and made many gallons of wine.[162]

This was illegal, of course, but German-Texans for long had placed home wine making and consumption among the basic rights of man. Few opinions had changed since 1909, when the National German-American Alliance, an anti-prohibition group, met in San Antonio and proclaimed: "We consider the right to drink our wine and beer as absolutely an attribute of human liberty as the right to consume any other food. Prohibition is a blow at a fundamental principle of righteousness."[163]

Wine and beer played a role in various recreations of late summer, as families gathered fodder crops to their haystacks and made preparations for the cotton-picking season just ahead. German families in particular managed to find time to attend all-day Fourth of July celebrations at area dance halls and to go on overnight fishing trips or visits to family members living in other communities. In fact, area farmers so successfully combined work and play in this brief period before the relentless labor of cotton picking began that teetotal Anglo-Americans sometimes referred to them as "carousing Germans."

The Fourth of July had been enthusiastically added to Mayfest, Octoberfest, and other traditional festive occasions by area Germans, who often surpassed Anglo-American communities at their own holiday. The German Fourth of July sometimes lasted twenty-four hours, beginning with formal readings of the Declaration of Independence in English and German; then a big picnic; then target shooting, foot races, and jumping competitions; then a dance; then speeches; then the main dance lasting all night long.[164] Certain dance halls specialized in putting on big Fourth of July celebrations, among them the Burton Hall and the Round Top Rifle Association Hall.[165] Constructed in 1912 for the "encouragement of innocent outdoor sports, such as bicycle riding, target and trap shooting, open air athletics, games, dancing, and others of a like character," the Round Top Hall lived up to its charter credo.[166] By 1927, the big cavernous hall, with its internal bandstand, had become surrounded by an outdoor bandstand, ice-cream stand, fruit stand, concession stand, barbecue pit, bowling alley, heavily used "saloon" and gallery, skeet range, rifle range, and carousel. Fourth of July at Round Top lasted all day and all night and featured a day band and a night band; a parade with floats, "comicals," and horseback riders; a barbecue dinner in the evening; and a dance until dawn. Most families stayed over until the next day, sleeping (if they slept at all) in and under their wagons. Every time during day or night that the replenishing Fayetteville beer wagon rolled into sight, Round Top patriots raised a big cheer.[167]

As July turned into August and the cotton bolls swelled in the dark-green fields, area families took late summer trips to visit distant family members, went fishing at the creeks or rivers, and played Sunday baseball while they still had the energy. After cotton picking began from can see to can't, Sundays truly became the "day of rest."

On the big sharecropper farms along the Brazos and Colorado, families had no fodder crops to get and few garden vegetables to preserve, so they had more time off between laid by and cotton picking. Small landowners and some thirds-and-fourths renters on the uplands, however, could not afford to take prolonged vacations to fish or visit—unless some family members remained behind to milk the cows and feed the chickens. Family visits often were Sunday afternoon affairs, only, as the traditional family afternoon "coffee" became a social event involving neighbors and visiting kinsmen. Participants consumed much more than coffee at these events, including jelly, sausage, and ham sandwiches, cookies, and various "coffee cakes."[168] Sometimes Howard Matthies's parents launched longer family visits in their 1919 Oakland, braving deep sand on their way to distant Walburg. A skeleton work force of older children always stayed behind to take care of the farm, however; vacation time or not, the cows still came up to be milked just the same.

Favored groups from other families also camped out on sandbars at well-known fishing sites along the Brazos River, Colorado River, Cedar Creek, and Yegua Creek. After Leola Tiedt's grandfather Hermann Eichler finished directing his hay crew: "Those men packed up on the wagon and went up to Flat Town, near Somerville, and camped there for a week. Drank beer, two keg of beer, and they had their fun, and the women still had to stay home and work and milk the cows and everything."[169] Eddie Wegner's sporting uncles sometimes "coon fished" in muddy Yegua Creek at such times, diving down to the bottom with big hooks lashed to their wrists in attempts to find and "foul hook" big catfish lurking under sunken logs. Eddie remembered a story told by one of his uncles: "Those big old cats would be under those snags, and they would ease up to him and hook them with that hook. But he said he got ahold of one one time, he kind of underestimated the size of the fish, and that booger like to drown him."[170] The Otto Fuchs family also went on overnight fishing trips to Yegua Creek, often visiting Flag Pond, a creek-bottom lake covered with water lilies, but they restricted their fishing techniques to trotlines and gill nets. The Fuchs spent the night camping out under their wagon and running lines and nets by paddle boat, and they consumed most of the catfish, shad, buffalo, "white perch," and "gaspergou" they caught in camp the next day to satisfy an accumulated "fish hunger." Water lilies bloomed magically at first light on Flag Pond every morning, presenting a rare vision of watery beauty to this family of blackland farmers from La Bahia Prairie.[171]

Grover Williams's family also fished Yegua Creek, usually finding that simple poles, corks, and hooks caught all the fish they could eat. These expeditions took place on Saturday afternoons, since Williams's grandmother strictly enforced Sunday blue laws. Sunday in this family was a day of worship and rest, with no working, cooking, laughing, playing, or whistling. Whistling was permitted on other days, but "it had to be a religious whistle, you couldn't whistle what they called a reel." Sundays were recreational, but all recreations were religious ones. A home "prayer meeting" preceded the walk to church, with the younger children reciting verses, the older children offering prayers. Singing at Williams's church was ferocious and impressive; clapping was forbidden, though one could shout "Amen!" and wave one's hands. As women in the congregation felt themselves overcome with emotion and about to begin "shouting," they often asked nearby persons to hold their purses or hats. This was a favor; a woman might say, "Well, here hold my purse for me," then begin to shout. Williams explained: "When they feel it coming on, some didn't want you to hold them when they were shouting, and some they had to hold because they looked like they was going to hurt themselves. They'd jump up and stand up in the seats, and they'd just run all down the aisles. The more they hollered and whooped, the more the preacher would try to make them."[172] After the family returned home, Grover Williams's grandmother allowed Grover and his siblings to "walk around the pasture," but that was all. Even if an emergency occurred and the cows got in the corn on Sunday afternoon, nothing could be done about it. At the African-American Hollow Springs Baptist Church, which Dave Taplin's family attended, little pasture-walking time remained, since Sunday school, first service, afternoon service, and evening service went on for seven or eight hours.[173] Black churches such as Taplin's and Williams's usually had July "associations," protracted meetings that lasted for a week or more.[174]

Baseball—although never played by Taplin and Williams on Sundays—was the dominant sport of late summer across the old counties along the rivers, and Grover Williams's Flat Prairie community, Howard Matthies's La Bahia community, and virtually every rural settlement fielded its own team. Boys (and some girls) began their sporting lives by playing serious mumbly-peg, marbles, and two-base versions of baseball, such as "town ball" and "one-eyed cat," then graduated to the formalized version of the national sport.

Mumbly-peg and marbles often preceded baseball as competitive sports. Mumbly-peg involved eye-hand coordination, sharp knives, and an element of danger, and so attracted early male interest, especially at rural schools. Kermit Fox explained: "The thrower from a variety of attitudes would attempt to throw the knife in such a manner to stick one blade into a circle crudely scratched on the ground. The experts would attempt to flip the knife from the tips of their fingers, from the point of an elbow, and even from the end of their nose."[175] Kids used large knives for mumbly-peg and were always searching for the perfectly balanced one that never failed to stick. Likewise, skilled marble shooters sought the perfect "taw" that would allow them to accumulate quart jars of captured marbles, taken "fair-and-square" on the field of play. Fox told: "I marveled at how these experts could impart so much English to these agates that upon impact with their target, the marble that was struck shot far outside the ring, whereas the agate remained frozen, wildly spinning at the precise site of impact. Such effective players usually bore the telltale hallmark of a shallow fractured indentation in their shooting thumbnail."[176]

By early teenage years, rural youths shifted their competitive interests to baseball. Kermit Fox began baseball games in childhood, using a homemade "carved paddle bat" and a "mushy string ball," then advanced to better things. Baseball needed little equipment, only some sort of bat and ball, and these could be jury-rigged at home. Grover Williams recalled: "We didn't have any balls like we know balls now. We had a homemade ball. You get a rock and wrap it around with material and sew it, and get you a big stick out there and trim it down. And that was it, no glove."[177] Like town ball, one-eyed cat required only two bases, and children often played it with these primitive balls and bats. The batter tried to hit the ball and run to the cat-eye base and back home again before a fielder retrieved the ball and impacted the batter's retreating backside with a stinging throw.

Later, childhood play ended, and young males from rural communities fiercely competed with other "nines" from nearby settlements. Mance Lipscomb and many others often walked several miles on Sunday afternoons to watch, or participate in, these games. Flat Prairie developed a good team, sometimes playing Ed Lathan's Mount Fall community in contests frequented by moonshiner gamblers with big money in their pockets.[178] Anglo-American followers of the sporting life showed up at some of these black baseball games, as well.[179]

Even when no money was involved, baseball games between rural teams could become combative. Commonly, no umpires were used, so when the contest between the Round Top "Scrubs" and the Wardeck "First Nine" stalemated in the fourth inning in a "squabble over the interpretation of Rule 51, Sec. 6," no one stepped forward to settle the dispute, and the Round Top boys quit in a huff and went home. The reporter of this event complimented the ladies present, apologized for the unseemly termination of the game, and opined that only their restraining feminine presence had kept the contest from following the not-uncommon shift from baseball to boxing.[180]

Howard Matthies and his brothers often took part in similar games at La Bahia Prairie south of Burton. Boys and men joined "baseball clubs" in late spring, contributing twenty-five cents for equipment and turning out with cotton hoes to whip the playing fields back in shape.

FIGURE 20 An early game of baseball at the farming community of Cedar Park, Fayette County. (Percy Faison album, Fayette Heritage Museum and Archives, La Grange)

At big games, the club also charged a small public admission to defray costs. Ten communities in the immediate vicinity fielded baseball teams, among them La Bahia's hated rival, Burton, so there was no lack of competition. The La Bahia team had some good athletes, running strongly along family lines—Matthieses, Krauses, Muhelbrads, Bodes, and Gerlands starred for La Bahia over the years. Harold and Walter Krause were tall, lanky men, both well over six feet in height, and they were outstanding pitchers. Howard recalled: "They could throw a ball as hard as Dizzy Dean. Walter, when he'd pitch, he'd lean back and make his fingers touch the ground and bring that ball in. Most of the time, they couldn't see it. That's where the word comes from, 'How in the world can you hit em if you can't see em?'"[181] Fritz Muhelbrad, a big slugger for La Bahia, batted cross-handed. On one occasion, Burton brought in a University of Texas pitcher as "ringer" for the annual Fourth of July match with La Bahia. Contemptuous of Muhelbrad's eccentric batting grip, the college pitcher announced, "I'm gonna make a monkey out of him," but Fritz got three hits, the last one winning the game for La Bahia.[182]

Sometime in August, however, the crack of the bat tended to fall silent, as the "fire-ball" Krauses and slugging Muhelbrads found other uses for their fine eye-hand coordination. By August in this summer of 1927, shiny cotton bolls hung heavy on dark-green cotton plants stretching far away across fields shimmering with heat. While the sons and husbands of farm families played baseball, farm women had been busy with summer sewing, making cotton field dresses, sunbonnets, canvas knee pads, and new cotton pick sacks in preparation for the fall picking season. Every day, farmers went outside at first light to view their fields, and on one of these mornings the first tufts of white appeared, low down on certain plants, scattered at long distances down the rows.

CHAPTER 6

Picking, Ginning, and Hog Killing

Since laid-by time, the farmer had anxiously watched the development of his cotton. "He looks out," Robert Dement recounted, "and thinks, 'My crop, I sure got a good-looking crop. They're putting on plenty squares, putting on cotton.'" Soon, the squares flowered into "kind of morning-glory blooms, a pretty bloom." Then, "that starts making a boll out there to get fertilized by the bees, a little old boll right there at the bottom of the flower—a little old bitty thing to start with, but it grows bigger and bigger. And then, when it gets ripe and the sun gets to it, it opens up, and then you're ready to pick your cotton. As soon as there was enough in there for us to get to it, we started on it."[1]

Painful complexities were involved in picking cotton, however. Kermit Fox explained:

> As the solid immature boll developed, it opened into five equal parts of the pod which cradled five fluffy locks of cotton. It seemed almost uncanny that the five movable digits of the human hand matched the five clefts of the boll so perfectly that it was possible to make a clean sweep with one grasp. However, the art lies in trying to pick the boll totally clean, avert grabbing the five sepals at the base—which is

FIGURE 21   A stand of tall cotton on the Percy Faison farm along Buckner Creek, Fayette County, 1894. In the foreground is one of numerous trees killed by girdling when the field was first cleared for cotton. (Percy Faison album, Fayette Heritage Museum and Archives, La Grange)

trash—and yet dodge the fine tines that mount the edge of the pod. Well, one never did completely, and this brought on the inevitable raw irritated fingernails and cuticles well recognized as "cotton pickers' hands.'"[2]

No sooner had three or four open bolls appeared on the bottom of each cotton plant than farm families donned field clothing and began

to pick, stooping or kneeling their ways down the rows in a crop harvest virtually unchanged since the eighteenth century. Now, for the first
time, the farmer clearly saw the full effects of all the vagaries of season
upon his crop—the number of bolls on the plants, the extent of weevil
damage (there a three-lock boll, here a two-lock boll), and the "staple"
of his cotton. Nothing determined the worth of the cotton so much as
staple, the length of the cotton fibers, and fiber length varied not just
with the kind of cotton the farmer grew, and the soil he grew it on, but
from season to season.

The farmer could do nothing about the staple length of his cotton
this late summer of 1927, but he could try to protect its "grade," another
major determinant of its value. Leaf and boll debris in the cotton from
careless picking, discoloration of the cotton from rainfall, and soil
stains or embedded sand caused by the cotton blowing off on the
ground during storms, all lowered the grade of the cotton, and the farm
family sought to pick clean, pick fast, and to "get that cotton in the
sack." At the end of a long gauntlet of seasonal dangers, the cotton
stood exposed in the fields, ready for harvest or destruction.

Hurricanes from the Gulf of Mexico had decimated area cotton in
1900 and 1915, and the possibility of a Gulf storm, or early fall thun-
derstorm, haunted farmers' minds. "Big thing you were always fighting
was to beat that first tropical hurricane from the Gulf," Eddie Wegner
recalled.[3] One year, Herman Schoenemann's family received word of a
possible storm in the Gulf, and "I'm gonna tell you, we almost killed
ourselves trying to get as much of our cotton picked before it got in and
destroyed the crops." Cotton blown off on the ground in the sandy land
often became so dirty that it could not be salvaged. Herman told:
"Storm just blow it out, and that's all of it. You're through."[4] Seed in the
cotton lints knocked off the plants by wind and rain soon germinated
in the sandy-land middles, ruining the cotton. "Them boogers, if it
rains on them and it's warm weather, in about three, four days them
things will sprout," Edwin Ebner told.[5] During Howard Matthies's boyhood, the only storm warning farm families had came over the telegraph to the Burton railroad depot; then, "everybody got up early and
picked late, even mother would help."[6] Some thought blackland cotton
discolored even worse on the ground than sandy-land cotton. Teddy
Keiler recalled:

Of course, if a big storm blow it out on the ground, you pick it up, whatever you could find, just as black as the land was. That storm would shake most of the lint out of the bolls—it'd be most of it on the ground, all hanging out this long, wrapped up. Well, you picked up what you could get, and that was it. Cotton looked black instead of white, and they didn't have the cleaners at the gins, either, like now. That was black cotton and cheap cotton.[7]

No wonder, then, that family field discipline peaked in cotton season, when the fields turned white. Everyone went to the field, where the rule was to "keep on picking," no matter how hot or painful the process became. A young picker complaining of the heat might hear the stock response, "It's never too hot to pick cotton," and one mentioning back pain might be told, "You ain't got no back." For most people, cotton picking hurt. One man tersely explained: "You'd pick standing up until your back hurt so bad you could hardly stand it, and you'd get down on your knees and go along until your knees got to hurting so bad you couldn't stand it, and you'd get back up and bend over again. Something was always hurting."[8] Nevertheless, disaster hung over the opening cotton, and all agreed with Eddie Wegner's father that "You'd best get after it and get it in the sack."[9] Robert Dement told:

> You was stooping over that old bag, and your back get to hurting so bad you raise up like this and try to straighten it up. And we'd be little kids out there, and Papa would say, "What you doing raised up all of a sudden?" And I'd say, "My back's hurting." And he'd say, "Ah, you don't have any back; get to picking." But he knew it was hurting and he knew what it was—getting that cotton and putting it in that sack, dragging that old sack behind, you know.[10]

Only the occasional "volunteer" watermelon in the field gave Bat Dement's sons a respite. J. M. Dement said, "Those were the best-tasting little old watermelons you ever saw. They didn't get very big. A lot of them were rotten on one end, but that just made them better. We'd get those things and put them all in a sack, and when we got to the end of a row under a shade tree, we'd stop and bust them open—just eat the heart, that's all."[11]

Unlike modern cotton, which grows low to the ground and ripens all at once, the old-style cotton varieties growing in area fields during the 1920s sometimes rose higher than a farmer's head and—given mild weather and generous autumn rainfall—put on "top crop" cotton into early December. This two- to three-month ripening schedule of the cotton determined farm families' picking strategies. Like the Dements, most began picking as soon as three or four bolls opened on each plant. At first, in the skimpy cotton of early season, pickers dumped their pick sacks into larger "stand sacks" stationed at the edge of the field, pulled the stand sacks to the barn each day on wooden sleds, and accumulated the seed cotton until fifteen hundred pounds was on hand, enough to make a five-hundred-pound bale at the gin. Later, at the height of the season, farmers often stationed cotton wagons in the field, dumped pick sacks directly into them, and tried to pick fifteen hundred pounds a day, ready for a trip to the gin early the next morning. Still later, the cotton grew sparse once more, and the stand-sack strategy again came into play to accumulate several days' picking into a bale. Finally, only "scrapping" of remnant cotton went on, as farm families tried to salvage every open top-crop boll from their winter fields.

Farmers prided themselves on how cleanly they picked their fields, and in this waste-not, want-not farming culture little cotton was lost. Partly, it was a matter of what the neighbors thought. Howard Davis recalled, "Aw, man, my daddy'd get on us for goose-tailing that cotton. 'Get them goose-tails out of there! Man, it looks bad,' he'd say."[12] Every day in October and November, when Bat Dement's sons came home from school, they took pick sacks to the field and scrapped cotton, though "you may pick a whole row back and forth and you wouldn't have ten, fifteen pounds in there," and the diligent John Skrabanek continued to send his children into the field until Christmas.[13] Teddy Keiler affirmed: "Here and there you'd be scrapping until Christmas. They'd pick as long as one boll was to be seen, somewhere. They could go to town with fifty pounds of cotton and sell it, even if we didn't get much money, but we got a few cents."[14] Even after frost had killed the cotton, the last mature but unopened bolls sometimes were pulled as "bollie cotton," stored in a shed to dry and partially open, then salvaged by lamplight on winter evenings.[15]

Picking time always was a stressful, exciting, and laborious period of the year for area farm families, but the intensity of these things depended on season—the way cotton ripened in the fields in a particular year. Sometimes, because of late summer rains and spells of cooler weather, the opening of the cotton bolls went slowly enough for family pickers to keep up, and not too much cotton became open—and vulnerable—all at once. In other years (as in this season of 1927), hot and dry weather at the end of the summer triggered an explosive opening of cotton in the fields, which literally turned white. Working from can see to can't (and sometimes by the light of the moon), and hiring anybody they could get to help pick, farm families desperately tried to gather the crop before rain fell or windstorm struck.[16]

Carrying flour sacks, pillowcases, or "croker" sacks, small children picked cotton beside their parents in the fields. Accompanying the adult pickers kept the children safe at a time when every family member had to work, and every pound of cotton they picked helped out. Like many others, Johnnie Loud had begun picking at around age seven, using a little customized pick sack, complete with shoulder strap, sewed from a fifty-pound flour sack.[17] Grover Williams began in a similar way, picking into a "little croker sack" to "get our trainings in," periodically dumping his cotton into the adult's sack with the least cotton in it.[18] Lydia Ehrigson, who began picking beside her mother at age five or six, recalled: "We had a little old flour sack with a little old strap on it around our neck, and we went besides Momma and helped pick cotton. I always grabbed the biggest bolls, Momma had the little ones. She didn't mind, I had to learn how. From then on, I never quit."[19]

As with the chopping, at a certain point in the picking adults imposed a harsher discipline on their child field hands. At first, Johnnie Loud picked when he wished and rested when he felt tired, but by 1927 those days had passed. As he told, "By then, that was a different story. I had to stay out there till time to quit, and that was night, you know."[20] Elvera Schmidt's father told each family member what his or her picking quota was, usually adding up to a fifteen-hundred-pound bale, and adults and children had to stay in the field until their quotas had been met.[21] Picking required good eye-hand coordination, rather than brute strength, and after two or three year's experience, a

FIGURE 22 Robert Wilhelmsen as a teenager (ca. 1953) driving
a slide to the barn loaded with stand sacks of seed cotton, picked
during that day's work in the field. (Robert Wilhelmsen, Washington
County)

precocious child's small hands could make major contributions.
Howard Davis recalled of his father: "Them days, it's just natural to go
do that, just start there when you're little right on. We didn't think
nothing about it. I recollect my daddy say he could pick a hundred
pounds of cotton when he was eight years old. You pick a-many a boll
to pick a hundred pounds of cotton; it's easy said but pretty hard to
do."[22] By age ten, Mance Lipscomb also could pick a hundred pounds
a day, but he still recalled his struggle to attain the landlord's assigned
quota of fifty pounds two years before.

> I worked, I worked. Sun was hot, and I was sweating. Kids
> had little old croker sacks they drug, not them old long sacks
> what the grown-ups toted. So, I picked that fifty pounds
> of cotton, and man, I was so tired. I tried to eat supper, and

look like I'd eat a little, lay the piece of bread down, pick it up again. And my arms was hurting, my legs was hurting, my back was hurting. Mama said, "You better eat your supper before you go to bed." But I didn't do nothing but set here at the table, half went to sleep and woke up, right there at the bread again. Went to bed hungry.[23]

By their mid-teens, children in cotton-farming families approached their peak picking capacities, which varied over a wide range of several hundred pounds a day. Good pickers prided themselves on their abilities and often made extra money picking for others; bad pickers tried hard to keep up, studied the techniques of successful pickers, felt guilty and inadequate, and made excuses. Mance Lipscomb picked a very respectable 300 to 350 pounds a day by age seventeen, but his older brother Charlie was a champion picker, totaling over 500 pounds any day and up to 650 pounds when he felt like it. Mance tried hard to match Charlie, but finally gave up, observing: "Ain't no use trying to be like nobody else, trying to do what the other fellow do. You come to find out what you can do best, and do that and be satisfied with it."[24]

Others had the same experience. Careful pickers, concerned to keep all trash from the pick sack, rarely went fast. Henry Jaeger gathered from 150 to 200 pounds of "clean cotton" a day, but a brother "could pick 400 pounds a day and laugh about it—he'd reach out and grab ahold of something, and whatever he had, that went into the sack."[25] Eddie Wegner, Robert Dement, and Robert Skrabanek all had "persnickety" fathers, who insisted on clean picking at all costs, and they picked amounts similar to Henry Jaeger's. Everybody knew outstanding pickers, however—the rare individuals that picked both clean and fast. Charlie Lipscomb was one such, and J. M. Dement remembered a Burton barber named Buster Hewett who often picked "two to three hundred pounds by nine o'clock in the morning," opening time for his barber shop. Will and Rosie Kieke, who lived near the Dement farm, also were outstanding pickers. Will Kieke pulled a long pick sack, longer than anyone else's, and he and his wife often rose at 3:00 a.m., after a certain train came through, and began to pick in the dark field. "If the moon was shining bright, you'd see him out there in the dark at night, picking cotton, he and Rosie."[26] Bubba Bowser's father timed him and his brother on one occasion, and, going as fast as he could, Bubba picked

111 pounds of cotton in one hour.[27] Eddie Wegner knew a remarkable cotton picker, a man named Archie Laws, who always picked two rows at a time. "I said, 'How can you pick so fast?' He always had pounds and pounds more every time he went to the scale than even the best of the rest. He said, 'Well, the best I can explain it to you, one hand must not know what the other hand is doing.'" Each of Laws's hands worked a row on each side as he faced directly up the middle, picking by peripheral vision. The hands full of cotton came together simultaneously with a clapping motion at the mouth of the open pick sack.[28]

Knowledge of such persons made things even worse for bad pickers such as J. M. Dement and Charlie Lincecum. Dement sometimes tried to convince his father to hire a replacement for him in the field, since almost everybody picked twice as much as he did, but Bat Dement refused to accept this option. Charlie Lincecum suffered from a painful back and could not pick over a hundred pounds a day, even under duress. Tolerant for a while, Lincecum's family finally lost patience with his bad picking and began to administer field punishments. His big sister Bertha, who picked four to five hundred pounds a day and was fifteen years older than Charlie, sometimes whipped him with a cotton plant, bolls and all, for bad picking. "They'd pull that cotton stalk and go to work on you," Charlie recalled. Lincecum's humiliations continued throughout his cotton-picking career, which included most of his life. Once, he worked on a man's farm where the cotton was full, white, and plentiful for three feet up the plant, but he still picked only a hundred pounds. "You must have just come down here to eat," the farmer told him.[29]

For the bad picker who still had to pick, fieldwork became a terrible mixture of pain and degradation. After a long day in the field "picking each separate boll by hand while crawling on knees, or stooping over each individual stalk, and pulling as much as fifty pounds of cotton in a sack hung by a strap on one shoulder, and the load getting heavier with each handful of cotton," Robert Skrabanek still had to endure what his father said about him at the supper table, when "Papa delighted in announcing that some young girl had picked more than I had on that day."[30] Born a slave, Bubba Bowser's grandfather had been sent out to the field every day with a split-oak cotton basket to fill before dark. Even with skipping lunch, Bowser could not accomplish this, and received a daily whipping for his cotton deficit. Finally, however, as his grandson told: "He said he got so he'd go to the field and find him a big old cocklebur or big stalk of cotton and lay up under there and sleep all day. Say, 'William,' his name William, 'Where your cotton?' Say, 'I ain't picked none.' Say, 'How come you ain't picked no cotton?' Say, 'Well, I pick all I can, y'all gonna whup me, I ain't gonna pick another damn stalk. Whup me, just whup me!' Said, he didn't whup him no more. Told him, 'Just pick what you get.'"[31] Oscar Adams, who left the cotton fields to become a newspaper editor, vividly recalled the scene of his picking experience as: "an enormous, treeless, sun-blistered field with plants either too short or too tall for comfortable harvest. With the short stalks we dropped to our knees and crawled down rows liberally land-mined with half-buried cockle-burrs. And the tall stalks were shrouded with dense foliage that were booby-trapped with stiffly-spined, stinging caterpillars and vicious striped spiders almost the size of a saucer. In either case the rows were more or less elastic with the far end completely indifferent about getting any nearer."[32]

Cotton picking was a meritocracy; from South Carolina to Texas, landowners paid hired pickers by the poundage picked, varying with the roller-coaster cotton economy from 30 cents to $1.50 a hundred-weight, and if a young female African-American picked more cotton than an adult male Anglo-American, she got more money. Albert Wilhelmsen recalled starting out beside a black picker on parallel rows. The black man, Jeff Hicks, fell behind Albert for a time, but soon remarked: "'That's alright. When that sun gonna hit this nigger on the back, I'm gone.' He got straddle over the row, them rows wasn't that high, and he picked over 400 pounds that day," leaving Albert far behind.[33] Cotton pickers varied more in technique and ability than in field clothing, which by 1927 had become virtually a uniform. Males wore straw hats, long-sleeve cotton shirts, overalls, and (after the weather turned cold) "jumper" jackets made from recycled cotton sacks. Shoes were optional, though on the blackest blacklands on the hottest days, ground surfaces burned even the horniest feet. Eddie Wegner recalled, "When you had green cotton stalks, when your feet got to that boiling point, you could kind of cool them under the shade of the cotton stalk a little, but when the cotton was dead, you made extra haste to get to the next green patch."[34] On the very hottest days, the picker tried to pick facing the sun, because in this position his hat shielded the back of his neck and kept him a little cooler. Hearing his son say, "Lord, I wish we could get some shade," Eddie Wegner's father replied, "'Well,

FIGURE 23 Members of the Johec family pose while picking cotton in the Nelsonville area of Austin County. (Fayette Area Heritage Museum, courtesy of Louis J. "Buddy" Polansky)

stand up straight and lift your hat and let the wind go through under it,' and sure enough a cloud would come."[35] It's never too hot to pick cotton, the old saying held, but one day the man Johnnie Loud picked for came to get him. The temperature had reached 114 degrees, and it "was just fire out there in that middle." The man said, "You coming out of the field. Ain't nobody gonna die on my place, not for me. It's too damn hot."[36]

Females wore long cotton dresses to cover the backs of their legs when they bent over, large slat-bonnets with neck-protecting curtains behind, and—rather often—long picking gloves with open fingers made from worn-out cotton sacks. Such "stove-pipe" field bonnets were big and deep, and, as Eddie Wegner told, "you had to look in there to see who that was."[37] Sometimes, women stuffed green cotton leaves into the tops of their bonnets to provide better insulation from the sun. A tanned skin marked the field hand, and most women tried to avoid this by covering every exposed inch of flesh. For every rule there was the exception, however. Outstanding cotton picker Leola Tiedt wore a straw hat instead of a bonnet and never wore gloves, since, as she explained, "I was always dark-skinned anyway, and if I was gonna pick cotton, I was gonna pick."[38]

As a picker, Tiedt stooped instead of knelt and picked the near halves of two rows at a time. Even as a "young kid" she could pick 350 pounds of cotton a day, but by her own admission she "picked dirty." When she emptied her sack at the wagon, "you could hear those dry leaves rustling in that pick sack." Explaining that "each one has his own method of picking," Tiedt recalled that some big strong men she worked beside picked only 150 pounds a day, while she picked 350. "Attitude" and technique explained some of the difference: "It was a rhythm, and whether your back would take it—I stooped all the time and my back never hurt."[39]

Like most pickers, Tiedt used her own special cotton pick sack, which she made herself. Sacks were made of heavy cotton ducking and were two to two-and-a-half feet wide and up to twelve feet long. Good pickers preferred long pick sacks, and "you didn't get a long pick sack unless you could pick." A bad picker with a long sack invited public derision, "cause there wouldn't be anything in it." The most important part of the pick sack was the strap, which Tiedt sewed "three levels thick and back and forth." The strap needed to be comfortable and to fit the individual picker so that the mouth of the sack came to just the right level for an easy reach with cotton-filled hands.[40] Cotton sacks were used for many chores besides picking cotton, including harvesting field peas, transporting shelled corn to the grist mill and cornmeal back, insulating blocks of ice being brought from town, and padding wagon and buggy seats. And, they served other, more personal needs, as well. Caught in a field by an unexpected shower, the picker draped the pick sack over his head to ward off the rain.[41]

Some pickers picked one row at a time, reaching over to feel for the half-seen cotton bolls on the other side, some picked astraddle of the row (at least in smaller cotton), and some picked half of two rows at a time, as did Leola Tiedt. There were family traditions about such things, as about picking by kneeling or stooping. Stoopers went faster, most thought, but their backs hurt more. Kneelers wore homemade knee pads of padded cotton sacks or recycled automobile tires, but the pads pinched behind the leg and sometimes got so hot they blistered the skin. One man recalled, "Your kneecap would alternately feel numb or like it was being pushed through your leg."[42] Grover Williams's parents eschewed knee pads and forbade kneeling, since this "wore out your duckings, the knee of your overalls." However, Williams said, his parents rules were not always obeyed: "If they weren't watching, if they were way down behind us, you know we'd get a little break, drag our sack up and pick on our knees and then get right back up. They couldn't see you like they do now, they had these big bonnets on. You had to turn your head to see behind all that bonnet. We knew when to get on our knees and when not to." Discovered kneeling, Williams would say, "Mama, my back's hurting," only to hear the standard response to this complaint, "Boy, you don't have a back, you just got a gristle."[43]

When caught up for a time with picking on their own farm, Grover Williams's family—his grandfather, grandmother, and two brothers— often picked on the neighboring farms of Germans and Anglo-Americans. Like so many other families, the Williamses picked as a family unit, with Williams's grandmother collecting the daily pay. "They got everything," Williams told; "We just got food, clothing, shelter, and beat up."[44]

Many other families did the same. As the cotton rapidly opened in the field in this hot, dry fall of 1927, farm families desperately picked from dark to dark and hired anybody they could to help. As one man recalled, in this sort of cotton year: "any sort of hand that can hobble about and drag a sack is in demand—high and low, men and women, big and little, young and old, they go after it. Every little bit is a help, they say—anything to relieve the stress—anything to get the precious staple out before the damaging rains come."[45] The farmer's problem was that every family's first priority was its own cotton. Teddy Keiler hired anyone he could to help pick—German neighbors, relatives, black families from the Round Top vicinity, school children, and the occasional group of passing Mexicans.[46] Mexican pickers had been following the ripening cotton northward along the Brazos valley since the 1880s and often worked at the big cropper farms, but small landowners in the uplands could not count on help from them.[47] Children also were hired, if their parents permitted it. Keiler made do with "children of school age, from seven, eight years old, they was all in the field— even if they didn't pick a whole lot—but they picked."[48] Gus Keiler hired "kinfolks and neighbor boys" to pick, sometimes nine or ten at a time, and Mrs. Keiler did double duty, getting up early enough to "have bread done at eight o'clock in the morning," then picking in the field, then preparing lunch, then returning to the field to pick until dark.[49] Far to the northeast, even Mrs. Cass Nation's blind brother Paul picked with his family in local fields during this peak cotton season of 1927. Nation recalled, "He could keep up with all as he crawled along from stalk to stalk. He would start at the bottom of the stalk and feel out the bolls, pick the cotton, and put it in his sack." Once, at the end of a row, blind Paul fell into an old cistern, but emerged unhurt.[50]

In countryside and county seat, African-Americans often came under social pressure to pick for others during this peak season of 1927. Black renters or small landowners, caught up for the time with their own picking (and the fact plainly visible in their fields), often found it difficult or impossible to refuse to pick for certain of their white neighbors, whose requests sometimes sounded more like commands. Editor B. F. Herrigel of the La Grange Journal regularly commented on "idle town Negroes" during chopping and picking seasons and sometimes reprinted stern editorials from his predecessors. One of these noted: "There is no excuse now for loafers of any kind in the streets. All such should be interviewed by the city marshal, and if they cannot give a satisfactory account as to their mode of obtaining a living, the vagrant law should be enforced."[51]

Especially across racial boundaries, the relationship between landowners and hired cotton pickers often engendered justifiable suspicions on both sides. Pickers and their employers were at economic cross-purposes. Otto Fuchs hired non-family members with reluctance, believing that "the quality of work by such hirelings would not usually fulfill desired standards,"[52] and John Skrabanek disliked "hired hands, who by his standards were sloppy and careless about not removing all the lint from the bolls."[53] From the landowner's perspective, pickers often picked too fast and too dirty, trying to accumulate the greatest weight of cotton in the shortest amount of time, no matter how much trash they put in the pick sack or how much cotton they skipped and left behind. Since weight was money, pickers rejoiced in dew-wet morning cotton, sand-covered fallen cotton (which they carefully placed in their sacks without shaking), and occasional weighty objects chanced upon in the field—stray "pine melons" or even rocks—which they

FIGURE 24 Ellis County cotton pickers weigh seed cotton before dumping it in the wagon, 1929, while the landowner records pickers' poundages and visits with the county agent. (Cushing Memorial Library, Texas A&M University)

sometimes included in their pick sacks. Another pickers' trick was to weigh the cotton at the scale, then fail to completely dump the sack, keeping some cotton to be weighed again, and weighers often were instructed to watch for suspicious "lumps" remaining after dumping.

Pickers did this sort of thing to compensate for anticipated cheating by the landowner at the cotton scale set up at the wagon in the field. As Grover Williams told, all too often the employer had "his pea weighted" for the scale to weigh light or resorted to other tricks: "The little weight you hang on the scale, up under the bottom it has a little recess in there. You could put lead in there, you could take lead out, or whatever. And most of the time, they never would let it settle. They had the weight and put it on, and it'd be in their favor all the time." Furthermore, employers sometimes cheated pickers by keeping crooked records or subtracting excessive poundages at the scales for the weight of the pickers' pick sacks. "The most I think they ever knocked off my sack would be eleven pounds, and I know it didn't weigh no eleven pounds," Williams recalled.[54]

In return, Williams and other pickers picked their sacks very full, cutting down on the frequency of bag-weight debits from their totals, and: "to compensate for that [the anticipated cheating at the cotton scale], when I'm picking, if we run up on some cotton in the middle that the wind's blown and the rain's knocked out, you didn't pick it up and shake off the dirt. You just picked it up, dirt and all and put it in there." Occasionally, a small watermelon or a rock went in the sack, as well, though "you emptied your own sack and didn't want to get caught." This might happen if "there was maybe five of them around there watching you, but if it was just the man we picked for and his wife, he didn't have a chance."[55]

Eddie Wegner often hired local black families to pick, and he was uncomfortably aware of the customary cheating on both sides at the cotton scales. Affirming that "there was skulduggery going on with weighing, I'm pretty sure I can be honest in saying that, because we got all kinds of people in this world," Wegner assumed his pickers did not trust him and acted accordingly. A fifty-pound weight remained with the field scale at the cotton wagon so that the hired hands could test its accuracy any time they wished, and Eddie selected a literate cotton picker, often a woman, to "write up the figures for my use and for most every hand." This powerful gesture of trust brought the same black pickers back to the Wegner farm, year after year.[56]

However, even Wegner could not keep his hired pickers from the main chance as his cotton diminished in the field. He explained: "When it gets down to the scrap, right over here, like the cow sees the pasture greener over there, neighbor has been unable to get any hands, he's got beautiful cotton over there. So, one evening you come up, all pick sacks full of cotton have been dropped off. The next morning, your hands won't show up. They're over at neighbor, where they can make more money."[57] Pickers had their own perspective on this matter, as well, and Mrs. Otis Dean well recalled the time she switched from one farmer to another as hired picker. The first employer offered her horrible chili and "bitter swamp coffee" for breakfast and allowed her to sleep free on cotton sacks on his slanting front porch—if she picked over five hundred pounds a day (which she sometimes did). Otherwise, he charged her $1.50 a night. The neighboring farmer who lured Dean away offered wonderful meals, a soft bed, snacks and water served in the field, a Delco lighting system, a bathtub with running water, and cotton of equal thickness. She told, "All I had to do was keep my head down, butt up, and pick one row at a time."[58]

Such a posture did not lend itself to song, however, and pickers in the field sang less than hoe hands or plowmen. Mance Lipscomb recalled occasional singing in the cotton field at the big Brazos valley plantation farms where he worked. Days spent picking cotton seemed endless, and only darkness brought release from the field. As Lipscomb recalled: "The sun was your bell. You know the sun down when it be turning into night, you don't supposed to work at night. So, they was crying for, 'Hurry up! Hurry up, let the sun go down.' And we sang that song about 'Hurry up, sun, go down, and hide yourself behind the western hill.' Maybe five or ten people get to singing that same song, trying to make the day go away. And sometime it'd make you feel better. Songs estimate on your mind, make your mind wander."[59] Ilo Ullrich of Carmine recalled black pickers singing in the fields when they picked. However, "We didn't sing; maybe close to night we'd sing a little."[60]

From time to time during the picking season, farmers finished picking a bale by "dusk dark" and prepared for a trip to the gin the next day. Forty-nine Fayette County gins and thirty-four Washington County gins were scattered across the countryside during this dry autumn of 1927, and it was a rare farm family that was not within a four-hour wagon ride of more than one.[61] A farmer chose a particular gin because of its closeness, speed of processing, the lack of damage it did to the cotton, the number of nearby cotton buyers, and the ginner's reputation. In Carmine, two gins operated, and some farmers believed one of them stole cotton seed. As the farmer and the lucky person chosen to accompany him rose and dressed in the dark, they heard the first whistles of the steam gins announcing they were "hot" and ready for farmers' cotton. Cotton had opened early and all at once in 1927, and gins were running long hours trying to service the lines of cotton wagons waiting in the "gathering yards" nearby. The farmer left home well before dawn in hopes of getting in line and getting "ginned off" before noon. The chosen son or daughter that rode the load of cotton with him got a break from the drudgery of cotton picking, half a day in town at Burton, Carmine, Round Top, or some other exciting place, and a chance to observe the dangerous and fascinating gin machinery in action, "a combination of the fiery pit and the mechanical juggernaut."[62] Those left behind donned cotton sacks at first light, entered the dew-wet fields, and returned to picking, dumping their pick sacks into stand sacks until the family cotton wagon returned.

In the gray light of morning, the farmer's wagon rolled into the gin yard and took a place in line behind the wagons of even earlier risers and the wagons left over from the day before. Some of these farmers had gone home for the night, others from farther away had slept in their wagons, comfortably half-buried in the loads of cotton. In 1927 most area gins still were powered by steam, and boilermen rose early to stoke their still-simmering boilers back to operating pressures. Only on Sundays were gin fires allowed to go entirely out, so the boilers could be cleaned and readied for the next week's run. Diesel-powered gins were harder to start in the morning, and Henry Wehring at the Burton gin and other master gin mechanics had become expert at coaxing the Bessemers, Tipps, and other engines into reluctant life. Starting a diesel required lengthy preliminary heating of the engine's external "firebox," as Robert Wilhelmsen recalled from observations of the Summerfield gin.

> We'd get there first in line, usually. And Summerfield'd come, and he'd get that old engine started. He'd put that fire up in front in there, get that firebox heated up, then he'd get that jack on that big flywheel, and that exhaust would go way in that pasture down there. First thing you'd hear, "kapung!," and the smoke'd fly, and the cows would move off. And finally it'd get going, and he engaged the clutch mechanism and it'd get that big belt going, and he'd go down the line and get those gins stands going good. Then, there was a racket, with all that stuff a-humming, you know.[63]

Diesel gins such as those at Summerfield and Burton made more noise than steam gins, especially at start up time. O. R. Carey recalled, "You could hear one of those old gas oilers running for ten miles on a good clear morning about sunup, every time it turned over."[64] At the

FIGURE 25   Loaded cotton wagons in line at the O'Quinn gin, Fayette County. During the height of the cotton-picking season, lines grew even longer, and farmers sometimes stayed with their wagons all night. (Percy Faison album, Fayette Heritage Museum and Archives, La Grange)

Farmers' Coop Gin in Burton, gin operator Henry Wehring had become a master at prodding the Bessemer diesel into action. Burton residents woke up around 7:00 a.m. when the Bessemer fired off, popping and backfiring, heard it thumping away like a big heart all day long, then sometimes woke up again at the silence late at night when Wehring shut it down.[65]

Farmers waiting in line to be ginned off socialized, visited nearby mercantile stores (planning what they might purchase with their cotton money later on), and otherwise amused themselves, though they also fretted at the delay, watched the sky for storm clouds, and worried about their vulnerable cotton back home in the fields. Farmers' children perhaps had more fun at their visit to the gin than the adults. While their fathers watched the cotton wagons, they went into the store, visited the blacksmith shop to watch the smithy at work (every gin had to have a blacksmith nearby), and—as much as they were allowed to do so—explored the gin.

Grover Williams usually accompanied his grandfather on the eight-mile trip from Flat Prairie to the gin at Burton, and he carried his shoeshine kit with him and tried to use the hours waiting at the gin to best advantage. He shined shoes at Heine's Barbershop for tips (though he could not go inside), helped Mr. Muhelbrad set up his tent for his "picture show" for a free admission, and swept the floor at Harding Harmel's cafe for a free hamburger. Grover also worked for the store-owning Knittel family, on one occasion mowing their yard, beating their rugs, and putting up little Thad Knittel's big trunk full of toys for "one quarter, one jelly sandwich, and a glass of milk."[66] Williams's problem in playing this role of helpful black boy was that he could not refuse any request, as when Mr. Bredthauer asked him to dig his potatoes and put them away in his potato house. Bredthauer compensated this service in potatoes, although young Williams had plenty of those back at Flat Prairie.

Sometimes local gins offered unique recreational opportunities. At the Moore family's gin near where the Washington-Navasota road crossed the Brazos, black employees of the Moores gambled immune from law enforcement officials, as Ed Lathan recalled.

> I've ginned a many a bale of cotton there, and on Saturdays, [at] Mr. Moore's, there's a big pecan tree back of there. Man, them people be round there like buzzards on a dead cow. Them people gambling, got a big blanket spread, some of em shooting craps. In the daytime! They might start Friday evening and shoot that till up in the midnight. Mr. Moore and them know there's gambling back there, wasn't no law going back there, "That's my negroes pleasure." He keep the law off em, "Let my folks alone."[67]

Some farmers' children had been forbidden to go near the dangerous gin (and, in truth, females rarely were allowed to accompany their fathers on trips there), but it held an endless fascination. Diesel or steam, gins belched smoke, dust, and cotton lint that blanketed the neighborhood around, soiling housewives' laundry on the clotheslines and accumulating on wire fences so they appeared to be fences made of

FIGURE 26   Burton gin workers wait to unload their cotton
at the Farmer's Cooperative Gin, ca. 1914. (Operation Restoration,
Burton, courtesy of Wanda Whitener)

cotton. Above all, gins made wonderful, thunderous noise—an industrial bedlam of sound to ears accustomed to the silence of the mule-
powered countryside. Beyond the thumping of the big engines was a
complexity of other noise, as one ginner's son recalled: "The multitude
of wheels all turning at once made a sound which I remember but can't
describe. It was a moan or whine coupled with the slapping of a loose-
laced drive belt and the rattle of an out-of-line screw type seed con-
veyor. Modern gins don't make this sound."[68] Rules normally kept
children from the gin, but these often were laxly enforced in the press
of ginning season. Farmers and their sons sometimes wandered around
among gin stands and slapping drive belts observing the machinery and
the progress of their cotton, and were little disturbed by the stories
they had heard about exploding boilers and "men ground up almost
altogether" in the gin stands.[69] "Safety first" attitudes rarely reached the
countryside in 1927. The steam-powered Clover gin had a huge
flywheel driving a belt that powered all the gin stands, and as one man
recalled, "When the steam got low, us kids would crawl out this old
iron beam, get on the belt, and just ride that belt," jumping off just
before it reached the gin stands.[70]

Veteran gin hands had few illusions about their dangerous work-places, however accustomed they might become to their friendly old diesels and the steam engines that "would sing a song to you if you knew what you were listening for."[71] Fires broke out in all the gins from time to time because of sparks in the cotton, and the wood-burning steam gins had even greater problems. These used two hundred or more cords of wood every ginning season, and their smokestacks belched smoke and sparks, which occasionally ignited cotton in the waiting wagons. "Keeping everything clean" was the rule of survival at steam gins. Sparks—originating from lost matches, careless tobacco use, or glass bottles focusing the sun—might start in the cotton, then be sucked up into the gin when the farmer emptied his wagon. Gin machinery generated its own sparks to start fires, often from flint rocks and other debris in the cotton, and many fires began from uncertain origins. Sometimes sparks in the cotton passed through the ginning process and became compressed deep within a bale, the dreaded "hot bale" that—undetected—might burst into flames days or weeks later at the storage area or compress. Strangely, only gasoline or kerosene poured into the bale over the deeply smouldering "hot spot" could put one of these out. Water would not penetrate the dense cotton.[72]

Ginner's son Joe Fred Cox remembered that experienced gin hands could smell fire in cotton long before the average person, and that people tested one old veteran from time to time by placing a tiny piece of smoldering cotton in a bucket during gin operation. Invariably, this man would begin to sniff the air, hone in on the source like a bird dog, and find it.[73] Ginners sometimes even paid attention to who brought in the particular cotton they were running. J. D. Bowman of Lone Oak recalled that one farmer became notorious for hiring "dirty pickers" who put rocks in the cotton and started fires. "Every time that we would see Rob Bronick come into Lone Oak under those scales to be weighed, the word went out to be on the alert, and there would be a fire."[74] Ginner Geoffrey Wills recalled, "We had to stay there, we couldn't leave the gin stands. We had to stay there and watch it, many things could happen. We had fires, big fires. Sometimes the cotton pickers, the youngsters, would put rocks in the cotton, and we'd suck them up and they would hit the machinery and start fires. We had to watch out for fire at all times."[75]

Every cotton season, various area gins had major fires and one or

FIGURE 27 A Fayetteville area group hauls wood to a local steam-powered gin, ca. 1912. Steam gins burned hundreds of cords of wood each operating season. (Fayette Area Heritage Museum, courtesy of Louis J. "Buddy" Polansky)

more burned to the ground. In this hot fall of 1927, the La Grange *Journal* reported smaller gin fires on a weekly basis, and by the end of August the William Wenke gin had experienced three fires, one started in the "condenser," one by a flint rock in the cotton, and one by pipe ashes from a black farmer. This man discovered fire in his seed cotton while waiting in line, threw the burning cotton out, decided he had thrown out too much, and put some back in. These smouldering remains were then sucked up with the rest of his cotton and started a fire in the gin machinery.[76]

When a local gin had a fire or broke down, everyone's cotton was at stake, and local farmers swiftly came to the rescue to get the gin up and operating. Fire began from lost matches at the little Ehrigson gin near Shelby and burned up most of the loading platform, but neighbors, desperate to get their cotton ginned, pitched in to get the gin going again. Lydia Ehrigson recalled: "Neighbors came. They all brought their hammers, this and that, and fixed everything up that was burned down as fast as they could. I believe that at three that afternoon we started ginning, and we ginned and we ginned—we didn't need no sleep."[77]

The veteran gin hand not only sniffed the air for the scent of burning cotton, he listened to the machinery to detect the first faint sound of mechanical trouble on the way. He was utterly familiar with all of the gin sounds and subsounds, a complexity of noises within noises that the uninitiated heard only as an undifferentiated, ear-shattering roar.[78]

The machinery brought its own dangers, no matter how deceptively familiar it became. Part of the problem was fatigue, since ginners worked up to fifteen hours a day during peak ginning season. Geoffrey Wills told, "When I'd leave out at night, twelve o'clock at night close down to get some rest, I couldn't hear nothing from all that noise. Fifteen hours, all that humming, the gins was humming, we had to stay there. And kick-off at four-thirty."[79] One morning after three hours sleep, Wills was clearing a "choke up," greasing a dry belt that fed cotton to one of the gins stands, when "I got too close to that cog, and I dropped that cog on me," mangling a hand and losing several fingers. Losing a hand or arm in a gin stand while trying to clear a choke up in a gin stand was the most common gin injury. Ginners reached in with "gin sticks" to do this and wore short-sleeve clothing or taped down their sleeves as additional precautions, but with the passage of time, over-familiarity with the machinery, and long hours, some people grew impatient, and impatience led to the loss of body parts. From South Carolina to West Texas, anyone who grew up in Southern cotton country knew a "one-armed man" or two, as Hall County resident Curtis Tunnell explained.

> There were a lot of one-armed men around town, just had one arm. The other arm is off up around the elbow. You always knew when you saw a one-armed man that he had worked in the cotton gin, because the boxes where the saws were, that removed the burrs, seeds, and things—those boxes get lint up in them, and you're supposed to wait until the gin shuts down, then you take a stick and clean the lint out, but they never would want to stop them. And so men would invariably take a stick and lift up the lid and go in there and clean out that lint, avoiding the saws. But when you're

working long hours, you're tired, and it's dark and noisy, and there's so much lint and dirt in the air in a cotton gin that it's like a fog. You can't see to the other end of the cotton gin, and you're breathing all that. And they'd reach in there, and occasionally it would grab that stick and jerk their arm into the saws, just like that. And it would mangle—cut the bone and flesh and everything up, and they'd have to have their arm taken off. I knew a dozen men around town that were one-armed from having lost their arm in the cotton gin.[80]

Robert Krinke, Otto Eichler, the son of William Ebner, and various others joined the ranks of one-armed men in Fayette and Washington counties, but they all survived. Stranger stories were told about gin deaths, and some of them were true. In the old days, gin boilers sometimes had exploded, demolishing the gins and killing the ginners, though by 1927 better metallurgy made such incidents less likely. Local ginners had read of a strange gin accident that happened in 1925 at Sweetwater, Texas. W. G. Owens, age fifty-five, had been working in a local gin late at night when he got his jumper caught in the line shaft and was "whirled to death."[81] As ginners also were well aware, back in August of 1912 young Harry Etzel of Round Top had died a horrible death at a local gin. "The young man was caught in the cotton press of the Round Top Gin and crushed to death," the newspaper account told. "His remains were laid to rest in the Florida Chapel Cemetery Thursday evening. He fell into the automatic cotton packer, and his body was crushed to a thickness of three inches. When rescued, he was still living, but died an hour later."[82]

Young Leola Tiedt attended Etzel's funeral, as she had the special ceremony held for her uncle Otto Eichler's arm, also lost in a gin accident. "I remember," she said, "when they took that limb that was cut off and put it in an apple box and took it to the cemetery and buried it on cemetery land. That was part of him."[83] The laying out of the "squashed young man," Harry Etzel, was a more somber affair. By the time of the laying out, the crushed body had begun to smell, despite the use of fruit jars of ice placed in the casket around the corpse. "They had the casket on two sawhorses in the home. They had a tub and some coals in it and put cedar limbs on it, green twigs, and that gave a sort of a smell. But his dog knew that he was in that casket, and he would not leave, he laid there on the floor. I was just a kid, but I can still see that dog, I can still see that tub, that cedar, smoldering."[84]

Kermit Fox, a classmate of Leola Tiedt at La Bahia School, perhaps thought of young Etzel's fate as he handled the gin's flexible pipe to suction his family's cotton from the wagon. Everything about the gin seemed intimidating, and handling the suction flue rattled Kermit's nerves. He disliked the deafening roar it made and its tendency to suck hats off heads, handkerchiefs from pockets, and jumpers, pocket knives, or other mislaid objects from the cotton.[85] Farmers suctioned their own cotton at most gins, though the Moore family gin stationed a gin hand at the suction tube, perhaps to avoid the common practice of "layering" the bale. Suctioners normally removed cotton from the top-front of the wagon to the bottom-back, and: "Some farmers, including my father, were therefore inclined, if possible, to put the best picked cotton on top in the front half of the wagon and on the bottom in the rear. This layered the best cotton on the sides of the bale from which the samples would be taken."[86]

Most farmers did this layering or "plating" of the bale. Picked from different parts of the field, by different pickers, and often on different days, the cotton in the farmer's wagon often varied in coloration, trash content, and even staple, and the farmer wanted his best product to end up on the outside of the bale. Children that picked fast and dirty and slowly and carefully all were useful, provided certain precautions were taken. Leola Tiedt's trashy cotton always went to the inside of her father's bales, while cotton from clean-picking siblings went where the sampler's crooked knife could get to it. Eddie Wegner's father was a shareholder in the Farmer's Coop Gin in Burton, but Mr. Wegner still plated his bales, not wishing to get "skinned." At Burton, the plating technique required a slightly different tactic than at the gins Kermit Fox's family frequented. At Farmer's Coop Gin one plated the bale by sucking up the best cotton rapidly at first so the gin stands filled up and overloaded, and the cotton spilled out on the floor. Thus, good cotton went into one of the curved sides of the bale, bad cotton went in the middle, and more good cotton went to the other side of the bale at the end of the run as the ginner upstairs used his suction tube to pick up the initial overload from the floor. Admitting that "you shouldn't put that good cotton on the sides of the bale," Wegner nonetheless thought the practice justified. "There were lots and lots of ways that the cotton

buyer, in one place or another, could skin you. Plating a bale wasn't especially hard, and I think everybody did that. You really weren't trying to
do anything illegal; on the other hand, you didn't want to get skinned."[87]

In every cash transaction involving cotton, from the field to the far-
away spinning mill, people worried about getting skinned—about "getting their plow cleaned" by cannier operators—and farmers were
especially suspicious of cotton buyers who appraised their cotton on
the basis of a complicated rating system well beyond easy understand-
ing. Public ginners were certified by the state, but many of them were
cotton buyers as well, and they also came under occasional suspicion.
Farmers thought that some gins "crowded the cotton" to compete with
the ginning times of larger, better equipped gins, a practice that damaged the cotton fibers and lowered the grade—and value—of the farmers' cotton, and some believed that ginners occasionally stole valuable
cottonseed. Both the Siebel and Eichler gins operated in Carmine, and
Henry Fuchs's father rarely ginned in one of them. Henry explained:
"One man would sell his cotton seed to the ginner, the next man would
take his home to feed his cows. And there was a trap [door] there. You
sell your seed, that trap was open, it'd go down in a hole. The next man
took his seed home, and maybe that trap wasn't closed for a little bit,
and fifty pounds or maybe a hundred would drop through. You never
did get it. That one ginner was apt to do that, my dad knew."[88]

Processing the farmer's fifteen hundred pounds of cotton from
wagon to bound bale normally took only twelve to fifteen minutes, and
Eddie Wegner often went inside the Farmers' Coop Gin to observe the
ginning. A fire started by sparks from the gin saws in the stands hitting
rocks and gravel always seemed possible, and this was his cotton. By
1927, all area gins used the pneumatic delivery system invented by
Robert S. Munger of Fayette County around 1883 in which no human
hands touched the cotton. Fan-driven air sucked cotton from the
wagon, cleaned the cotton of dust and dirt, transported it to the gin
stands, fed it into the stands that separated lint from seed, and then
sent the lint cotton to the bale press.[89] Kermit Fox described: "At the
gin, through a system of ducts the seeded cotton and lint were con-
veyed by air. In the series of gin-stands, spinning fine-toothed saws and
whirling brushes separated the lint from the seeds. The fluffy lint was
compressed into bales which were wrapped in hemp bailing and
secured by six metal bands about one and one-fourth inches wide. The

average load of seeded cotton usually yielded about 500 pounds of lint and 1,000 pounds of seed. The compacted bale measured 54" x 27" x 46" and had a density of 22 1/2 pounds per cubic foot."[90]

During the ginning, cottonseed separated by the gin stands fell into a "scale bin" from which a ginner diverted it either into the farmer's waiting wagon, or, if the farmer wished to sell it to the gin, the "seed house." Farmers commonly "tolled" their seed, using a portion of it to pay the several-dollar ginning costs and saving the rest for planting, animal feed, or resale to nearby cottonseed mills, which ran night and day during ginning season.[91]

Cottonseed had to be processed swiftly and close to the gins that produced it, so the Carmine mill ran twenty-four hours a day in cotton season. Steam-powered and burning cordwood, the Carmine mill generated its own electricity. Kermit Fox recalled it as "a huge, multi-storied, virtually windowless structure encased in corrugated sheet metal" with mountains of cotton seed outside and "loud and offensive" operating noises. The mill's whistle was powerful and deep, very unlike the whistles of nearby steam gins and passing trains. "In a small village like Carmine it appeared strange to see a giant plant operate throughout the night under the sprinkling of eerie, yellow lights."[92] Like other cottonseed mills, the one at Carmine processed the highly perishable seed into valuable oil, cake, hulls, meal, and "linters"—fine cotton fibers adhering to the seed and often destined to become smokeless powder for rifle cartridges.

At the Burton gin, Eddie Wegner often watched action at the "compressor" after his cotton had been ginned and his seed separated, as he described, the lint cotton became a bale:

> First, a tamper tamps it down as it comes in, then the hydraulic ram comes from underneath and compresses it to bale, and the top part of the press already has the bagging on it, and there's a bagging on the lower part which comes up with the ramp. And then they lap it over and put the bands around it. The oldtimers tied it by hand: one pushed the band, the other one grabbed it and put it through the buckle, which had a slot, bent over, and when it released the pressure, it sucked those bands down into the bale.[93]

Then, Wegner's bale was "kicked out" of the compressor, weighed on the "big balance scale" beside the compress, had a sample cut out of it, and was pushed down the inclined stairway to the small loading platform, at that point becoming the Wegner family's bale to sell, warehouse, or store at home.

The Wegners usually sold their cotton in Brenham, but most farmers were like Grover Williams's grandfather and sold their cotton to a local buyer near the gin on the same day they ginned it. They knew they might get a little more for their cotton at the county seat towns of Brenham or La Grange, but such places were a long day's wagon ride away, and farmers usually felt they needed to hurry home and get the rest of their cotton in from the field. Every mercantile store in Burton bought cotton, and Williams's grandfather took his cotton sample, wrapped in brown paper with the gin and bale number on it, around to each in turn. Each buyer would "go through it and tear around on it" and make an offer based on the staple length, grade, character, and current market value of cotton.[94]

Most farmers found this a mysterious and unsettling process. They could measure staple length, which ranged from seven-eighths inch to one-and-one-eighth inch in Texas cotton, but grade involved a complex judgment about color, trash content, and amount of ginning damage that assigned cotton to nine categories, ranging from "middling fair" at the top to "good ordinary" at the bottom. Few farmers chose to argue with a buyer who thought their cotton graded only "good middling" but, instead, went on their way to find someone who thought it was the grade above, "strict good middling." Beyond the mysteries of grade were the even more esoteric mysteries of the cotton's "character," which involved factors of strength, smoothness, silkiness, body, uniformity and "spirality of fibers," and was even harder to judge.[95] Usually, every buyer the farmer visited made an offer on his cotton, and if minimally satisfied he took the highest bid, bought a few items in the store, and went home. Grover Williams's grandfather kept things just that simple: he ginned his bale, sold the bale to the highest bidder, and went to the store to pay any outstanding bill he might have and to purchase flour, sugar, "whatever Mama had on that note—maybe some material, or he got him a new work suit, a jumper, and some overalls, socks, shoes, maybe another hat, and a bottle of whisky."[96]

As farmers often suspected, many complexities went on behind the scenes in local cotton buying. Eddie Wegner's family believed in "cash and carry or starve to death," but other farmers—landowners and renters—relied on store credit for several months of the year between cotton seasons.[97] These people, who paid credit prices from 10 to 60 percent higher than cash ones, were one reason the merchants' credo was, "Everything will be O.K. in September."[98] Henry Fuchs's father was another cash and carry man, selling his cotton to merchants in Carmine, where "every one was a cotton buyer," but "there were a lot of em [farmers], when those first bales of cotton come in, they didn't get too much cash out of that—I know that."[99] For obvious reasons, the cotton buyers from these stores often gave the debtor farmers the best prices for their cotton. Being the highest bidder in a real bidding competition cost money, however, and in some communities rival merchants–cotton buyers struck secret agreements to let the cotton go to the merchant who had the farmer in greatest debt. Other merchants deliberately underbid that farmer's cotton, knowing they would profit in turn when their own champion debtors brought their cotton in. At one community, a merchant's putting a foot on the farmer's wagon wheel while examining his bales of cotton signaled to other merchants–buyers that "this man is mine."[100] Farmers might suspect that something was going on, but with the next crossroads community and its cotton buyers miles and hours away, they still tended to sell near where they ginned.

Farmers also knew that their local cotton buyers were only the bottom rungs of a ladder of ever-larger cotton entrepreneurs terminating far away at the great international cotton markets of New York, Paris, and London.[101] Some local buyers in Fayette and Washington counties were true independents—"spot buyers" or "scalpers," people called them—but most served as local agents for major "cotton brokers" in La Grange and Brenham. Such men got on the telephone or telegraph every morning and told their agents among local ginners and store-owners how much and what kind of cotton they needed and how high the agent buyers could bid to get it. The local buyer whose cotton broker needed cotton the most was likely to give a farmer the best deal on that particular day, but the next day his broker's quota might have been filled and he might be making only token offers. Local agents rarely made a lot of money on these deals, but the transactions were safe and profitable, provided they did not make major mistakes in judging staple and grade. Even at the bottom of the cotton ladder, the buyer's eye had to be keen. One man explained: "You had to know how to look at it. And don't never buy cotton under artificial light. You get under some electric light and it'll fool the shit out of you!"[102]

When farmers took their baled cotton from gins to local buyers, sometimes they did not like what the buyers had to say, and those who could afford the option chose not to sell. Having run the gauntlet of season, past threats of killer frosts, hailstorms, weeds, worms, and weevils, farmers now faced the perils of international economics. Cotton prices varied greatly from year to year because of complex economic forces farmers could neither predict nor fully understand, and in the early ginning season of this year of 1927, local cotton sold for just under twenty cents a pound—not enough, some farmers thought.

Henry Jaeger's father sold the family bales "just as they came" during 1927, as he had in other years, reasoning that he might get a low price for the first one, a high price for the last one, and that all would average out in the end. Jaeger never held his cotton back or stored it in a warehouse, waiting for the price to rise, and repeated cautionary tales about those who did. One man had held fifteen bales at his farm, but they caught fire and burned up, and "he didn't get nothing." Having gambled all year with weather and weevils, additional chance-taking with the precious cotton bales did not make sense to the Jaegers.[103]

Other farmers—bigger gamblers, or perhaps with greater resources—felt differently, though few men were as brave or as foolhardy as thirds-and-fourths renter Joe Tatum, who once piled seventeen bales of seed cotton on his turnrow, watched the sky, and waited for the price to go up. Like many other renters, Tatum had no large barn in which to store his baled cotton, so when he took it to the distant gin he had to sell it; in order to "speculate," he had to store his cotton loose and in the open.[104] Farmers ginning in larger communities sometimes had the option of storing their cotton in government-approved cotton warehouses, such as the one run by Frankie Jaster in Burton. After receiving, weighing, and tagging each bale, Jaster issued a receipt of ownership, which the farmer could immediately use as security for loans of up to 80 percent of the current value of his cotton while he waited for prices to rise.[105] A good many farmers, however, did not have access to such a warehouse (or did not wish to pay the warehousing fee) and took their bales back to their farms for storage.

Sometimes this worked out, and sometimes it didn't. Teddy Keiler recalled one man who stockpiled bales at forty cents a pound, waiting for the price to return to forty-five cents, and "got caught with it," watching his cotton deteriorate in the barn and the price fall over several years until he eventually sold at six cents.[106] Howard Matthies knew an old German farmer who had stored twenty-one bales in his barn in 1914 and still had them there thirteen years later (and would die with them in his barn during World War II).[107] Some spot dealers, such as Elenora Manske's husband and brother, would travel the countryside trying to strike deals with cotton-hoarding farmers like this man.[108] Shrewder farmers also stored cotton, however. If the price was acceptable, Otto Fuchs sold immediately to the highest buyer; if it was not, he often gambled on the price going up. As Kermit Fox recalled: "We often kept our cotton bales in various places around our farm, hoping and at times gambling for better future prices. We had at one time accumulated over 50 bales which robbed our barns, sheds, and outhouses of every conceivable storage nook." Some of the bales deteriorated significantly "from weathering and varmints," but in the end Otto Fuchs sold for over twenty cents a pound, netting more than six thousand dollars.[109]

As bale after bale was ginned and sold during this autumn of 1927, area farmers went about their business in a sometimes complicated "settling up" with banks, landowners, and mercantile stores. Thirds-and-fourths renters normally sold their own cotton, then paid their landowners either the value of every fourth bale or that of one-fourth of each bale, as the landowner wished. The landowners' one-third of the field corn often went directly into their cribs. Sometimes renters had operated cash-and-carry, like frugal landowners, but more often than not they had negotiated small bank loans to "make a crop" or else had been "furnished" during the year by credit stores. Sometimes these furnishing deals were made through the landowner, who established the line of credit, up to so much a month, at a certain store; sometimes the renters established their own credit at a store of their choice.

Such arrangements were fraught with peril. As researchers had firmly established back in 1915, many slings and snares for Texas farmers lay embedded in the complicated credit system, which varied greatly from community to community and county to county. Resolute believers in "cash and carry or starve to death," Eddie Wegner's family had good reasons for this policy, among them a Burton storeowner's ominous dictum to his employees, "it's better on credit business to note twice than forget once."[110]

During the economic crisis associated with the drastic fall in cotton prices at the beginning of World War I, Walton Peteet and other researchers from Texas Agricultural and Mechanical College had surveyed the practices of farming credit in Texas and discovered many shocking facts. Peteet reported in 1917, "Texas debtor farmers have been paying to banks 10 to 40 percent interest per annum, or to credit merchants 10 to 60 percent above cash prices."[111] In some areas, banks dominated farm credit; in other areas, credit stores dominated; but researchers discovered that in each case debtor farmers often did not know credit price mark-ups in the stores or the rates they paid to banks and landowners for their yearly loans to make a crop.[112] Besides the ferocious rates of interest and elevated credit-store prices, various tricks and scams commonly were used to put farmers even farther in the hole. An abuse of uncertain frequency was the credit merchant paying the landowner-furnisher a "commission" on the sale of supplies to his tenants—this for requiring the tenants to buy in the merchant's store. Big landlords also sometimes got "kick-backs" from wholesalers on high-priced goods sold to croppers in the landlords' commissary stores.[113] As previously noted, some farmers who owed a merchant could not get bids on their cotton from other buyers without consent of the merchant. Furthermore, credit stores often tried to keep their profitable credit customers permanently on credit, no matter how good a crop they made. One black farmer told: "If a negro makes a good crop, the merchants tempts him to buy wagons and buggies on credit and sometimes will refuse to accept cash in order to keep him in bondage next year."[114] Storeowners kept records, many farmers did not, and much chicanery followed from that simple fact. One black woman told the 1915 investigators:

> They robbed you. They always would write and give my daddy a receipt, you know, for what he got. You know my daddy didn't have no kind of education. They give him a receipt. He didn't pay no attention to that receipt, he'd throw that receipt down, you know. Then, they'd say, "John, you bring up your receipt." Well, my daddy couldn't find

no receipt. He done lost it and the man with the receipt got your money. [115]

Landowners also sometimes took advantage of black renter-debtors, especially when the latter had something they wanted—fine cotton crops or handsome work animals. In a story similar to many others from across the South, historian Neil Foley told of "one Texas landowner [who] made a practice of renting to Black tenants, securing their notes for supplies, and then running them off his property just before the crop was gathered."[116] In such situations, blacks often had little legal recourse, since the local sheriff was just another white landowner, and blacks did not even vote.

No wonder, then, that when Grover Williams's grandparents discussed money matters they took certain precautions. Landowners with valuable work stock and equipment that might be coveted by whites, they sent Grover and his brothers outside when they talked "business." Or, if the weather precluded this, Grover's grandmother issued a stern warning, "If a word of this gets out, and I find out about it, I'm gonna bust you down to the ground."[117]

After surveying hundreds of primary accounts, historian Jack Temple Kirby flatly stated that "country stores and plantation commissaries were the principal agents of credit and chiseling."[118] It was a rare crossroads cotton town without at least one mercantile store about which accusations accumulated, and Burton was no exception. In the store where the Williams family usually traded, Grover noted that black people's purchases automatically were "put on the book," on credit, even if they did not ask for credit. He opined: "They'd put it on the book almost automatic, cause they was going to pad the book. See, they didn't give you a receipt, and you don't know what he put in his book. Like, if you got a bottle of snuff and some other stuff, and it cost a dollar and eighty-five cents, when you got ready to pay it might have been two dollars and three cents. There's no way you could question it." Credit, "putting it on the book," was the primary method for charging blacks higher prices, Williams thought.[119] Local Anglos and Germans often had their suspicions about this store, or perhaps another one. Oliver Whitener told how one local merchant "always put the year, say 1921, just above the figures to be added, and to always add the year in with the figures," and also to "always have an axe or a broom or some-like item on the counter, and to include them in the purchases the farmer would make."[120] Gilbert Buck's grandfather caught this particular storekeeper trying the trick of adding in the year "three or four times" and thought that other creative bookkeeping went on, as well. "A lot of people never look at their bill and just paid whatever he put down. And I think a lot of these stores around here, they added a little because they were holding for the year—they added a little more to it. And who knows what happened nine months ago? Did I buy this nine months ago, this wash tub or something like that? They paid for stuff they never got."[121]

During the fall cotton pay-off of 1927, the greatest social and economic divide of all lay between thirds-and-fourths renters, who sold their own cotton, and the sharecroppers—mostly blacks—who did not. Black cropper families along the Brazos and Colorado valleys watched bale after bale of their seed cotton roll away in landowners' wagons and learned only at the end of the year how they had fared. Families normally did not know how much "furnishing" money they owed the landlord for the year, or how much he had sold their cotton for. Each family was due half the value of the cotton, minus the landowner's costs, and more often than not the settling up he reported failed to fulfill their hopes and dreams. Elnora Lipscomb tersely summed up one such year, "Well, we made 31 bales of cotton that year, and the Man said we'd made a clear receipt."[122]

Willie Lipscomb explained how the system worked along the Brazos. If a sharecropper family had to go to the owner for something it had to have during the crop year, he would pay for it,

> but you had to pay him double back. If you had a sweep sharpened for you, you paid for that out of your crop. In the end of the year they come to a settlement, they called it. And like, he gonna tell you how much you owed him, how much he owe you—how much you clear out of your crop. Your advances, all that, took out—everything, doctor bills, clothing bill. The bossman kept the record, the colored people didn't keep none. You got to do all the picking, you got to do all the hauling, but you don't sell nothing, you ain't got no rights to sell anything. He sell all the cotton. You don't know how much you get a bale for that cotton or how

much it was a pound. You had to go by what he tell you. You never seen a paper to know what it was, didn't have it in black and white, how you gonna 'spute him?[123]

Disputing the owner's word with a rival set of records was not a good idea for a black sharecropper in the Brazos bottoms—was, in fact, quite an unthinkable act. Davis Washington told:

There's nothing you can do about it. Of course you wouldn't want to lose no friendship, get the law, about your crop. You wouldn't want to lose no friendship with em, and you druther make that crop. And you know what's happening, you can move away from there. Course, you don't know whether you going from better to worse.[124]

For sharecroppers like Davis, day hands, thirds-and-fourths renters in the uplands, and landowners large and small, the cotton season of 1927 wound toward a close, with a dry, hot, early fall and a swift ripening of the cotton. Finally, the weather began to turn cool, and farmers knew that this year there would be no hoped-for "top crop" of cotton, spurred by fall rains and unseasonable warmth, to add additional bales to their productions and bring in welcome Christmas money. Over the short span from 1924 to 1927, cotton production had varied from 40,697 bales to 11,963 bales in Fayette County, and from 38,596 bales to 11,544 bales in Washington County. Fayette's 1927 crop of 33,056 bales and Washington's crop of 30,525 bales fell somewhere in between—not bad, not good, with a so-so price ranging around twenty cents a pound most of the season.[125] However, across the alluvial bottomlands, blacklands, sandy lands, and post-oak belts of the diverse countryside along the rivers, such judgments meant little. On individual family farms, cotton fortunes had waxed and waned with the season each had experienced, the unique play of local circumstances: frosts or near frosts; hailstorms or saving rains; weeds, worms, and weevils or their relative absences; clean harvests or cotton blown into the dirty middles by fall thundershowers. Gamblers all, whether they wished to be or not, cotton families found out by October how the year's game had played out, and as one farmer said, "on the average, you could expect anything."[126]

As the leaves turned and the corn went into the crib, circuses came to market towns in the old counties along the Brazos and Colorado, and house parties and dance-hall affairs were held, as in many autumns before. Farm families rarely visited their county seats, but they often went in to town to see the fall circuses. The grown-ups remembered when "Buffalo Bill" Cody's Wild West Show last visited the area in 1915, with the famous scout's entourage of private railroad car, chef, valet, masseur, and "private tent on the circus grounds with a davenport, carpet, rugs, decks, and every other possible convenience which would be found in the living room of a home."[127] That great show had ended with Cody's death, but other circuses, "traveling vaudeville companies," "street carnivals," and "medicine shows" still made their rounds. Like Buffalo Bill's extravaganza, the Gentry Brothers' Dog and Pony Show arrived by special train, then formed ranks for the obligatory street parade of circus performers, caged animals, uncaged animals, and a steam piano playing "Good Old Summertime" and "Dixie." A man preceded the parade, crying out dramatically, "Hold your horses, the elephants are coming!" which was no idle warning, since, as one man recalled, "local horses were liable to act up even at the smell of these monsters."

Medicine shows played courthouse towns such as Brenham, La Grange, Sealy, and Giddings, but they also reached farther into the countryside than the major circuses, visiting smaller market towns such as Burton, Round Top, and Fayetteville. One medicine show, which drew big crowds to a platform set up near the Lee County courthouse, was recalled as "a two-hour program of slapstick comedy interspersed with the doctor's sales pitch." Medicines were few in number but made up for it by the numbers of maladies each claimed to cure. Comedians at this show sang such songs as, "Mama, Get the Hammer, There's a Flea on Baby's Nose," and the "doctor" making the pitch for his product often lapsed into fluent German to better appeal to that part of his audience. As usual, local authorities let the show go on, despite misgivings about the "medicine," sold for one dollar a bottle, which turned out to be colored rainwater, possibly fortified with epsom salts.[128]

After the cotton was in, and before the roads became too muddy to travel or it got too cold to stand around outside, blacks, Germans, Czechs, and Anglo-Americans held "house parties"—affairs at private homes in which the guests danced, sang, drank, talked, and gambled. Dancing and music were central to all house parties in the old counties along the rivers, and hosts normally removed furniture from all or part of their houses to facilitate dancing. Often, they put up temporary board seating around the edges of their rooms to accommodate resting dancers and spectators, and on special occasions, such as big weddings, they sometimes even removed their floorboards and used them to build temporary dance platforms outside the houses.[129] Ethnic groups stepped to somewhat different drummers at these affairs, but at all house parties one strong pattern held sway: young unmarried persons did most of the dancing, older married women sat and watched them dance, and married men and boys roamed about outside, conversing with other males, drinking, and occasionally gambling.

Gambling was especially important at the partly commercialized African-American house parties, which along the Brazos usually were called "Saturday night suppers." Typically, hosts let it be known to the community at large a week ahead of time that they were giving a Saturday night supper and that a certain musician would be there to play. The host family prepared roast or barbecued pork, cakes, pies, candy, home brew, and other foods for the supper, which were sold on the premises. Music and dancing were provided free by the hosts, but the food and drink cost money, though not very much; a barbecue dinner plate might sell for twenty cents in 1927 and a bottle of potent home brew for a nickel or a dime. Saturday night suppers, sometimes aptly called "protracted suppers," since they lasted all night and into the next day, had begun after emancipation. Born a slave, Harriet Smith had held such suppers during the late nineteenth century, noting that "then, sometimes, I'd have a supper at the house and cook three or four possums and sell em."[130]

Holding a supper involved a lot of hard work for the host family, especially the women. One supper host recalled that she began getting ready for a supper after coming in from the field on Friday—cleaning the house, cooking, getting together parched peanuts, candy, cakes, pies, chickens (caught off the roost), and usually a whole hog, which she sometimes barbecued but usually cooked in her big wood stove. Most suppers were given in the fall of the year, during and after cotton-picking time, because people had money then, and a host family at a successful supper might expect to make from fifty dollars on a bad night to ninety on a good one. According to one supper host, preparing the hog always took longest:

We'd have a hog and sometimes chickens. I'd run out and catch the chickens off the roost and kill em. Hogs a-weighing bout two hundred pounds over, you could get it and kill him on a Saturday morning. Had me big washpots where I could parboil him with salt and black pepper and red pepper, and season it. Then take him out and put him in a great big stove pan, and bake him and mop him—just bake him in that wood-burning stove I had.[131]

At the Saturday night suppers, food, music, and gambling attracted the most attention. People began to show up at the house in the late afternoon, ate a meal, then turned to more exciting things—dancing, drinking, and gambling. By dark: "Wouldn't hardly be nothing in the house but womens and girls and boys what danced, and all the mens'd be out around the gambling game. And the womens inside the house be just setting down looking at the girls dancing."[132]

Ed Lathan offered this unmatched description of a Washington County Saturday night supper in action, especially the men's precincts outside:

Them protracted suppers, it was several classes: some was gambling, some was bootlegging liquor, some was courting, some was dancing with the girls, and some was so drunk they couldn't dance, and some was hunting something to steal— stealing one another's liquor. They's a corn crib out there at the man's house that was having the supper, they'd be stealing his corn, or stealing his chickens. They's all type of people that visit them suppers, I'm telling you what I know. And lot of em, if I knowed a lot of bad people was coming there, I wouldn't go. They'd kill folks and shoot folks and cut folks, all that kind of stuff. That didn't happen ever time, but I pretty well picked my places to go to.

[The host] had a tub of beer iced down, and maybe a man or lady back there to tend to the beer. And maybe another man or woman, they's cutting the pork. Another lady or something, maybe she's cutting the cakes or pies. The biggest food they served in them days was pork.

In them days, man, people'd come from far and near to
a big supper, you know what I mean? Big hustlers, gamblers,
he'd come there with the intentions of winning the money.
Lots of times, they didn't have a house they'd go in. If it was
getting late in the fall and was kinda cool, the man giving the
supper would go down there in the woods hauling a big load
of wood. And they get out there by the wood pile in a great
big ring, they'd have a big piece of quilting or cotton-sack duck,
and that what they be dealing and shooting crap on. And
guys used to take these soda bottles and fill em with kerosene,
and get a rag and twist it plumb down in there and light em.
And they have a big fire made right off there, and the light of
that fire would help give light so they could see the cards
while they gamble. I'm telling you what I saw, I ain't telling
you what somebody told me.[133]

The gamblers sometimes started trouble, but they were economi-
cally important to the hosts, since they stayed around the longest and
some of them had money to spend the morning after. A supper host
explained: "I have made ten dollars out of two can of salmon to mens
they call gamblers. Where they done gambled all night long and sold
out of everything Sunday morning, then I'd make them salmon balls,
and they'd buy em, fifty cents apiece."[134] Some men had no money left
for salmon balls, however, and James Wade told a sworn-as-true story
about a gambler friend returning home after an unsuccessful all-night
gambling session to hear a mockingbird singing at first light: "Gamble!
Gamble! Gamble! Sho'nuff! Sho'nuff! Sho'nuff! He broke! He broke!
He broke!"[135]

By his own admission "the ace man in the county," Mance Lipscomb
played his guitar and sang at Saturday night suppers for over fifty years,
and Mance was in heavy demand to deliver his customary all-night per-
formance for $1.50 or $2.00, only occasionally changing from "G code to
F code to C code" to rest his fingers. Mance's ex-slave father Charlie
played the fiddle at suppers, and Mance's brothers and sisters also were
musical, as he explained. "Eleven kids in the family, and ever one of em
could play some kind of music. They played ahead of me, one was two
years older'n me, they was real good guitar players. But when I did get a
guitar, I passed them like a pay car passing a tramp. Into my fingers!"[136]

Mance's normal Saturday night began when party hosts for that night's supper came to get him around six o'clock in the evening. Mance mounted the horse provided, and he and the partygoers rode through the countryside on their way to the host's house, picking up other riders as they went along. He told:

> Man, I been in the middle of somewhere long of fifteen or twenty horses—some behind me, some in front, and some beside me. And when I got there, first thing they said, "I'll get down and hold your guitar till you get down. I don't want this guitar broke. I can dance behind your music." Them people would do all kind of dances behind my music: waltz, slow draw, two step. And then the one step, swing out, balling the jack, buzzard lope, wringing the chicken's neck. Cakewalk come in somewhere in the midst of all that, can't forget the Charleston in there. And then we had the blues, the blues was an original type of dance, see. You was out there in the woods dancing.
>
> For all the people for fifty-nine years, I was the big ace of this country. My wife'll tell you, if somebody couldn't get me, they didn't have no to-do going on, it wasn't no supper. They followed me, walking miles and miles behind me, to play for Saturday night dances. A lot of people say, "I heard you way down the road. Man, I couldn't get here fast enough!" Played all night till four o'clock in the morning, sometimes eleven o'clock on a Sunday, sitting right in one chair. When I gets to playing I go out of the bounds of reason. As long as it look like they paying attention to me, I can play all night for em. Finally, somebody had to die ever Saturday night, somebody had to get kilt. Long about twelve or one o'clock, you hear a gun somewhere—in the house or out the house—"Boom!," somebody died.[137]

Although gambling seemed much less important to the German families, their house parties otherwise rivaled African-American ones in their long hours and exuberance. Like Mance Lipscomb's family, Howard Matthies's and other German families were musically inclined. When the Matthieses held house dances one whole floor of the house would be cleared of furniture, and Howard's father and uncle Arthur Neutzler provided traditional German dance music with accordion and fiddle.[138] Older male relatives of Eddie Wegner also played the fiddle, and the Wegner's tenant, a man named Pusches, played the concertina and "was a real live wire for dances." The Wegners would have big neighborhood dances "and dance to the wee hours of the night or morning."[139] Beer, "German soda water," was much in evidence at the Wegner's parties, and before, during, and after National Prohibition one of Eddie's uncles provided powerful home brew in special three-cornered bottles. Typically, at the house parties people would drink for a while, then the older ones would begin to sing the old songs—religious songs, beer hall songs, all kinds of songs. As the night wore on, the singing grew stronger, the musicians played louder, the dancers polkaed harder, and the revelers entered a state of *Gemutlichkeit*, something basically untranslatable but explained by Eddie Wegner as "having a good old time with good old companions to a good hour of the night, with lots of beer."[140]

Saturday night dance-hall affairs were larger versions of the same thing, drawing families from miles around. In the Burton, Carmine, and Round Top area, the major halls were the Cedar Creek Schuetzen Verein ("Shooting Club") Hall of Carmine, the La Bahia Turn Verein ("Dancing Club") Hall, the Round Top Rifle Association Hall, and the Burton Hall. Early recollections of events in these vast, barnlike wooden buildings, echoing with music, song, and thundering feet, fixed themselves in people's minds for the rest of their lives. Kermit Fox recalled of the Carmine Hall, "I still remember when only kerosene lamps were bracketed from the walls and columns and crude suspended chandeliers provided a yellowish flickering glow."[141]

Special autumnal events, especially the "King's Shoot," took place at certain dance halls, as the year turned once again toward the season of cold and dark. Like Carmine's, Round Top's hall had begun as a rifle club, and in autumn the yearly Schutzen Fest took place for members only. Beginning in the morning, riflemen competed in shooting at a target, putting money into a pot with each shot, until finally one man won the competition, took the money, and became *Koenig* ("King"). Round Top riflemen shot at a bull's-eye on a rifle range, and when they hit the target a metal rooster triggered by a mechanism sprang up.[142] Miles to the south, members of the even older Schutzen Verein at little Biegel's

FIGURE 28 Beer was the social beverage of choice for many local farmers, as for these Czech-Americans at the Frank Klimek farm on Cummins Creek. (Fayetteville Area Heritage Museum, courtesy of Louis J. "Buddy" Polansky)

Settlement also held their king's shoot, firing their rifles long range at: "a four-foot wooden bird painted blue, green, and other various colors with outstretched wings pegged to the body, the head in profile, and a tail. The bird was attached to a wooden pole, which resembled a candle."[143]

At Round Top, after a big feast at noon, ladies bowled in the afternoon in a winner-take-all event similar to the men's target match, competing until one won the prize. Finally, at six in the evening, the assembled riflemen crowned the King with a wreath of cedar entwined with flowers, the band played, and club members—dressed in brown and black uniforms—staged a parade with the King and his consort leading. Then, the all-night dance began, and whenever the beer wagon from Fayetteville came into sight, the traditional cheer went up.[144]

Oblivious of the celebrations of early autumn, doomed swine wandered the fall woods, fattening on acorns, or were penned near farmhouses to gorge on newly gathered field corn. Corn and pork were the dietary mainstays of the farm families along the rivers, and—whatever its cotton season had been—no family felt prepared for the coming winter until its crib overflowed with corn and its smokehouse with pork. At Verlie Wegner's farm, wagonload after wagonload of corn came in from the field until the sixteen-by-sixteen-foot room in an old house they used for a corncrib filled to its twelve-foot ceiling, and some of that corn swiftly became transformed into hog flesh.[145] "In the old days, the old German people, they didn't think a hog was a hog until he weighed about five or six hundred pounds," Eddie Wegner told, and farm families used all of the hog but its eyes, the hard portion of its hooves, and a scrap or two more—"everything but the squeal," the familiar saying proclaimed.[146] During this autumn of 1927, as in so many autumns before, corn became hog and hog became farmer in a ritual food cycle as old as American agriculture.

German-, Czech-, African-, and Anglo-American farm families gathered their field corn and took part in neighborly rituals of hog-killing time in much the same ways. Farmers "broke" corn in intervals between cotton pickings and after cotton had reached the "scrapping" stage. Very often, harvesters used the same "four rows in one middle" method earlier used for corn tops. In the afternoon, when the ears of corn were dry and easily broken from their stalks, two people moved through the cornfield, each pulling corn on two rows at one time and throwing the ears into the middle between them. Later, someone drove a "half-bale-bed" wagon through the field between these four-on-one "heap piles," while harvesters on either side tossed the corn in from the piles.[147] In another common method, someone drove through the field knocking down one row with the wagon, while two gatherers broke and tossed corn from rows on either side, and a less-fortunate harvester, often a child, "pulled the down row" flattened by passage of the wagon.

Corn harvest was light field labor compared to cotton picking, but hog-killing was different—both a critical work event in the yearly food cycle and an enjoyable social occasion involving neighborly help; everybody looked forward to it. Normally, farmers killed one or two hogs after the first good norther of autumn, sharing much fresh meat with the neighbors who came to help kill and butcher. One woman recalled the seasonal aspect of the event: "Neighbors took turns at butchering and sharing fresh meat. Not until dependable winter weather came—

usually not before Thanksgiving and some years as late as Christmas—did butchering and curing meat for future use take place."[148]

Some farmers kept their hogs penned up all the year, some penned and fattened them only in autumn. Farmers living in the post-oak belts or along wooded bottoms often ranged their hogs out for several months of the year, allowing them to fend for themselves and wander back and forth across property lines, scavenging for food and mixing with the hog herds of neighbors, who ranged their hogs "outside" just the same. In a few remote precincts of Fayette and Washington counties, this "free range" hog raising remained legal; at other places the "near neighbors" simply allowed matters to take their natural course for mutual benefit.[149] As long as stock stayed off the highways and no one complained, county sheriff's departments rarely got involved in such matters. Most of these free-ranging "woods hogs" had ear marks to allow neighbors to tell whose hog was which, but some did not. Some woods hogs were doubly outlaws—violating both county laws and landowners' wishes—and these animals went unmarked. Eddie Wegner explained: "It used to be, in the old days when I was first around, very little of this country had what they know as stock law; everybody ran their stock—cattle, hogs, whatnot—wild. Because, in places like that old Washington river bottom down there, there were a lot of poor people, tenant farmers, they had run everything wild because they weren't given a lot of land to keep them on. If the landowner didn't furnish it, well, they just made out the best they could, because they wanted to eat a little sausage and pork, too."[150]

Legal or illegal, as autumn acorns began to fall, the lean hogs of summer prospered on the windfall mast, and at some point most owners went out with stock dogs to gather them in and pen them for further fattening on corn. A few outlaw hog rangers made do with acorn-fattened hogs, killed in the woods, and some people even preferred the taste of acorn-flavored pork. At Biegel's Settlement in earlier times, ginner Joe Tschiedel, assisted by black gin hands, had gone to the woods with hog dogs to bay and shoot his hogs and wagon them to his steam gin for steam-scalding, scraping, and butchering.[151]

Most families, like Grover Williams's, preferred to corn-fatten their hogs in pens. "The first hog killed in the fall, that was a big community affair, then. That was when the blue norther came, big blue norther. We always had two, three fattening hogs, or maybe five or six—feed them special, you know."[152] Sometimes the Williams's fattening pens were built "in tiers," with uneaten food from the hogs on top falling down into the pen of the hogs on the bottom, thence to be consumed. Top hogs or bottom hogs, all were doomed, though there might be preliminaries. As Oliver Whitener recalled, before hog killing time the condemned boars often were encouraged to "breed the sows and set the pigs" as one of their last earthly acts; "that was just part of the program."[153]

Finally, toward the end of November, farmers began to watch for signs of the first norther of the season, a cold snap foretold by the passage of wild geese in the night and signaled by blue-black clouds approaching from the north. "The geese and the clouds told Papa when to butcher hogs," one person remembered.[154] Before this time, farmers had readied knives, scalding barrels, block-and-tackles, and wooden sleds to transport hogs from pens to butchering areas. Now, as the norther swept through, they filled cast-iron washpots with water and set the firewood under them, ready for lighting early the next morning. The word went out to neighbors, "We're butchering tomorrow."[155]

At first light the neighbors appeared, and work was planned and allotted; this person to kill the hog, this person to stick him and drain his blood, these two to scald and scrape him, this man to cut him up, and so on; a lot of labor was involved and some of it had to be done fast. Women often stationed themselves inside the house, ready for their part of the hog processing.

Then, hog killing began. Only just awakened, the first hog of autumn was led out, then swiftly shot, stabbed, or bludgeoned to death. Robert Skrabanek's and Eddie Wegner's families shot their hogs, Ed Lathan's stuck theirs, Grover Williams's used an axe: Williams told, "You put a little corn out there, and while he was there getting that corn, rared back and let him have it. 'BOOM!'"[156] Then, the hog was stuck and bled. African-Americans rarely tried to catch the blood, but German and Czech families almost always did, since nothing must be wasted and they liked blood sausage. The Wegners allowed the hog blood to flow into a pan that had a large mixing spoon and a good bit

FIGURE 29   August Oltmann (left) and Gus Ahlrich (right) butcher a hog at the Fayette County settlement of Warrenton, ca. 1922. Hog butchering began with the first strong norther of early winter. (Winedale Historical Center Photo Collection, Winedale)

of salt in it. As the blood flowed, someone continually stirred it with the spoon to keep it from clotting. Then, the pan of blood went into the house and passed into the hands of the women to begin processing into blood sausage, which would be encased in the hog's large intestine.[157]

Outside, things moved quickly. Men rolled the hog on a wooden sled and dragged it with a mule to the scalding kettles, where another man had been carefully watching the water for the pattern of bubbles denoting proper scalding temperature. If the hog was large, scalding water was poured on it and it was scraped clean of hair right on the sled, first the belly, then each side in turn. Water too cold failed to loosen the hog hair, water too hot "set" the hair and made shaving necessary. A smaller hog might be briefly thrust into a tilted barrel to scald it, as Ed Lathan described: "Kill that hog and just chuck him in that barrel head down, pull him out. Say, 'Turn him, boy! Turn him, man! Let's turn him while the water's hot.' Then, stick that other end in there, and run your hand down there and test that hair. Say, 'It's coming, let's get him out of there 'fore it's set.' And drag him out there on that scaffold, then bout three men, and have the hair off that hog fore you could say 'Jack Robinson.'"[158]

Scraped clean and "white as that piece of paper," the hog was dragged on the sled to the block and tackle attached to tree limb or scaffolding, where workers thrust a singletree used as a "gambling stick" through the hog's "leaders," then hoisted him upside down ready for butchering.[159] The man assigned to butcher placed a washtub under the hog and "opened him up." Internal organs were carefully saved, especially the intestines, which were immediately taken to the women for processing.

Working fast, the women cleaned and scraped the intestines while they were still warm. Lydia Ehrigson explained: "We put them on a table and separated them. And then we'd empty all the waste out, pour water through them a few times. Wash em real clean, turn em inside out, and then scrape them like real thin paper, real clean. And then, we would wash them again. They were so nice and clean."[160] The large intestine would become the container for the blood sausage or the liver sausage, the small intestine for the regular meat sausage, which families made in large quantities. Blacks often chose to process the large intestine as "chittlings." Bubba Bowser remembered the process: "You just wash them big guts, then you just hung em up and let em dry. And, boy, after they dry good, you just reach up there and get you a long gut and just eat it. It'd be just dried up."[161]

FIGURE 30 Sausage making immediately followed hog killing. Members of the Recknagel family of Round Top prepare sausage for smoking, ca. 1897, as a family cat watches with interest. (The Institute of Texan Cultures, San Antonio, courtesy of Mr. and Mrs. E. W. Ahlrich)

Outside, men dismembered the hog, and nothing was lost or wasted. They boiled and readied the head meat for hog-head's cheese or "head souse," saved the feet for pickling, accumulated the hog fat for lard, and extracted the brains for scrambling with eggs at the noon meal. Livers, kidneys, "melts," "sweet meats," and other organs not consumed fresh went into the liver sausage. Cooked hog lungs became dog food. Greasy hog scrotums cured on barn walls to lubricate saw blades. Even the hog's bladder was saved, inflated by blowing into it with a turkey quill, and after drying became a child's kick ball or volleyball. Boys in Grover Williams's family inherited each season's hog bladders, saved them until Christmas eve, then put them to good use. Grover told: "See, Christmas time come, didn't have firecrackers like you got now. You'd put it some-where and you get up on something and you'd jump down on it. 'POW!' Down here in Flat Prairie we didn't get firecrackers, you had to make your own stuff."[162]

After the hog carcass had been cleaned out, the Wegners "split every-thing open down to the backbone," spread the carcass with a stick, and left it to cool a few hours in the north wind. "Then it was taken down and quartered, and you commenced to cutting. First, the hams were cut off, then the ribs were cut off, and then the front shoulder was cut off, and you cut off all the salvageable meat that you wanted for sausage and cut it in pieces where it would go into the grinder."[163] Grinding this much hog meat "by manpower" was a big task, but some sausage mak-ing was mechanized. Herbert Beinhorn's grandfather, "had a power grinder that was powered by jacking up a rear wheel on his Model A and running a belt from a mandrel to a pulley bolted to the car wheel. The mandrel turned the handle of the large grinder."

The swine was the quintessential Southern meat animal, but the Beinhorns and other German families outdid Anglo- and African-American Southerners at consuming the whole hog; for example, besides the usual edibles, Herbert's grandmother prepared "pot wurst," a tasty dish composed of hog blood and grits, and Herbert's grandfa-ther enjoyed hog lard on bread sprinkled with a little sugar.[164] At the end of a long day's hog processing, sausage, hams, bacon, and other meat hung curing in the Beinhorn's and Wegner's smokehouses over ritual fires of hickory or oak that would not be extinguished for days. Besides this, large amounts of fresh sausage and pork chops were cooked, then preserved under lard in big crocks.

Often, however, the first hog of autumn almost disappeared into the mouths and hands of the neighbors to assuage a pent-up pork hunger. At Grover Williams's farm on hog-killing day, ribs normally were con-sumed as the main meal for the work group. He explained:

> Pork ribs, and cornbread, and syrup, and that light, thirty-weight gravy they had on them ribs, little thickening in there, and all that liver and other scraps of meat we put on the fire and ate. Next night, you'd be sick as a dog. Now, you didn't take them all, because everybody got some of that first hog, everybody in the neighborhood was there. They had brought

their little crock, little flour sacks and things; they carried little pans. They carried that home from that first hog, so they have the first meat. But certain parts you kept, like the middling and the jowls and most of the sausage.[165]

Soon, the neighbors would stage their own first hog killings of winter and the gift meat would be reciprocated. As fall shifted into winter once again, most farm families in the old counties along the Brazos and Colorado still lived two different lives: one life of self-reliance, subsistence farming, and neighborly reciprocities, and one of cash-crop cotton agriculture that sometimes pitted neighbor against neighbor, landowner against renter, and hired hand against employer. These incongruities would persist until the older rural world itself ended. In any case, at farm after farm during this cool November of 1927, smokehouses filled with meat, corncribs with corn, and hundreds of gallon jars of preserved garden vegetables stood ringing household walls, as one more farming season passed into the time of "winter on the land."[166]

A World Ends

Spring followed winter in its annual course, and Fayette and Washington County farmers in 1928 planted fields and gardens as in all the years before. Cycles of plowing and planting and cultivating and harvesting followed seasonal rhythms for decades more, but storms of change from world economics and politics soon altered the lives of farm families far more profoundly than weed, or weevil, or the wandering hailstorms of spring.

Accustomed to occasional disasters rising from the ground or falling from the sky, farmers at first faced the great downturn in cotton prices, which began in 1929, with customary stoicism. The all-time record Southern cotton crop of 14.8 million bales brought only an average of 16 cents a pound, and the next year a slightly smaller crop brought 9 cents a pound.[1] Cotton prices had vacillated wildly in the past, but this time they plummeted to rock-bottom levels and stayed down—hovering at around 5 cents in 1931 and 1932. Average farm income from cotton and cotton seed fell from $735 in 1928–1929 to $216 in 1932–1933.[2] By 1933, area farmers accepted that the so-called Great Depression applied to them as much as to industrial workers in distant Houston and Dallas.

Small landowners of Fayette and Washington counties reacted characteristically to the fall of their traditional cash crop's value below the costs of its production—they relied upon the subsistence side of their farms for survival, recycled everything, and stubbornly continued to raise cotton. Diversified farmers already, with chickens, turkeys, milk cows, bee hives, two-acre gardens, and rows of field peas in the corn, they took advantage of cautious practices like that of Eddie Wegner's family, "Don't put all your eggs in one basket, have a little bit of everything."[3] By 1932, many families' store purchases had shrunken to "pepper and salt, flour and sugar and coffee," and in Howard Matthies's family such things often were paid for with live chickens. Olefa Matthies's mother remarked that the family would "have to live a little bit closer," meaning, among other things, that dresses now were re-dyed several times before discarding, not just once.[4]

For a time, at least on the surface of things, the depression seemed to impact very little on the small blackland and sandy-land farms of the Fayette and Washington County uplands. Gardens increased in size, chicken flocks grew, open-range turkeys became more important, people planted more land in the survival crops of corn and field peas, but families still raised cotton. "Waste not, want not" could hardly have been practiced with greater rigor, but now it was. People relied more on their neighbors for help and recreation and less on their automobiles, which now often sat on blocks in garages for lack of gas. Trying to explain that early 1930s world, Howard Matthies told: "People weren't all that excited about things that they are now. People were more concerned about the everyday life than money. As long as they had something to eat, had something to drink, and had a good bed to sleep in, and had this and that, they weren't concerned. They visited amongst the neighbors—neighbors knew neighbors and helped neighbors."[5] Many people, like Bat Dement of La Bahia Prairie near Burton, faced the great economic downturn with the farmer's characteristic battlefield humor. Dement claimed that—for him, at least—the Great Depression was nothing more than business as usual.[6]

Beneath the surface, however, lay much anxiety. Despite the new federal programs beginning in 1933 that paid farmers to take cotton lands out of production, prices rose only slightly during the middle 1930s then fell again to below ten cents a pound. Small landowners paying off debts for new farms or farmhouses, acquired during the prosperous 1920s, struggled to keep from losing them to the banks, and renters struggled merely to survive.[7] Some landowners could not save their farms, and by early in 1933 the "sheriff's sale" section of the La Grange *Journal* had expanded to half a page.

Federal intervention had begun with a shock with the "plow up" program of 1933. The Agricultural Adjustment Act (AAA) of that year, which sought to raise cotton prices by paying farmers to take land out of production, had been passed too late to stop a record crop from going in the ground, so farmers joining the program had to destroy excess cotton. A few farmers did not mind doing this, but for many others the destruction of part of a growing crop in late summer violated deeply held tenets of frugality and husbandry. Farmers loathed waste, and they gritted their teeth as they plowed under row after row of flourishing cotton plants. Echoing the statements of many others, Eddie Wegner told: "I remember we had to plow out an acre or two. I can still see that stuff. You took a plow and just jerked it out. It layed there along that furrow—the beautiful white bolls laying there—it made me sick. The thing is, we dearly needed that cotton."[8] Howard Matthies's father felt the same. The government cut-backs came at just the wrong time for Mr. Matthies, who had a house full of big sons ready to work the field and—like many other local farmers—chafed under the new regulations. On one occasion, a neighbor turned Matthies in for planting too much cotton, and he had to send his sons to the field to plow up ten rows just as the bolls were opening. Participation in federal programs became compulsory in 1934, when the Bankhead Cotton Act imposed penalties on farmers who produced cotton over their assigned quotas, and one year Mr. Matthies paid over six hundred dollars for his stubbornness.[9]

Like other critics of AAA and USDA programs, area farmers believed that government programs little profited small cotton farmers—renters and owners alike. Despite farmers' sacrifices of plow-ups and reduced acreages, cotton prices did not rise much above costs of production for many such farmers throughout the 1930s, and removing one-fourth to one-half of their scarce cotton lands from production reduced their cash incomes. Government programs favored the "big farmers," Albert Wilhelmsen of the Salem community thought, and historian Gilbert Fite noted: "It soon became evident that farmers who had larger land holdings and substantial production would be the principal beneficiaries of the New Deal agricultural legislation. Any program that tied benefits to acres of land taken out of cultivation and price supports on production would inevitably be most helpful to those who possessed property."[10] By three years into the AAA program, "it was clear that the program was run by and for landowners and better-off commercial farmers."[11] A small farmer who took 10 of his 30 cotton acres out of production in 1933 might receive less than $100 from the government, based on his previous yields per acre. Conversely, 307 large landowners contracted with the AAA in 1933 to remove 182,792 acres from production and received an average payment of $15,500.[12]

The larger one's acreage, the more "not growing cotton" became a profitable enterprise. Charles Jacoby, retired manager of a Navasota cottonseed mill, affirmed that only the big plantation farms of the Brazos valley really benefited from government programs. "The only way you could survive in raising cotton was to just have a whole lot of acres—I mean, lots of em!," Jacobs said. "And when they came along with this government program that paid you for not planting, boy, that was a good deal—if you had a lot of acres. That's the way you could really make some money, just get paid for not planting your land. That's the total answer."[13]

Owners of big farms along the Brazos used the government money to put in new irrigation systems, to modernize their operations, and—as elsewhere across the South—to replace sharecropper families with tractors. Tenants of large landowners repeatedly complained that their landlords had failed to pass along their fair shares of government payments, had demoted them from thirds-and-fourths renters to half renters (thus pocketing a larger portion of the government money), or had evicted them from their places.[14] Landlords played other economic games, as well; since payments were calibrated to average yield of the land per acre, owners often placed their best acres in the government program and let renters till their worst. If the renters soon chose to pack up and leave, so much the better. Howard Matthies recalled several farms with twenty or more tenants on the Washington County side of the Brazos where, after crop-reduction programs began, the owners "kept the good land for themselves and put the tenants on the upland where they couldn't produce any, and so they all disappeared."[15]

All across the South, cotton renters were "disappearing." Renters suffered the most during the depression 1930s, and as time went on some of them began to leave the land. Even the more prosperous cotton

renters operated closer to the economic precipice, with little subsistence-crop backup, and now some of these people got in trouble.
Plagued by unforeseen medical bills and staggered by the bad cotton
prices of 1930, Howard Davis's father went under; the elder Davis's long-
patient bankers seized his six fine cotton mules and all his equipment.[16]
Roughly one-third of all Texas rental farms changed hands every year,
and now many of these peripatetic farm families moved into town,
rather than to another place—the beginning of the vast "Southern exodus" from the land that peaked during the 1940s and 1950s.[17]

As the years passed and the depression did not end, the noose tight-
ened on small landowners and renters, no matter how frugal their
lifestyles and how stoically they endured. Having put himself through
college during the early years of the depression, farm-boy-turned-
schoolteacher Howard Matthies saw his students dwindling away, year
by year, at little Hohenwalde School near Burton, as desperate renter
families moved into town. When the trustees informed Matthies that
they had to reduce his salary from eighty-five dollars to seventy dollars
a month because of decreased tax revenues, Howard gave up teaching
and followed his students.[18] Southwest of Hohenwalde, at the Czech
community of Hostyn in Fayette County, the Czech farmers who had
erected "Our Lady Shrine" after the drought of 1925 "as an offering to
God, thanking him for past blessings and asking that such a drouth
never reoccur," now erected several additional shrines in hopes that
God (or the Virgin) would end the Great Depression. [19]

With or without divine intervention, World War II and not New
Deal programs finally cured the Great Depression. Cotton still was
worth only 9.9 cents a pound in the fall of 1939, but by 1943 textile mills
ran night and day, cotton brought over 20 cents a pound, and the government had removed all acreage allotments. Millions of farm boys and
farm girls left the countryside for military service or war-industry
employments, but farm families that retained enough labor to work
their fields made money for the first time in over a decade. Tractors
doubled in numbers during the labor-poor war years, and all farm
machinery increased greatly. Big cotton farms continued their shift
from cropper families and mules to day hands and tractors.[20]

Far away from Washington and Fayette counties, other great
changes were afoot during the war years. Encouraged by the fall-off in

American production during the 1930s and the war demands of the 1940s, Brazil, India, and certain African countries became major cotton producers. U.S. production percentage of world cotton fell from 72 percent in 1911 to 38 percent in 1943, synthetic fabrics were developed and improved, and in the United States cotton farming moved west and mechanized.[21] Dr. A. B. Conner of the Texas Agricultural Experiment Station observed: "The man in the bottoms can't compete with the western cotton farmer who can produce cotton for six cents a pound. The old system of tenancy is doomed, I believe. The best thing for the tenant is to jump in and become a machinery operator. Two years ago I was talking to Ward Templeman down at Navasota. He sold all his mules and bought tractors. He just put it up to them and told them the best tractor operators would get the jobs."[22]

Dimly aware of these great changes underway, the mule-powered farmers of the Fayette and Washington County uplands nonetheless breathed a sign of relief during the war-boom 1940s. Sons joined the service and German ceased being spoken in the rural schools—occasions for further worry—but many of the farms were saved from bank foreclosure by the return of 20-cent cotton. By 1943, John Skrabanek knew he would keep his fifty-acre blackland farm near Snook. After twenty-three years of renting, the Skrabaneks had bought a farm for $5,000 during the 1920s, when cotton brought over 25 cents a pound, then watched it fall to under 5 cents in 1932. The Czech credit union allowed John and Frances Skrabanek to get by with paying only the interest owed on their loan during the depression, and so the farm was saved, and at the end of the war all their debt had been paid.[23]

By 1950, however, John Skrabanek worked his long-sought blackland farm in a rapidly changing countryside. Snook and hundreds of other rural communities of small landowners in the counties along the rivers had closed ranks, helped each other, and endured the Great Depression with few changes, but they were drastically affected by World War II. The great world conflict and its aftermath shattered the rural world into a thousand pieces that—like Humpty-Dumpty—never quite got back together again. As rural mailman Kermit Blume drove his Lee and Washington County routes during the 1940s and 1950s, day-by-day and year-by-year he watched the countryside change. Farms fell untended or became pastureland as sons failed to return after the war; roads improved; country schools, gins, and crossroads stores declined and disappeared; "cattle and coastal" spread across lands where cotton plants had grown; and a new kind of countrymen, people with jobs in town, built new homes along the rural roads.[24]

Road improvements hastened many changes, though mud for long remained dominant over motor car. Rural mailmen began to run their routes by horse power around the turn of the century, though sometimes even they could not get through. The "Good Roads" movement flourished in county newspapers for decades before roads actually were much improved. John Banik saw his first car at Round Top in a characteristic condition—broken down and stuck in the mud. Most early car owners carried an important bit of primitive technology with them wherever they went, a shovel to dig themselves out.[25] For long, cars were fully useful only for the lucky people who lived in "gravel country," though by 1932 in Fayette County gravel from such areas was being spread on roads in muddier ones to provide the first short stretches of "all weather" road.[26]

Increasingly, during the 1940s, rural roads were graveled or paved, setting off a chain of unforeseen consequences that transformed rural life. As roads improved, people could drive farther to shop, gin, sell cotton, socialize, or attend church, and they began to do so, setting off a wave of consolidations in country stores, gins, churches, and finally schools. Remote crossroads stores had specialized in running the roads for supplies when nobody else could get through to town. As Howard Matthies recounted: "Those little rural stores, when the roads were muddy [they] used four horses. They'd drive to Brenham, get the supplies, and bring it in."[27] Now, anybody could get to Brenham, or at least to Burton or Fayetteville, and the small stores began a long decline. Peddlers had also depended on rural isolation for their customers, and now—virtually unnoticed—they began to disappear from country roads. Gradually, larger, faster-running and more-modern gins—now readily accessible by road—won out over older, more primitive gins, and larger churches triumphed over smaller ones.[28]

With the decline and consolidation of institutions, came the decline of rural communities—a wave of change that moved inward from the remote countryside toward the county-seat towns. Having the least to keep them together, after roads improved, dispersed communities such as little Biegel's Settlement in Fayette County declined first. Then came the smaller crossroads hamlets, with their characteristic infrastructures of gin, blacksmith, post office, store, and school, then the larger market towns such as Round Top, Fayetteville, Carmine, and Burton. Burton and others for a time had bustled with new economic life drawn from dead or dying hinterland communities, but soon they also began to decline. The Burton Farmer's Gin for long had triumphed over countryside competitors with its new machinery to clean cotton and process "bollie cotton," but now it also began to lose out to trucks, cotton trailers and bigger and better gins in the county seat of Brenham. By 1955, Burton residents did most of their shopping at Brenham, fourteen miles away down highway 290, and Carmine residents traded at Giddings, forgetful of their community's grand days of mercantile stores, meat market, gins, blacksmith shops, broom factory, creamery, telephone system, cotton-oil mill, automobile dealerships, bakery, bank, and newspaper. Carmine had begun with a depot on the new railroad, but by 1955 the depot had closed, and in the end even the railroad would pull up its tracks.[29]

As rural institutions consolidated inward toward the county-seat towns, so did the schools, though Carmine managed to join forces with nearby Round Top in a rear guard action against encroaching La Grange Independent School District. "When the school dies, the community dies," rural people once said, speaking the literal truth, but by 1950 and the passage of the Gilmer-Akin Act rural schools could no longer be maintained. Gilmer-Akin set new, higher standards for buildings and programs that—as lawmakers had intended—virtually put the common school districts (CSDs) out of business. Two decades of gradual consolidation of rural schools ended around 1950 in a survival-of-the-fittest battle for territory, students, and tax dollars, as county-seat independent school districts (ISDs) absorbed neighboring CSDs and larger CSDs coalesced with smaller ones in efforts to survive by attaining ISD status.[30] Thus, little Snook CSD incorporated surrounding districts (some of them non-Czech) to become Snook ISD, and Round Top and Carmine joined forces to do the same. Teacher Leola Tiedt and other rural teachers came in with their students and school buildings to form the new Carmine-Round Top ISD at Carmine. For a time, a two-room school moved in from the countryside became the lunchroom, and other former country schools were set up as classrooms in a long line, termed "school alley." Meanwhile, thirty miles away at the county seat, consolidationists, who had dreamed of a county-wide La Grange ISD, languished in disappointment.[31]

At the same time that rural communities diminished or died and economic life consolidated into the courthouse towns, cotton agriculture perfected itself—in the end leaving small room for four-mule (or one-tractor) cotton farmers on hundred-acre farms. Successful mechanical cotton pickers had been around since 1941, but by 1950 only 5 percent of cotton grown in the United States was picked by machine, and most of that in Arizona and California. To be fully efficient, cotton pickers needed to be employed on several-hundred-acre irrigated farms to gather low-growing cotton that opened its bolls all at once. USDA scientists worked to develop new strains of cotton, better fertilizers, improved pesticides, defoliants, and herbicides that worked as "chemical hoes" to suppress weeds and grasses; by 1965, a cotton industry for the industrialized "New South" had been perfected.[32] By then, pickers harvested 96 percent of U.S. cotton, and "because each two-row picker replaced approximately 80 workers, the machine displaced at least a million men and women in the harvest fields."[33]

Not much of this new mechanized cotton raising, however, looked familiar to a retired mule farmer driving past the fields on his way into town. As one 2,000-acre cotton farmer informed participants in a conference on mechanization, cotton farming had become very much like factory work. "We start with shredding our stalks and subsoiling in the fall," the farmer began, in the new language of farming. Then, in the spring they applied potash and phosphate sparingly in fields where soil tests indicated a need. "We disk once, then row out land and apply anhydrous ammonia at the same time, then we knock down the rows and plant and apply pre-emergency herbicides." After planting, "we cultivate and apply directed post-emergency herbicides approximately three times. This is followed with a layby herbicide application and insect control treatments." Tractors did the fieldwork, chemicals did the weeding, and airplanes sprayed insecticides, fertilizer, and—just before picking—defoliants over the crop.[34]

Outside the Brazos and Colorado valleys, few cotton farms were large enough to attain this evolved agribusiness level of cotton production. At Allenfarm on the Brazos, however, William Terrell, Sr., took over from his father in 1953, gradually abolished the remaining croppers and mules, drained and leveled the land, and began fully mechanized cotton farming. Where patchwork plots of twenty- and thirty-acre cropper fields had juxtaposed in a crazy-quilt pattern, broken by drainages and swampy lowlands, rows of cotton now stretched straight and level for three-and-a-half miles to the horizon.[35]

Mechanized operations such as Allenfarm required relatively few hired hands, compared to the old days, and those needed to be adept with machinery. Mule-farmer Mance Lipscomb worked at various Brazos valley farms into the early 1960s and learned to drive a tractor, but he reported that things were not the same. Lipscomb and other hands had always sung in the field, but now "you couldn't hear no songs going on in the field, cause they use machinery, and you couldn't sing much around on a tractor—it would drown out your voice, and it keep you always in motion thinking what you was doing with that motor, you see."[36] Jack Temple Kirby observed of the great change in farming experience suggested by Lipscomb:

> The passing of animal power from agriculture meant a profound change in culture. Not only were multitudes displaced from rural life by machines, but life for those remaining changed fundamentally. Timing of the cycle of farm work remained about the same. But now one labored in din and dust (not to mention debt) undreamed of before. Fuel replaced fodder. Accounting supplanted estimation. Farmers became mechanics who worked sitting down. And those who lived through the transformation never forgot the feeling of loss especially of the *company* of an animal.[37]

With mules or tractors, west of the Brazos valley during the 1950s and 1960s stubborn families continued to practice old-style row-crop agriculture, while neighbors all around them converted to cattle and Bermuda hay. Eddie Wegner bought a tractor at the end of World War II and developed a productive cotton agriculture for his small farm using no pesticides, herbicides, or commercial fertilizers, only deep plowing, manure, and alternate crops of clover.[38] Other farmers believed that tractors were not in proper economic scale with the size of their farms and continued to farm with horses and mules. Well-off Otto Fuchs, with a larger-than-average blackland farm of 242 acres, bought a manure spreader, a mechanical hay loader, an expensive disk plow, and other modern machinery, but not a tractor, since he did not feel that it made cost-benefit sense.[39] Herman Schoenemann and Ed Lathan felt the same, but Lathan had additional reasons not to go into debt to buy a tractor. Being in debt to white people was dangerous, Lathan thought.

> That man I renting from, he tried to encourage me to buy a tractor. But I wouldn't buy it because I'd of had to go in debt, and he might get up tight with me, and then I'd be beholden to work his land and take his pushing round. I'd always hire somebody with a tractor to break my land and prepare it, and I would then plant it and cultivate it with one mule. A lot of colored people round here bought tractors, used em, and now they setting in branches, chimney corners, some of em had to sell em, and they ain't no better off than me.[40]

Whether they were mule men or tractor men, at some point between 1950 and the early 1970s most of the hundred-acre upland farmers of Fayette and Washington counties finally abandoned their traditional crop of cotton and reluctantly converted their farms to cattle, hay, feed sorghum, and—increasingly, as time went on—weekend house sites for refugees from Houston.

Government programs and school consolidation drove Teddy Keiler into cattle, "coastal"—and hated Johnson grass. The small farmer was more hurt than helped by government cotton quotas, Keiler believed, while "the plantations got bigger and bigger—all them big cotton countries." Keiler's section around Oldenburg was "little cotton country" and had "almost been put out of business" by government regulations. Furthermore, after local schools consolidated and so many people moved into town, Keiler could no longer get adequate help at the crucial chopping and picking times, and on more than one occasion his cotton wasted in the field. Finally, since he no longer could get assistance to control Johnson grass, he gave up on cotton, allowed the grass to take his fields, and brought in cattle to eat it—so humiliating a defeat for this dedicated row-crop farmer that he abruptly terminated his 1974 interview after admitting this.[41]

Other farmers told similar stories. Small farmers, even if they wanted tractors, often could not afford this one "improvement," let alone spindle pickers and herbicides, and by the 1950s human choppers and pickers were hard to obtain. New minimum wage laws and child-labor laws precluded the hiring of whole families to pick and chop, as in decades past.[42] Year after year, the government lowered the Wilhelmsen family's cotton quotas, until around 1956 it got down to an allotment of only twelve acres. That was not enough, so in 1958 the family quit cotton farming, and Robert Wilhelmsen—who had wanted to stay on the farm—joined the U.S. Navy.[43] Along the Washington County side of the Brazos valley, harassment from big landowners and government men finally forced other farmers to quit and sell out. Plantation-owner Tom Moore told Bubba Bowser: "'You got to spray that cotton and then fertilize or quit planting.' That was the government, the white man's the government—said we wasn't doing nothing on this side of the river but raising boll weevils, that kept coming over in theirs." Bowser farmed into the late 1950s, but the combined pressure from big farmers, the USDA, and county tax officials finally made him quit. Participating in the compulsory cotton-allotment program, Bowser suffered harassment from the government men, once paying a USDA official "ten or fifteen dollars" to come out from Brenham only to be informed, "there's two stalks you didn't get, you got to get them two stalks." According to Bowser, another fee had to be paid for the government man's return visit to check on the demise of the two stalks. Such pressures, a lack of ready labor, the incursions of neighbors' cows into his unfenced ninety-acre field, and rapidly rising land taxes finally forced Bowser to sell out, getting only $500 an acre for this prime Brazos bottomland, a price he knew was not good. He told: "If they [the white purchasers] sell it, they'd of got $1,500 an acre for that good rich bottomland."[44] In truth, though some families persisted in the farming life, by the 1960s the real estate value (and accompanying taxes) of much of the land in Washington and Fayette counties had risen to exceed its agricultural worth, forcing many to sell out, often to real estate speculators or Houstonites in search of weekend homes.[45]

Bubba Bowser's friend Mance Lipscomb, who never owned any land, retired from rent farming during the 1950s by finally taking his long-dead father's advice, "If you can't pay a man in full, pay him in distance." Tired of the abuses of his Washington County landowner, John Sommers, and despairing of ever getting out of debt to him, Lipscomb stealthily packed wife, family, and possessions into his car and ran away to Houston—a traditional sharecropper's escape. After about a year, he returned to the Brazos bottoms but not to the farming life. Lipscomb was mowing roadside grass for the county during the 1960s when Anglo folklorists discovered his extraordinary musical talents, thus beginning Mance's final career as nationally known folk artist.

A decade of life as a famous musician failed to shake Mance Lipscomb's personal identity as sharecropper and cotton farmer, formed during a half century on the land. In his seventies, he often dreamed about farming and woke with a start: "thinking I got to go to the field. I lay there and get myself reckomasized, I say, 'Aw, the devil! I ain't got to go to the field this morning.' Boy, talk about pulling some hard days, I pulled em." But after this feeling of relief that he did not have to go to the field, came a sense of loss that he could not; he had enjoyed his old life as much as he had hated it. Lipscomb (with an ambivalence characteristic of many) told his young friend Glen Alyn:

> I like farming, cause I understood it and knowed how to farm. Every near cut in a farm, I knowed how to take that right angle on it. Man, I was at home on a farm, but I was treated so bad on it that I never could inherit nothing. Every year I'd get in debt a little deeper and deeper. They just kept me in debt so they could work me, you know. We had a lot of fun and a lot of worrynation. It's a whole lot in farming. If I was able to farm, that's the happiest life that I ever lived in my life, even if I didn't get nothing out of it, because, see, I was nated to farming. I knowed exactly what steps to make to make a farm."[46]

A few farmers around Burton felt the same way and stubbornly practiced the traditional cotton-farming craft until 1974, the last year that the Burton Farmer's Gin operated. Lawrence and Elvera Schmidt on La Bahia Prairie produced part of the seven bales ginned that year, and Gus Draeger contributed the last, hauled into Burton in his old cotton wagon.[47] After that, only a few stubborn souls separated by miles of countryside continued with row-crop agriculture in the old way—horse and mule man Herman Schoenemann at the Sand Town community, tractor farmer Henry Fuchs near Carmine, and a few more.

Fuchs still broke land for cotton in 1995, but he practiced a lonely trade. Fuchs explained: "This whole area here, large area, at La Grange, down in the river bottom, there's a lot of farming, but from La Grange this way, 24 miles, all those old farms they got Johnson grass and cattle—and weeds, a lot of weeds. The older people, they're gone; the younger people, they have jobs in the city, live in the cities. Some live on the farm and work in nearby towns. A lot of people from Houston have bought weekend places and rent their land out to local cattlemen."[48]

Thousands of families in the lands along the Brazos and Colorado told stories of the end of the farming life—and of a stubborn reluctance to leave the land. Agricultural censuses of 1954 and 1964 revealed a transforming countryside akin to many others across the cotton South—a land of declining farm numbers, increasing farm size, row-crop reductions, and decreasing subsistence crops—but in the counties along the rivers these trends moved more slowly than elsewhere. The Agricultural Census of 1964 enumerated 2,873 Fayette County farms—down from 3,271 in 1959 but still the largest number in any Texas county.[49] Another statistic showed the altered nature of these farms and the compromise most found necessary to stay on the land; over 2,600 of the farm operators reported significant nonfarm income from working part-time or full-time in town.[50] Milk cows, chickens, turkeys, potatoes, and garden vegetables also had declined from 1954 to 1964, but they still stood at the highest levels in the state. And scattered across the countryside, die-hard farmers on 899 Fayette County farms in 1964 still produced 10,900 bales of the gambler's crop of cotton.[51]

Historians of the decline and fall of the Southern farmers' world have written much about the reasons for its transformation, little about its stubborn persistence in scattered places such as Fayette and Washington counties. Persistence in the face of massive forces making for change is hard to explain—not just for historians, but for farm families themselves, still living upon the inherited land. Asked directly, Gus Draeger could not tell why he had farmed cotton so long, only that "We just toughed it out."[52] No land seemed quite as familiar as family land, tilled for generations. As Linda Roscher told of her family's farm, "You know what the land is like, you know where certain different soils are. When you've lived on a piece of land like that, you know what the land is going to do."[53] For the Roschers and other area families—Germans

FIGURE 31   Established in 1914, the Burton Farmer's Cooperative
Gin continued to gin cotton until the 1970s. It now serves as the
focal point for Burton's annual Cotton Gin Festival. (Eric Long and
Jeff Tinsley, Smithsonian Institution)

and Czechs and Anglos and blacks—family land was an extension of
the family itself, a legacy from the past and an obligation to the future.
Believing that "we are getting too greedy, we want to get too much out
of the land," Frank Janish explained: "The oldtime people say that when
I inherit a farm from my daddy, that I shall improve it, so that it is better than when I did get it, to give it to my offsprung."[54]

Terry Jordan, in his 1966 study *German Seed in Texas Soil*, sought for
evidence of German uniqueness in the old counties along the rivers, but
even as early as the mid-nineteenth century, such differences proved elu-
sive. German settlers built log houses, raised cotton and corn, and lived
much like nearby Anglo-Americans, but they also sought landownership more diligently, farmed more intensively, and stayed in place longer.
They had a "more intimate attachment to the land," Jordan concluded.[55]
Czechs also came from a land-poor peasantry in the Old World, and the

older people Robert Skrabanek grew up among "ate, drank, and slept farming" and talked about it almost to obsession. "Land was almost worshipped. Success, to the Snook Czechs, meant the ownership of a farm with the necessary buildings and equipment."[56]

But many Southerners—and not just those from Czechoslovakia and Germany—had felt like this about the farming life, though few of them were lucky enough to remain on the farm. Swept aside in the transformation of the Southern countryside were thousands of communities where, as at little Biegel's Settlement in Fayette County, "the love of the land" had fallen "like a benediction upon every heart."[57]

Notes

CHAPTER ONE

1. La Grange *Journal*, October 10, 1907.

2. Daniel, "The Transformation of the Rural South, 1930 to Present" 231. See also Kirby, "The Southern Exodus, 1910–1960," 600.

3. Foley, "The New South in the Southwest" (1990), Sharpless, "Fertile Ground, Narrow Choices" (1993), Wilkison, "The End of Independence" (1995).

4. Daniel, "The Transformation of the Rural South," 244.

5. Fite, *Cotton Fields No More*, 144. See also Fite, "The Agricultural Trap in the South," 38–50.

6. Fite, *Cotton Fields No More*, 34.

7. Daniel, *Breaking the Land*, 156.

8. Ibid., 296.

9. Ibid., 297.

10. Ibid., xv.

11. Kirby, *Rural Worlds Lost*, 116.

12. Rosengarten, *All God's Dangers*; E. Brown, *On Shares*; C. Brown, *Coming Up Down Home*; Crews, *A Childhood*; Crenshaw, *Texas Blackland Heritage*; Goode, *Passing This Way But Once*; Owens, *This Stubborn Soil*; Stimpson, *My Remembers*; Howard, *Dorothy's World*; Vaughn, *The Cotton Renter's Son*; Skrabanek, *We're Czechs*; Fox, *A Son of La Bahia Remembers*; Lipscomb and Alyn, *I Say Me For a Parable*.

13. Crews quoted in Daniel, *Breaking the Land*, 67.

14. J. M. Dement interview, September 13, 1992.

15. Kirby, *Rural Worlds Lost*, 45.

16. Fayette County had 2,873 farms in that year, down from 3,271 in 1959. Washington County had 2,077, down from 2,290. *U.S. Census of Agriculture, 1964*, 319, 379.

17. Wilkison, "The End of Independence," 52–54; *U.S. Census of Agriculture, 1924*, 73.

18. *U.S. Census of Agriculture, 1954*, 161.

19. Gus Draeger interview, May 5, 1995.

20. *Dallas Times Herald*, March 4, 1990.

21. John Henry Faulk taped interviews, University of Texas Folklore Center Archives, Center for American History, University of Texas at Austin.

22. Lipscomb-Myers Collection, Center for American History, the University of Texas at Austin.

CHAPTER TWO

1. Cune Gutierrez interview, January 1, 1994.

2. Ibid.

3. Evans, "Texas Agriculture, 1880–1930," 2.

4. Calvert and De Leon, *A History of Texas*, 225.

5. Moulton, *Cotton Production and Distribution in the Gulf Southwest*, 3.

6. Ibid., 4.

7. Foote, "Horton Foote," 18.

8. Vance, *Human Factors in Cotton Culture*, 21.

9. Henry L. Fuchs interview, October 21, 1994.

10. Howard H. Davis interview, December 8, 1994.

11. Teddy R. Keiler interview, October 3, 1974.

12. *The Paris News*, July 15, 1948.

13. Howard Matthies interview, September 9, 1994.

14. Jordan, *German Seed in Texas Soil*, 8.

15. Britton, *Bale O' Cotton*, 20.

16. Tarlton, "The History of the Cotton Industry in Texas, 1820–1923," 4.

17. Ibid., 7.

18. Britton, *Bale O' Cotton*, 20.

19. Padilla, "Texas in 1820," 61.

20. Barker, *The Life of Stephen F. Austin*, 37.

21. Jordan, *German Seed in Texas Soil*, 23.

22. Barker, "The Influence of Slavery in the Colonization of Texas," 4.

23. Doughty, *At Home in Texas*, 22.

24. Quoted in Doughty, *Wildlife and Man in Texas*, 15.

25. Barker, "The Influence of Slavery in the Colonization of Texas," 33.

26. Britton, *Bale O'Cotton*, 23.

27. Tarlton, "The History of the Cotton Industry in Texas, 1820–1923," 22.

28. Curlee, "History of a Texas Slave Plantation, 1831–1863," 87; Tarlton, "The History of the Cotton Industry in Texas, 1820–1923," 33–57.

29. Almonte, "Statistical Report On Texas," 198.

30. Jordan, *German Seed in Texas Soil*, 26–27.

31. Hogan, *The Texas Republic*, 18.

32. Jordan, *German Seed in Texas Soil*, 12.

33. Lowe and Campbell, *Planters and Plain Folk*, 89.

34. Jordan, *Trails to Texas*, 25–58; Sitton, *Backwoodsmen*, 194–232. For an excellent case study of a slave-owning backwoods stockman, who listed his occupation as "hunting and fishing" in the 1860 Census, see Otto, "Slaveholding General Farmers in a Cotton County," 167–178.

35. Curlee, "A Study of Texas Slave Plantations, 1822–1865," 246.

36. Ibid., 248.

37. Quoted in Curlee, "History of a Slave Plantation, 1831–1863," 91.

38. Edward F. Wegner interview, September 9, 1992.

39. Jordan and Kaups, *The American Backwoods Frontier*, 123; Henry L. Fuchs interview, October 21, 1994; Edward F. Wegner interview, February 12, 1992; La Grange *Journal*, November 12, 1925.

40. Sinks, *Chronicles of Fayette County*, 36; Burnam, "Reminiscences of Capt. Jesse Burnam," 12–18.

41. Smithwick, *The Evolution of a State*, 24.

42. Hinueber, "The Life of German Pioneers in Texas," 229.

43. Kleberg, "Some of My Early Experiences in Texas," 299.

44. Institute of Texan Cultures, *Czech Texans*, 15–16.

45. Ibid.

46. Jordan, *German Seed in Texas Soil*, 47.

47. Carter and Ragsdale, *Biegel Settlement*, 25.

48. Jordan, *German Seed in Texas Soil*, 69.

49. Ibid., 75.

50. Ibid., 69.

51. Jordan, *Texas: A Geography*, 92.

52. Skrabanek, *We're Czechs*, 17; Sinks quoted in Carter and Ragsdale, *Biegel Settlement*, 68; Lich, *The German Texans*, 32.

53. Jordan, *German Seed in Texas Soil*, 106.

54. Skrabanek, *We're Czechs*, 12.

55. Grider, *The Wendish Texans*, 182.

56. Carter and Ragsdale, *Biegel Settlement*, 66.

57. Weyand and Wade, *An Early History of Fayette County*, 56.

58. Carter and Ragsdale, *Biegel Settlement*, 54–72.

59. Ibid., 101.

60. Ibid., 99.

61. Ibid., 92.

62. Lotto, *Fayette County*, 67.

63. Lowe and Campbell, *Planters and Plain Folk*, 9.

64. Strong, "Cotton Production in Rural Washington County, 1820–1941," 31.

65. Winfield and Winfield, *All Our Yesterdays*, 3.

66. Curlee, "A Study of Texas Slave Plantations, 1822–1865," 232.

67. Ibid.

68. Ibid.

69. Tarlton, "The History of the Cotton Industry in Texas, 1820–1923," 67–69.

70. Moore, *Rekindled Embers*, 17.

71. Curlee, "A Study of Texas Slave Plantations, 1822–1865," 132.

72. Ibid., 68.

73. Ibid., 304.

74. Ibid., 173.

75. Wallis, *Sixty Years On the Brazos*, 23–39.

76. Winfield and Winfield, *All Our Yesterdays*, 4.

77. Strong, "Cotton Production in Rural Washington County, 1820–1941," 23–39.

78. Winfield and Winfield, *All Our Yesterdays*, 5.

79. Jordan, *German Seed in Texas Soil*, 95.

80. Ibid., 57.

81. Brenham *Banner-Press*, "Historical Edition," 1934.

82. William J. Terrell interview, May 9, 1995.

83. Kirby, *Rural Worlds Lost*, 30.

84. Ed Lathan interview, November 28, 1976.

85. Howard Matthies interview, October 13, 1994; Grover Williams interview, November 25, 1991.

86. Kirby, *Rural Worlds Lost*, 237–243.

87. Strong, "Cotton Production in Rural Washington County, 1820–1941," 5–7; Dugas, "A Social and Economic History of Texas in the Civil War and Reconstruction Periods," 649.

88. Fischer, "Florence Fischer Talks about Old Time Burton," 2.

89. *Fayette County Record*, "Progress Edition," 1938.

90. Skrabanek, *We're Czechs*, 17.

91. Gilbert Buck interview, June 28, 1993.

92. A. Banik, "Mr. Albert Banik," 9.

93. Ora Nell Wehring Moseley interview, January 22, 1992; Gilbert Buck interviews, June 28 and July 1, 1993; Robert Dement interview, June 28, 1993.

94. Edward F. Wegner interview, January 22, 1992.

95. La Grange *Journal*, September 23, 1909.

96. Dugas, "A Social and Economic History of Texas in the Civil War and Reconstruction," 674.

CHAPTER THREE

1. Howard Matthies interview, October 13, 1994. Huebner and his route

and mode of operating are real. The description of roads, communities, settlements, and countryside draws on over 75 oral history interviews, as well as other printed primary accounts.

2. Ibid.

3. Brenham *Banner-Press*, "Centennial Edition," March 2, 1936.

4. Selected interview sources on roads and mud include: James Wade interview, June, 14, 1977; Edward F. Wegner interview, February 20, 1992; Nona Mae Tatum Gilley interview, June 22, 1994; Howard Matthies interview, September 9, 1994; Kermit Blume interview, November 4, 1994; Edwin Ebner interview, November 4, 1994; and Howard H. Davis interview, October 27, 1994.

5. Lotto, *Fayette County*, 67; Lawson, "The Schiege Cigar Factory Still Standing After 110 Years," 5.

6. Edward F. Wegner interview, February 20, 1992.

7. Ayers, *The Promise of the New South*, 207. For the best discussion of the dimensions of Southern agricultural diversity before World War 2, see Kirby, *Rural Worlds Lost*, especially p. 45.

8. Domasch, "Lydia Domasch," 6.

9. Herman Schoenemann interview, October 13, 1994. For additional details on the Washington and Fayette County free range, see: Edward F. Wegner interview, February 12, 1992; Albert F. Wilhelmsen interview, May 5, 1995; Henry L. Fuchs interview, October 21, 1994; J. M. Dement interview, August 13, 1992. An announcement of an approaching Fayette County stock law election (Justice Precinct No. 4) occurred as late as November 12, 1925, in the La Grange *Journal*.

10. Grover Williams interview, May 8, 1992.

11. Ed Lathan interview, November 28, 1976.

12. Skrabanek, *We're Czechs*, 38–39. For East Texas open range practices, see: Jordan, *Trails to Texas*, 103–124; Sitton, *Backwoodsmen*, 194–232.

13. Robert Dement interview, June 28, 1993.

14. Ibid.

15. Herbert Wegner interview, June 9, 1995.

16. Daniel, *The Shadow of Slavery: Peonage in the South, 1901-1969*.

17. Herman Schoenemann interview, October 13, 1994.

18. Foley, "The New South in the Southwest," 227–267. As Jonathan M. Weiner noted, in many places across the South by 1920 large plantation farms were returning to the practice of using supervised gang laborers paid as day hands, instead of using sharecroppers. Many had tried wage gangs as the first labor adjustment after slavery, then had converted to sharecropping because of freedmen resistance. See Weiner, "Class Structure and Economic Development in the American South, 1865-1955," 970–1006.

19. William J. Terrell interview, May 9, 1995.

20. Ibid.

21. Mance Lipscomb transcripts, File 2K197, Lipscomb-Myers Collection, Center for American History, the University of Texas at Austin. See also the other taped interviews in the collection.

22. Evans, "Texas Agriculture, 1880–1930," 308–333; Wilkison, "The End of Independence," 12–54; Vance, *Human Factors in Cotton Culture*, 153–154; Fite, *Cotton Fields No More*, 7–27; and Johnson, Embree, and Alexander, *The Collapse of Cotton Tenancy*, 5–60.

23. Wilkison, "The End of Independence," 204.

24. Evans, "Texas Agriculture, 1880–1930," 310.

25. Moulton, *Cotton Production and Distribution in the Gulf Southwest*, 130–131.

26. Foley, "The New South in the Southwest," 6–9.

27. Ibid., 170–181; Evans, "Texas Agriculture, 1880–1930," 318–340.

28. Howard Matthies interview, September 9, 1994.

29. Robert H. Wilhelmsen interview, July 22, 1995.

30. Edward F. Wegner interview, February 12, 1992.

31. Ora Nell Jacobs Fuchs interview, October 24, 1994.

32. Henry L. Fuchs interview, October 21, 1994.

33. Howard H. Davis interviews, October 27 and December 8, 1994. For an excellent recent study of an Ellis County thirds-and-fourths renter who not only survived but prospered during the 1920s and 1930s, see Gruver, "Surviving the Agricultural Holocaust."

34. Skrabanek, *We're Czechs*, 17.

35. Howard H. Davis interview, October 27, 1994.

36. Johnnie Loud interview, December 2, 1994.

37. Mance Lipscomb transcripts, Lipscomb-Myers Collection, File 2K197.

38. Elnora Lipscomb transcripts, Lipscomb-Myers Collection, File 2K197.

39. Bubba Bowser interview, August 11, 1977.

40. Willie Davis interview, July 17, 1977.

41. Descriptions of life on Brazos valley plantation farms, as given in the interviews in the Lipscomb-Myers Collection (Center for American History, the University of Texas at Austin) parallel in nearly every detail John Dollard's description of landowner-tenant relationships in his classic 1937 study of the Mississippi Delta, *Caste and Class in a Southern Town* (see especially 109–125).

42. Willie Lipscomb interview, July 17, 1977.

43. Mance Lipscomb transcript, Lipscomb-Myers Collection, File 2K197.

44. Ed Lathan interview, November 28, 1976.

45. Grover Williams interview, May 8, 1992.

46. Ed Lathan interview, November 28, 1976.

47. Bubba Bowser interview, August 11, 1977. A black man named Willis Sorrells told John Henry Faulk in a 1941 interview how he was recruited in Austin to work on a Brazos valley cotton farm near Hearne, Texas, then was kept in virtual penal servitude for months. Bells signaled all daily activities on

this farm, and "If you didn't get up and eat by em, they'd whup you till you couldn't see."

48. Edward F. Wegner interview, February 20, 1993.

49. Howard Matthies interview, January 22, 1992.

50. Olefa Matthies interview, January 22, 1992.

51. Leola K. Tiedt interview, November 11, 1994; A. Matthies, "Pop," 16.

52. Fox, *A Son of La Bahia Remembers*, 13–14.

53. Dietrich, "German American Pioneers in Washington County and Their Influence," 123–125; Brenham *Morning Messenger*, May 21, 1921; *Austin American-Statesman*, May 21, 1921.

54. Reich, "Soldiers of Democracy," 13; Crenshaw, *Texas Blackland Heritage*, 85–86.

55. Neville, "Backward Glances," *The Paris News*, August 30, 1946.

56. Fite, *Cotton Fields No More*, 10.

57. Fite, "The Agricultural Trap in the South," 38–50.

58. For example, chosen from many similar editorializings, see the La Grange *Journal*, July 8, 1909; July 15, 1909; July 22, 1909; September 1, 1909; October 21, 1909; November 25, 1909; and April 23, 1931.

59. Fite, *Cotton Fields No More*, 92.

60. Peteet, *Farming Credit in Texas*, 54.

61. Fite, *Cotton Fields No More*, 94–107.

62. La Grange *Journal*, January 1 and February 5, 1925. All subsequent dates in this discussion refer to *Journal* news items from 1925.

63. Skrabanek, *We're Czechs*, 36.

64. Ibid, 155.

65. Leola K. Tiedt interviews, November 11, 1995, December 1, 1995.

66. Henry C. Jaeger interview, October 28, 1994.

67. Brenham *Banner-Press*, August 7, 1925.

68. Ibid., April 22, 1925; May 25, 1925; July 16, 1925; July 20, 1925; July 29, 1925; August 10, 1925; August 17, 1925; August 20, 1925; August 25, 1925.

69. Herbert Wegner interview, May 9, 1995.

70. National Fibers Information Center, "The History of Cotton In Texas, 5.

71. Skrabanek, *We're Czechs*, 155.

72. Fayette County *Record*, "Progress Edition," 1938.

CHAPTER FOUR

1. Skrabanek, *We're Czechs*, 18.

2. J. M. Dement interview, August 13, 1992.

3. Skrabanek, *We're Czechs*, 32.

4. Grover Williams interview, November 25, 1991.

5. Skrabanek, *We're Czechs*, 21.

6. Howard, *Dorothy's World*, 149.

7. Bubba Bowser interview, September 11, 1977.

8. William J. Terrell interview, May 9, 1995. A sharecropper house from Allenfarm remains on permanent display at the Institute of Texan Cultures, the University of Texas at San Antonio.

9. Kirby, *Rural Worlds Lost*, 175.

10. Elnora Lipscomb transcript, Lipscomb-Myers Collection, File 2K197.

11. Edward F. Wegner interview, March 25, 1992.

12. Sharpless, "Fertile Ground, Narrow Choices," 143.

13. Prudie B. Crumley interview, May 24, 1995.

14. Herman Schoenemann interview, October 13, 1994.

15. George Lester Vaughn, quoted in Ayers, *The Promise of the New South*, 201.

16. Vaughn, *The Cotton Renter's Son*, 35.

17. Skrabanek, *We're Czechs*, 17.

18. Lotto, *Fayette County*, 64.

19. Fox, *A Son of La Bahia Remembers*, 117.

20. Ibid., 119.

21. Howard Matthies interview, December 21, 1991.

22. Fox, *A Son of La Bahia Remembers*, 122.

23. Grover Williams interview, June 5, 1992.

24. Nona Mae Tatum Gilley interview, June 22, 1994; Olivia ("Chang") Ewing interview, October 10, 1976.

25. Ibid.

26. Frank Janish interview, January 9, 1975.

27. Albert F. Wilhelmsen interview, May 5, 1995.

28. Whitener, "Memoir."

29. Robert H. Wilhelmsen interview, July 22, 1995.

30. Edward F. Wegner interviews, January 22, 1992, and February 20, 1992.

31. Robert Dement interview, June 28, 1993.

32. Edward F. Wegner interview, January 22, 1992.

33. Fox, *The Otto F. Fuchs Story*, 29.

34. Howard H. Davis interview, December 8, 1994.

35. Elnora Lipscomb transcript, Lipscomb-Myers Collection, File 2K197.

36. Howard H. Davis interview, December 8, 1994.

37. Lotto, *Fayette County*, 64.

38. Arning, "Arning Tells Her Story," 182; Harriet Smith interview, 1941.

39. Skrabanek, *We're Czechs*, 156.

40. Ibid., 61.

41. Ibid., 50.

42. Henry C. Jaeger interview, November 4, 1994.

43. Edward F. Wegner interview, September 16, 1994.

44. Skrabanek, *We're Czechs*, 161.

45. Blume, "The First Hundred Years of the Blume Family of Fayette and McClennan County Texas, 1853 to Date," 9.

46. Howard Matthies interview, December 21, 1991.

47. Ibid.

48. Edward F. Wegner interview, February 20, 1992.

49. Grover Williams interview, May 22, 1992.

50. Ibid.

51. Grover Williams, May 8, 1992.

52. Howard Matthies interview, December 1, 1994.

53. Howard Matthies interview, October 13, 1994.

54. Howard H. Davis interview, December 8, 1994. For a discussion of long-range drives, see W. Windicott, "Annual Drive Had Gobblers On the Go," *Austin American-Statesman*, November 14, 1994, pp. 1, 20.

55. Ed Lathan interview, December 8, 1994.

56. Grover Williams interview, May 8, 1992.

57. Ed Lathan interview, December 8, 1994.

58. Howard Matthies interview, October 13, 1994.

59. Ed Lathan interview, December 8, 1994.

60. Annie Schmidt interview, September 19, 1974.

61. Fox, "Thoughts On Which I Wrote"; Verlie Wegner interview, September 1974.

62. Verlie Wegner interview, September 1974; Kermit Blume interview, November 4, 1994.

63. Ibid.

64. Tiedt, "My Grandmother's Garden," 39–43.

65. Skrabanek, *We're Czechs*, 148.

66. Howard, *Dorothy's World*, 107.

67. Evans, "Texas Agriculture, 1880–1930," 333.

68. Howard H. Davis interview, December 8, 1994.

69. Vance, *Human Factors in Cotton Culture*, 152.

70. Wilkison, "The End of Independence," 195.

71. Dollard, *Caste and Class in a Southern Town*, 117.

72. Lily Lipscomb Davis interview July 16, 1977; Willie Lipscomb interview, July 16, 1977.

73. Mance Lipscomb transcript, Lipscomb-Myers Collection, File 2K197.

74. Evans, "Texas Agriculture, 1880–1930," 17.

75. Frank Janish interview, January 9, 1975.

76. Herman Schoenemann interview, October 13, 1994.

77. Henry L. Fuchs interview, October 21, 1994.

78. Bubba Bowser interview, August 11, 1977.

79. Skrabanek, *We're Czechs*, 47.

80. Robert H. Wilhelmsen interview, July 22, 1996.

81. Grover Williams, personal communication, April 22, 1995.

82. Grover Williams interview, November 25, 1992.

83. Gus Keiler interview, October 3, 1974.

84. Knutzen, "Blacksmithing," 16.

85. Brenham *Daily Banner-Press*, June 2, 1925.

86. H. Matthies, "I'm Going To Do My Talking Standing Up," 37.

87. Sharpless, "Fertile Ground, Narrow Choices," 168.

88. Grider, *The Wendish Texans*, 84.

89. Sharpless, "Fertile Ground, Narrow Choices," 175.

90. Ibid.

91. Lawrence Schmidt interview, July 22, 1995.

92. Johnnie Loud interview, December 2, 1994.

93. Earnest Hancock, personal communication, October 28, 1994.

94. For example, see La Grange *Journal*, October 24, 1907.

95. Evarilla Harrell Sitton interview, July 15, 1977.

96. Quesenberry, "Witching for Water and Oil," 193–202.

97. Blasig, *The Wends of Texas*, 59.

98. Edward F. Wegner interview, March 18, 1992.

99. Fox, *A Son of La Bahia Remembers*, 87.

100. Violet Hoermann interview, October 21, 1994.

101. Edwin Ebner interview, November 4, 1994.

102. Kotter et. al., "Final Report of Cultural Resource Investigations at the Cummins Creek Coal Mine, Fayette County, Texas," 78.

103. Howard Matthies interview, January 22, 1992; Whitener, "Memoir."

104. Ed Lathan interview, November 28, 1976.

105. Ibid.

106. Carr, *The Second Oldest Profession*, 1–32.

107. Ed Lathan interview, November 28, 1976.

108. Robert H. Wilhelmsen interview, July 22, 1995.

109. Howard Matthies interview, September 9, 1994.

110. Ibid.

111. Ibid.

112. Edward F. Wegner interview, September 9, 1994.

113. Mance Lipscomb transcripts, Lipscomb-Myers Collection, File 2K197.

114. Skrabanek, *We're Czechs*, 28.

115. Albert F. Wilhelmsen interview, May 5, 1995.

116. Edward F. Wegner interview, September 9, 1994; Grover Williams interview, May 22, 1992; Howard, *Dorothy's World*, 16.

117. Ferris, *You Live and Learn and Then You Die and Forget It All*, 5.

118. Henry C. Jaeger interview, October 28, 1994.

119. Harriet Smith interview, 1941; Edna Ebner interview, November 4, 1994; Johnnie Loud interview, December 2, 1994; Earnest Hancock interview, October 28, 1994.

120. Johnnie Loud interview, December 2, 1994.

121. Henry L. Fuchs interview, October 21, 1994.

122. Earnest Hancock interview, October 28, 1994.

123. Howard Matthies interview, September 9, 1994.

124. Ibid.

125. Johnnie Loud interview, December 2, 1994.

126. Howard H. Davis interview, November 27, 1994.

127. Massey, *Bittersweet Country*, 77.

128. Robert H. Wilhelmsen interview, May 5, 1995.

129. Skrabanek, *We're Czechs*, 30.

130. Ibid., 24.

131. Robert H. Wilhelmsen interview, May 5, 1995; Howard H. Davis interview, November 27, 1994.

132. Edward F. Wegner interview, September 9, 1994.

133. Howard H. Davis interview, November 27, 1994.

134. Skrabanek, *We're Czechs*, 24.

135. *U.S. Agricultural Census of 1935*, 741.

136. Johnnie Loud interview, December 2, 1994.

137. Albert F. Wilhelmsen interview, July 17, 1995.

138. Evans, "Texas Agriculture, 1880–1930," 19.

139. Robert H. Wilhelmsen interview, May 5, 1995; Skeeter Stolz interview, May 30, 1980.

140. Robert H. Wilhelmsen interview, May 5, 1995; Henry C. Jaeger interview, October 28, 1994; Fox, *The Otto F. Fuchs Story*, 26.

141. Brooks, *Cotton*, 129.

142. Grover Williams interview, November 25, 1991. Oral history accounts describing use of the lister buster and turning plow for bedding up are: Kermit Blume interview, November 4, 1994; Harold H. Davis interview, October 27, 1994; Gus Draeger interview, May 5, 1995; Kermit W. Fox interview, December 1, 1994; Henry L. Fuchs interview, October 21, 1994; Henry C. Jaeger interview, October 28, 1994; Johnnie Loud interview, December 2, 1994; Elenora Manske interview, October 3, 1974; Howard Matthies interview, September 9, 1994; Fritz Meinen interview, October 2, 1974; Lawrence Schmidt interview, July 22, 1995; Herman Schoenemann interview, October 13, 1994; Edward F. Wegner interview, September 9, 1994; Albert F. Wilhelmsen interview, May 5, 1995; Robert H. Wilhelmsen interview, May 5, 1995; Grover Williams interview, May 22, 1992.

143. Henry L. Fuchs interview, October 21, 1994.

144. Howard Matthies interview, September 9, 1994.

145. Albert F. Wilhelmsen interview, May 5, 1995.

146. Ibid.

147. Evarilla Harrell Sitton interview, July 15, 1977; Susie Davidson Gipson interview, October 31, 1981.

148. Domasch, "Lydia Domasch," 5.

149. Georgie Lee Wade interview, June 14, 1977.

150. Ed Lathan interview, November 28, 1976.

151. Herbert Wegner interview, May 9, 1995.

152. Mance Lipscomb transcripts, Lipscomb-Myers Collection, File 2K197.

153. James Wade interview, June 14, 1977.

154. Fox, *A Son of La Bahia Remembers*, 24.

155. Grover Williams interview, November 25, 1991.

156. Roy Schmidt interview, July 22, 1995.

157. Lawrence Schmidt interview, July 22, 1995.

158. Brenham *Daily Banner-Press*, September 10, 1925; Texas State Board of Education, *A Report On the Adequacy of Texas Schools*, 591.

159. Sitton and Rowold, *Ringing the Children In*, 38–47.

160. Leola K. Tiedt interview, November 11, 1994.

161. Fox, *A Son of La Bahia Remembers*, 24.

162. Ibid.

163. H. C. Henninger interview, n.d.

164. Sitton and Rowold, *Ringing the Children In*, 203–212.

165. Fox, *A Son of La Bahia Remembers*, 26.

166. Leola K. Tiedt interview, November 11, 1994.

167. Grover Williams interview, November 25, 1991.

168. Howard Matthies interview, October 13, 1994.

169. Howard H. Davis interview, December 8, 1994.

170. Domasch, "Lydia Domasch," 6.

171. Ed Lathan interview, December 8, 1994.

172. Mance Lipscomb transcripts, Lipscomb-Myers Collection, File 2K197.

173. Grover Williams interview, May 9, 1992.

174. La Grange *Journal*, February 19, 1925.

175. Mance Lipscomb transcripts, Lipscomb-Myers Collection, File 2K198.

176. James Wade interview, June 14, 1977.

177. H. Matthies, "I'm Going To Do My Talking Standing Up," 32.

178. Howard Matthies interview, December 21, 1991.

179. Ibid.

180. Fox, "Thoughts On Which I Wrote."

181. Grider, *The Wendish Texans*, 59.

182. Ed Lathan interview, November 28, 1976.

183. Edna Ebner interview, November 4, 1994.

184. A. Matthies, "Pop," 16.

185. Ibid.

186. Ibid., 18.

187. Joswiak, quoted in Wassermann, *The Common School Districts of Washington County, Texas, 1909–1967*, 175.

188. McCauley, quoted in Wassermann, *The Common School Districts of Washington County, Texas, 1909–1967*, 101.

189. Howard Matthies interview, September 9, 1994.

190. Fox, *A Son of La Bahia Remembers*, 13.

191. Oliver Whitener interview, March 25, 1992.

192. Howard Matthies interview, January 22, 1992.

193. Edwin Ebner interview, November 4, 1994.

194. Nona Mae Tatum Gilley interview, June 22, 1994.

195. Mance Lipscomb transcripts, Lipscomb-Myers Collection, File 2K198.

196. Howard Matthies interview, January 22, 1992.

197. Fox, *A Son of La Bahia Remembers*, 111.

198. Mance Lipscomb transcripts, Lipscomb-Myers Collection, File 2K197.

199. La Grange *Journal*, January 24, 1907.

200. Ibid, February 18, 1909.

201. Ibid., January 24, 1907.

202. Ibid., August 19, 1909.

203. Ibid., September 16, 1909.

204. Grider, *The Wendish Texans*, 73.

205. Bayer, "Not Too Bad, Not Too Good," 4; Guelker, "Born Not for Ourselves, But for the Whole World," 21.

206. Grider, *The Wendish Texans*, 77.

207. Bubba Bowser interview, August 11, 1977.

208. Fox, *A Son of La Bahia Remembers*, 111.

209. Ibid., 114.

210. Olefa Matthies interview, January 22, 1992.

211. "A Brief History of Concordia Gesang-Verein During the First 125 Years of Its Existence," 168.

212. Howard Matthies interview, September 9, 1994; Henry L. Fuchs interview, October 21, 1994.

213. Jonnie Bauer interview, October 17, 1974.

214. Fayette County *Record*, "Progress Edition," 1938.

215. Ibid.

216. Kermit Blume interview, November 4, 1994.

217. Grover Williams interview, May 22, 1992.

218. Howard Matthies interview, January 22, 1992.

219. Edward F. Wegner interview, March 25, 1992.

220. Fox, *A Son of La Bahia Remembers*, 15.

221. Ora Nell Jacobs Fuchs interview, October 21, 1994; Mrs. Herman Schoenemann, personal communication to Thad Sitton, October 14, 1994.

222. Goode, *Passing This Way But Once*, 84.

223. Skrabanek, *We're Czechs*, 81.

CHAPTER FIVE

1. Skrabanek, *We're Czechs*, 49.

2. Bubba Bowser interview, August 11, 1977.

3. Ibid.

4. Frank Janish interview, January 9, 1975.

5. Howard Matthies interview, October 13, 1994.

6. Ibid.

7. Mrs. Otis Dean interview, November 21, 1994.

8. Howard Matthies interview, October 13, 1994; Mance Lipscomb transcripts, Lipscomb-Myers Collection, file 2K197.

9. La Grange *Journal*, February 8, 1933.

10. Gus Keiler interview, October 3, 1974.

11. Dietrich, *The Blazing Story of Washington County*, 41.

12. Edward F. Wegner interview, March 18, 1992; Henry C. Jaeger interview, October 28, 1994.

13. Black, quoted in Sitton and King, *The Loblolly Book*, 183.

14. Howard Matthies interview, October 13, 1994.

15. Henry C. Jaeger interview, October 28, 1994.

16. Frank Janish interview, January 9, 1975.

17. Edward F. Wegner interview, March 18, 1992.

18. Skrabanek, *We're Czechs*, 55.

19. Ibid., 57.

20. Evans, "Texas Agriculture, 1880–1930," 14.

21. Verlie Wegner interview, September 1974.

22. Evans, "Texas Agriculture, 1880–1930," 14–17.

23. Brooks, *Cotton*, 144.

24. Herman Schoenemann interview, October 13, 1994.

25. Edwin Ebner interview, November 4, 1994.

26. Teddy R. Keiler interview, October 3, 1974; Howard H. Davis interview, October 27, 1994; Otto Treybig interview, October 17, 1974.

27. Verlie Wegner interview, September 1974.

28. Skrabanek, *We're Czechs*, 63.

29. Edward F. Wegner interview, March 18, 1992.

30. Robert Dement interview, June 28, 1993.

31. Grover Williams interview, May 22, 1992.

32. Mance Lipscomb transcripts, Lipscomb-Myers Collection, file 2K197.

33. Curtis Tunnell interview, January 27, 1995.

34. Herman Schoenemann interview, October 13, 1994.

35. Mance Lipscomb transcripts, Lipscomb-Myers Collection, file 2K197.

36. Wallie Schmidt interview, September 19, 1974.

37. Robert H. Wilhelmsen interview, May 5, 1995.

38. Skrabanek, *We're Czechs*, 59.

39. Fox, *A Son of La Bahia Remembers*, 66.

40. Henry L. Fuchs interview, October 21, 1994.

41. Evans, "Texas Agriculture, 1880–1930," 38.

42. Elvera Schmidt interview, July 22, 1995.

43. Edward F. Wegner interview, March 18, 1992.

44. Mance Lipscomb transcripts, Lipscomb-Myers Collection file 2K198.

45. Herman Schoenemann interview, October 13, 1994.

46. Edward F. Wegner interview, January 22, 1992.

47. Howard Matthies interview, September 9, 1994.

48. Ora Nell Jacobs Fuchs interview, October 21, 1994.

49. Vaughn, *The Cotton Renter's Son*, 48.

50. Susie Davidson Gipson interview, October 31, 1981.

51. Sharpless, "Fertile Ground, Narrow Choices," 289.

52. Whitener, "Memoir."

53. Albers, "Emil Albers," 3.

54. Willie Lipscomb interview, July 16, 1977; Lily Lipscomb Davis interview, July 16, 1977.

55. Skrabanek, *We're Czechs*, 65.

56. Willis Sorrells interview, 1941.

57. Mance Lipscomb transcripts, Lipscomb-Myers Collection, file 2K197.

58. Ibid.

59. Willis Sorrells interview, 1941.

60. Laura Smalley interview, September 27, 1941.

61. Howard Matthies interview, September 9, 1994.

62. Ora Nell Jacobs Fuchs interview, October 21, 1994.

63. Domasch, "Lydia Domasch," 5.

64. Susie Davidson Gipson interview, October 31, 1981.

65. Evarilla Harrell Sitton interview, July 16, 1977.

66. Chism, "Fannie Chism," 101.

67. Howard H. Davis interview, October 27, 1994.

68. Leola K. Tiedt interview, December 1, 1994.

69. Howard Matthies interview, December 1, 1994.

70. Fox, *The Otto F. Fuchs Story*, 24.

71. A. Banik, "Mr. Albert Banik," 10.

72. Skrabanek, *We're Czechs*, 92.

73. Edwards, "Grandmother's Apron," 237.

74. Edward F. Wegner interview, March 18, 1992.

75. Mrs. Otis Dean interview, November 21, 1994.

76. Teddy R. Keiler interview, October 3, 1974.

77. Henry C. Jaeger interview, October 28, 1994.

78. La Grange *Journal*, September 1, 1909.

79. Robert H. Wilhelmsen interview, May 5, 1995.

80. Edward F. Wegner interview, March 18, 1992.

81. Johnnie Loud interview, December 2, 1994.

82. Evans, "Texas Agriculture, 1880–1930," 53.

83. Robert Dement interview, June 28, 1993.

84. Herman Schoenemann interview, October 13, 1994.

85. Howard Matthies interview, September 9, 1994.

86. Edward F. Wegner interview, March 18, 1992.

87. Ibid.

88. Evans, "Texas Agriculture, 1880–1930," 53–54.

89. Laura Smalley interview, September 27, 1941; Gladys J. Krause interview, December 2, 1994.

90. Evans, "Texas Agriculture, 1880–1930," 55.

91. Ibid., 58.

92. Fritz Meinen interview, October 2, 1974.

93. Albert F. Wilhelmsen interview, July 22, 1995.

94. Gus Draeger interview, May 5, 1995.

95. Evans, "Texas Agriculture, 1880–1930," 63.

96. Gus Draeger interview, May 5, 1995.

97. Harold H. Davis interview, October 27, 1994.

98. Fox, A Son of La Bahia Remembers, 55.

99. Grover Williams interview, November 25, 1991.

100. La Grange Journal, June 24, 1909.

101. Herman Schoenemann interview, October 13, 1994.

102. Teddy R. Keiler interview, October 3, 1974.

103. Howard H. Davis interview, October 27, 1994.

104. Gus Draeger interview, May 5, 1995.

105. Britton, Bale O'Cotton, 79.

106. Evans, "Texas Agriculture, 1880–1930," 75.

107. Robert H. Wilhelmsen interview, May 5, 1995.

108. Skeeter Stoltz interview, May 30, 1980.

109. Nona Mae Tatum Gilley interview, June 22, 1994.

110. Grover Williams interview, November 25, 1991.

111. Wilkison, "The End of Independence," 162.

112. Nona Mae Tatum Gilley interview, June 22, 1994.

113. Bubba Bowser interview, August 11, 1977.

114. Ibid.

115. Ed Lathan interview, December 8, 1994.

116. Goode, Passing This Way But Once, 97.

117. Hahn, "Hunting, Fishing, and Foraging," 42.

118. Williams, "Backward Glances," Wolfe City Sun, November 21, 1947.

119. Wanda Gipson DuBose interview, July 30, 1994.

120. Skrabanek, We're Czechs, 86.

121. Fox, A Son of La Bahia Remembers, 108.

122. Lawrence Schmidt interview, July 22, 1995.

123. J. M. Dement interview, August 13, 1992.

124. Howard Matthies interview, December 21, 1991.

125. Edward F. Wegner interview, February 20, 1992.

126. Fox, A Son of La Bahia Remembers, 76.

127. Skrabanek, We're Czechs, 45.

128. Edward F. Wegner interview, September 16, 1991.

129. Howard Matthies interview, October 13, 1994.

130. Skrabanek, *We're Czechs*, 8.

131. Wallie Schmidt interview, September 19, 1974.

132. Ed Lathan interview, December 8, 1994.

133. Robert H. Wilhelmsen, personal communication to Thad Sitton, July 26, 1995.

134. Howard Matthies interview, October 13, 1994.

135. Frank Janish interview, January 9, 1975.

136. Wallie Schmidt interview, September 19, 1974.

137. Fox, *A Son of La Bahia Remembers*, 68.

138. Wallie Schmidt interview, September 19, 1974.

139. Fox, *A Son of La Bahia Remembers*, 68.

140. Elvera Schmidt interview, July 22, 1995.

141. Johnnie Loud interview, December 2, 1994.

142. Skrabanek, *We're Czechs*, 60.

143. Otto Treybig interview, October 17, 1974.

144. Frank Janish interview, January 9, 1975.

145. Ibid.

146. Fox, "Thoughts on Which I Wrote."

147. Skrabanek, *We're Czechs*, 33.

148. Grover Williams interview, June 5, 1992.

149. Ibid.

150. Jordan, *German Seed in Texas Soil*, 70–73. German settlers immediately adopted the unfamiliar sweet potato after arrival, only later switching back to the familiar white potato after learning how to grow it in the hot Texas climate.

151. Mrs. Gus Keiler interview, October 3, 1974.

152. Ed Lathan interview, December 8, 1994.

153. Skrabanek, *We're Czechs*, 83; Edward F. Wegner interview, March 18, 1992.

154. Sharpless, "Fertile Ground, Narrow Choices," 206–214.

155. Wilkison, "The End of Independence," 116.

156. William J. Terrell interview, May 9, 1995.

157. Willie Lipscomb interview, July 16, 1977.

158. Bubba Bowser interview, September 11, 1977.

159. Howard H. Davis interview, December 8, 1994.

160. Herbert Wegner interview, May 9, 1995; Gertrude Wegner Krinke interview, May 9, 1995.

161. Skrabanek, *We're Czechs*, 41.

162. Herbert Wegner interview, May 9, 1995; Gertrude Wegner Krinke interview, May 9, 1995.

163. La Grange *Journal*, September 16, 1909.

164. Lich, *The German Texans*, 171.

165. Fox, "Thoughts on Which I Wrote."

166. Krause, "Round Top Rifle Association Hall," 381.
167. Ibid., 383.
168. Fox, "Thoughts on Which I Wrote."
169. Leola K. Tiedt interview, December 1, 1994.
170. Edward F. Wegner interview, February 12, 1992.
171. Kermit W. Fox interview, March 8, 1995.
172. Grover Williams interview, May 22, 1992.
173. Taplin, "Picking and Pulling," 28.
174. Olivia ("Chang") Ewing interview, October 8, 1976.
175. Fox, "Thoughts on Which I Wrote."
176. Ibid.
177. Ibid.; Grover Williams interview, June 12, 1992.
178. Ed Lathan interview, November 28, 1976.
179. Grover Williams interview, June 12, 1992.
180. La Grange *Journal*, August 19, 1909.
181. Howard Matthies interview, February 2, 1992.
182. Ibid.

CHAPTER SIX

1. Robert Dement interview, June 28, 1992.
2. Fox, *A Son of La Bahia Remembers*, 62.
3. Edward F. Wegner interview, March 18, 1992.
4. Herman Schoenemann interview, October 13, 1994.
5. Edwin Ebner interview, November 4, 1994.
6. Howard Matthies interview, September 9, 1994.
7. Teddy R. Keiler interview, October 3, 1974.
8. Curtis Tunnell interview, January 27, 1995.
9. Edward F. Wegner interview, September 16, 1994.
10. Robert Dement interview, June 28, 1992.
11. J. M. Dement interview, August 13, 1992.
12. Howard H. Davis interview, December 8, 1994.
13. Robert Dement interview, June 28, 1992; Skrabanek, *We're Czechs*, 73.
14. Teddy R. Keiler interview, October 3, 1974.
15. Bea Ruth Tatum Collier interview, June 6, 1995; Edna Ruth Gilley Reed interview, May 30, 1995.
16. General references to the cotton season of 1927 derive from news items in the La Grange *Journal* and Brenham *Daily Banner-Press* of that year.
17. Johnnie Loud interview, December 2, 1994.
18. Grover Williams interview, November 25, 1991.
19. Lydia Ehrigson interview, February 9, 1995.
20. Johnnie Loud interview, December 2, 1994.
21. Elvera Schmidt interview, July 22, 1995.
22. Howard H. Davis interview, December 8, 1994.

23. Mance Lipscomb transcripts, Lipscomb-Myers Collection, file 2K197.

24. Ibid.

25. Henry C. Jaeger interview, October 28, 1994.

26. J. M. Dement interview, August 13, 1992.

27. Bubba Bowser interview, August 11, 1977.

28. Edward F. Wegner interview, September 16, 1994.

29. J. M. Dement interview, August 13, 1992; Charlie Lincecum interview, August 28, 1992.

30. Skrabanek, *We're Czechs*, 71.

31. Bubba Bowser interview, August 11, 1977.

32. Commerce *Journal*, September 28, 1955.

33. Albert F. Wilhelmsen interview, May 5, 1995.

34. Edward F. Wegner interview, March 18, 1992.

35. Ibid.

36. Edward F. Wegner interview, December 2, 1995.

37. Edward F. Wegner interview, March 18, 1992.

38. Leola K. Tiedt interview, December 1, 1994.

39. Ibid.

40. Ibid.

41. Fox, "Thoughts On Which I Wrote."

42. Coltharp, "Reminiscences of Cotton Picking Days," 541.

43. Grover Williams interview, November 25, 1991.

44. Grover Williams interview, June 5, 1992.

45. Jeffries, quoted in Evans, "Texas Agriculture, 1880–1930," 42.

46. Teddy R. Keiler interview, October 3, 1974.

47. Foley, "The New South in the Southwest," 84.

48. Teddy R. Keiler interview, October 3, 1974.

49. Gus Keiler interview, October 3, 1974; Mrs. Gus Keiler interview, October 3, 1974.

50. Mrs. Cass Nation, letter to James H. Conrad, September 13, 1991.

51. La Grange *Journal*, October 4, 1927.

52. Fox, *A Son of La Bahia Remembers*, 52.

53. Skrabanek, *We're Czechs*, 73.

54. Grover Williams interview, June 5, 1992.

55. Ibid.

56. Edward F. Wegner interview, March 18, 1992.

57. Edward F. Wegner interview, September 16, 1994.

58. Mrs. Otis Dean interview, November 21, 1994.

59. Mance Lipscomb transcripts, Lipscomb-Myers Collection, file 2K197.

60. Ilo Ullrich interview, November 4, 1994.

61. Moulton, *Cotton Production and Distribution in the Gulf Southwest*, 78–79.

62. Coltharp, "Reminiscences of Cotton Pickin' Days," 542.

63. Robert H. Wilhelmsen interview, May 5, 1995.

64. Carey in Britton, *Bale O'Cotton*, 87.

65. Gilbert Buck interview, June 28, 1993.

66. Grover Williams interview, November 11, 1991.

67. Ed Lathan interview, November 28, 1976.

68. Cox, *Bale O' Cotton*, 22.

69. Howard Matthies interview, December 2, 1994.

70. James Burton interview, June 22, 1994.

71. Quoted in Britton, *Bale O' Cotton*, 64.

72. Curtis Tunnell interview, January 27, 1995.

73. Joe Fred Cox interview, March 7, 1995.

74. J. D. Bowman interview, May 4, 1994.

75. Wills, "Geoffrey Wills," 37.

76. La Grange *Journal,* August 18, 1927; August 25, 1927.

77. Lydia Ehrigson interview, February 9, 1995.

78. Joe Fred Cox interview, March 7, 1995.

79. Wills, "Geoffrey Wills," 37.

80. Curtis Tunnell interview, January 27, 1995.

81. Brenham *Daily Banner-Press,* October 1, 1925.

82. La Grange *Journal,* August 29, 1912.

83. Leola K. Tiedt interview, December 1, 1994.

84. Ibid.

85. Fox, *A Son of La Bahia Remembers,* 60.

86. Ibid., 61.

87. Edward F. Wegner interview, March 18, 1992.

88. Henry L. Fuchs interview, November 21, 1994.

89. Britton, *Bale O'Cotton,* 60.

90. Fox, "Thoughts On Which I Wrote."

91. Edward F. Wegner interview, March 18, 1992.

92. Fox, "Thoughts On Which I Wrote."

93. Edward F. Wegner interview, March 18, 1992.

94. Ibid.

95. Moulton, *Cotton Production and Distribution in the Gulf Southwest,* 181.

96. Grover Williams interview, June 6, 1992.

97. Edward F. Wegner interview, September 16, 1994.

98. Peteet, *Farming Credit in Texas,* 3.

99. Henry L. Fuchs interview, October 21, 1994.

100. Peteet, *Farming Credit in Texas,* 27.

101. Moulton, *Cotton Production and Distribution in the Gulf Southwest,* 190–195.

102. Howard Matthies interview, December 2, 1994.

103. Henry C. Jaeger interview, October 29, 1994.

104. Booth Tatum interview, June 22, 1994.

105. Britton, *Bale O'Cotton,* 91; Vance, *Human Factors in Cotton Culture,* 170.

106. Teddy R. Keiler interview, October 3, 1974.

107. Howard Matthies interview, December 2, 1994.

108. Elenora Manske interview, October 3, 1974.

109. Fox, *A Son of La Bahia Remembers*, 58.

110. Edward F. Wegner interview, September 16, 1994.

111. Peteet, *Farming Credit in Texas*, 3.

112. Ibid., 13.

113. Ibid., 18.

114. Ibid., 29.

115. Quoted in Wilkison, "The End of Independence," 132.

116. Foley, "The New South in the Southwest," 175.

117. Grover Williams interview, June 5, 1992.

118. Kirby, *Rural Worlds Lost*, 149.

119. Grover Williams interview, May 11, 1992.

120. Whitener, "Memoir."

121. Gilbert Buck interview, June 28, 1993.

122. Elnora Lipscomb transcripts, Lipscomb-Myers Collection, file 2K197.

123. Willie Lipscomb interview, July 16, 1977.

124. Davis Washington interview, June 24, 1977.

125. Moulton, *Cotton Production and Distribution in the Gulf Southwest*, 78–79.

126. Teddy R. Keiler interview, October 3, 1974.

127. Brenham *Daily Banner-Press*, October 12, 1915.

128. Giddings *Times and News*, "Centennial Edition," June 24, 1971.

129. Howard Matthies interview, January 22, 1992.

130. Harriet Smith interview, 1941.

131. Elnora Lipscomb transcripts, Lipscomb-Myers Collection, file 2K197.

132. Ibid.

133. Ed Lathan interview, November 28, 1976.

134. Elnora Lipscomb transcripts, Lipscomb-Myers Collection, file 2K197.

135. James Wade interview, June 14, 1977.

136. Mance Lipscomb transcripts, Lipscomb-Myers Collection, file 2K197.

137. Ibid.

138. Howard Matthies interview, January 22, 1992.

139. Edward F. Wegner interview, February 20, 1992.

140. Ibid.

141. Fox, "Thoughts On Which I Wrote."

142. Krause, "Round Top Rifle Association Hall," 381–382.

143. Carter and Ragsdale, *Biegel Settlement*, 193.

144. Krause, "Round Top Rifle Association Hall," 383.

145. Verlie Wegner interview, September 74.

146. Edward F. Wegner interview, January 22, 1992.

147. Ed Lathan interview, December 8, 1994.

148. Howard, *Dorothy's World*, 119.

149. Grover Williams interview, May 8, 1992.

150. Edward F. Wegner interview, February 12, 1992.

151. Carter and Ragsdale, *Biegel Settlement*, 92.

152. Grover Williams interview, May 8, 1992.

153. Oliver Whitener interview, March 25, 1992.

154. Howard, *Dorothy's World*, 119.

155. Skrabanek, *We're Czechs*, 87.

156. Grover Williams interview, May 8, 1992.

157. Edward F. Wegner interview, January 22, 1992.

158. Ed Lathan interview, December 8, 1994.

159. Grover Williams interview, May 8, 1992.

160. Lydia Ehrigson interview, February 9, 1995.

161. Bubba Bowser interview, September 11, 1977.

162. Grover Williams interview, May 8, 1992.

163. Edward F. Wegner interview, January 22, 1992.

164. Beinhorn, "Beinhorn Family Reminiscences," 180.

165. Grover Williams interview, May 8, 1992.

166. Johnnie Loud interview, December 2, 1994.

EPILOGUE

1. Fite, *Cotton Fields No More*, 124.

2. Johnson, *The Collapse of Cotton Tenancy*, 47.

3. Edward F. Wegner interview, March 18, 1992.

4. Howard Matthies interview, February 12, 1992.

5. Ibid.

6. J. M. Dement interview, August 13, 1992.

7. Kermit Blume interview, November 4, 1994; Skrabanek, *We're Czechs*, 27.

8. Edward F. Wegner interview, September 16, 1994.

9. Howard Matthies interview, February 12, 1992.

10. Albert F. Wilhelmsen interview, July 17, 1995; Fite, *Cotton Fields No More*, 139.

11. Ibid., 142.

12. Ibid., 139.

13. Charles Jacoby interview, July 13, 1977.

14. Daniel, *Breaking the Land*, 101.

15. Howard Matthies, interview, December 2, 1994.

16. Howard Davis interview, December 8, 1994.

17. Vance, *Human Factors in Cotton Culture*, 153; Kirby, "The Southern Exodus," 588–600.

18. Howard Matthies interview, October 29, 1992.

19. Fayette County *Record*, "Progress Edition," 1938.

20. Fite, *Cotton Fields No More*, 169.

21. Ibid., 174–175.

22. Johnson, *The Collapse of Cotton Tenancy*, 43.
23. Skrabanek, *We're Czechs*, 27.
24. Kermit Blume interview, November 4, 1994.
25. Banik, "Mr. John Banik," 13.
26. Eichler, "Reflections," 14; Kermit Blume interview, November 4, 1994.
27. Howard Matthies interview, October 13, 1994.
28. Lydia Ehrigson interview, February 9, 1995; Kirby, *Rural Worlds Lost*, 181.
29. Fayette County *Record*, "Sesquicentennial Edition," March 4, 1986.
30. Sitton and Rowold, *Ringing the Children In*, 188–202.
31. Leola K. Tiedt interview, November 11, 1994.
32. Fite, *Cotton Fields No More*, 180.
33. Ferris and Wilson, *Encyclopedia of Southern Culture*, 26.
34. Daniel, *Breaking the Land*, 252.
35. William J. Terrell interview, May 9, 1995.
36. Mance Lipscomb transcripts, Lipscomb-Myers Collection, File 2K198.
37. Kirby, *Rural Worlds Lost*, 195.
38. Edward F. Wegner interview, March 18, 1992.
39. Kermit W. Fox interview, December 1, 1994.
40. Ed Lathan interview, November 28, 1976.
41. Teddy R. Keiler interview, October 3, 1974.
42. Howard Matthies interview, October 29, 1992.
43. Robert H. Wilhelmsen interview, May 5, 1995.
44. Bubba Bowser interview, August 11, 1977.
45. Strong, "Cotton Production in Rural Washington County, 1820–1941," 9.
46. Mance Lipscomb transcripts, Lipscomb-Myers Collection, File 2K198.
47. Lawrence Schmidt interview, July 22, 1995; Elvera Schmidt interview, July 22, 1995; Gus Draeger interview, May 5, 1995.
48. Henry L. Fuchs interview, October 21, 1994.
49. *U.S. Agricultural Census, 1964*, 319.
50. Ibid., 460.
51. Ibid.
52. Gus Draeger interview, May 5, 1995.
53. Dallas *Times Herald*, March 4, 1990.
54. Frank Janish interview, January 9, 1975.
55. Jordan, *German Seed in Texas Soil*, 193.
56. Skrabanek, *We're Czechs*, 17.
57. Julia Sinks, quoted in Carter and Ragsdale, *Biegel Settlement*, 68.

Bibliography

ABBREVIATIONS USED IN BIBLIOGRAPHY

BU   Baylor Institute for Oral History tapes, Baylor University, Waco, Texas.

CAH   University of Texas Folklore Center Archives, Center for American History, University of Texas at Austin.

ETSU   East Texas State University Oral History Program tapes, East Texas State University, Commerce.

LCRA   Lower Colorado River Authority archive, Austin, Texas.

LMC   Lipscomb-Myers Collection tapes, Center for American History, University of Texas at Austin.

WHC   Winedale Historical Center, Winedale, Texas.

WRITTEN SOURCES

"A Brief History of the Origin, Activities and Development of Concordia Gesang-Verein During the First 125 Years of Its Existence." *German-Texan Heritage Society Journal* 7, no. 2 (Summer 1985): 167–168.

Adams, Oscar C. "File 13." *Commerce Journal*, September 28, 1955.

Albers, Emil. "Emil Albers." In *Cummins Creek Chronicle*, pp. 3–4. Round Top–Carmine High School, 1979.

Almonte, Juan N. "Statistical Report on Texas." *Southwestern Historical Quarterly* 28 (1924–1925): 177–222.

Ankli, Robert E., and Alan L. Olmstead. "The Adoption of the Gasoline Tractor in California." *Agricultural History* 55 (1981): 213–230.

Arning, Henrietta Remmert. "Arning Tells Her Story." *German-Texan Heritage Society Journal* 15 (1992): 179–182.

Austin County Historical Commission. *Dance Halls of Austin County.* Austin County Historical Commission, 1993.

Avis, Annie Maud. *The History of Burton.* Wolfe City: Henington Press, 1974 (v.1) and 1985 (v.2).

Ayers, Edward L. *The Promise of the New South.* New York: Oxford University Press, 1992.

Azadian, Dee, ed. *Earth Has No Sorrow.* Austin: Voluntary Action Center of Caldwell County, Texas, 1977.

Banik, Albert. "Mr. Albert Banik." In *Cummins Creek Chronicle,* pp. 9–11. Round Top–Carmine High School, 1979.

Banik, John G. "Mr. John Banik." In *Cummins Creek Chronicle,* pp. 4–5, 13. Round Top–Carmine High School, 1979.

Barker, Eugene C. "The Influence of Slavery in the Colonization of Texas. *Southwestern Historical Quarterly* 28 (1): July 1924: 1–33.

———. *The Life of Stephen F. Austin.* Nashville and Dallas: Cokesbury Press, 1925.

Barth, Felicia Beth. "Oldtime Farm Equipment." *German-Texan Heritage Society Journal* 4 (1982): 66–76.

Bayer, Ernest. "Not Too Bad, Not Too Good." In *Hidden Memories,* edited by Pamela McGlaun, pp. 4–8. Burton: Burton High School, 1978.

Beinhorn, Herbert L. "Beinhorn Family Reminiscences." *German-Texan Heritage Society Journal* 12 (1990): 180–182.

Blasig, Ann. *The Wends of Texas.* Brownsville: 1954.

Blume, Irwin H. "The First Hundred Years of the Blume Family of Fayette and McClennan County, Texas, 1852 to Date." Privately published, 1975.

Britton, Karen. *Bale O'Cotton.* College Station: Texas A&M University Press, 1993.

Brooks, C. P. *Cotton: Its Uses, Varieties, Fibre Structure, Cultivation.* New York: Spon & Chamberlain, 1898.

Brown, Cecil. *Coming Up Down Home: A Memoir of a Southern Childhood* Hopewell: Ecco Press, 1993.

Brown, Ed. *On Shares: Ed Brown's Story.* New York: Norton, 1975.

Brown, Harry Bates. *Cotton: History, Species, Varieties, Morphology, Breeding, Culture, Diseases, Marketing, and Uses.* New York: McGraw-Hill, 1938.

Brundage, W. Fitzhugh. "A Portrait of Southern Sharecropping: The 1911–1912 Georgia Plantation Survey of Robert Preston Brooks." *Georgia Historical Quarterly* 77 (Summer 1993): 367–381.

Bugbee, Lester G. "The Old Three Hundred." *Quarterly of the Texas State Historical Association* 1 (1897): 108–115.

Burnam, Capt. Jesse. "The Reminiscences of Capt. Jesse Burnam." *Quarterly of the Texas State Historical Association* 5 (1901–1902): 12–18.

Calvert, Robert A., and Arnoldo De Leon. *A History of Texas.* Arlington Heights: Harlan-Davidson, 1990.

"Carmine Has Very Colorful History." *Fayette County Record, Sesquicentennial Edition*, March 4, 1986, 14.

Carr, Jess. *The Second Oldest Profession: An Informal History of Moonshining in America*. Englewood Cliffs: Prentice-Hall, 1972.

Carter, Emily S., and Crystal S. Ragsdale. *Biegel Settlement: Historic Sites Research, Fayette Power Project, Fayette County, Texas*. Texas Archeological Survey, Research Report 59. University of Texas at Austin, 1976.

Cat Spring Agricultural Society. *Century of Agricultural Progress, 1856–1956: Minutes of the Cat Spring Agricultural Society*. Cat Spring, Texas: 1956.

Chambers, William T. "Life in a Cotton Farming Community." *Journal of Geography* 28 (1930): 141–147.

Chism, Fannie. "Fannie Chism." In *When I Was Just Your Age*, edited by Robert Flynn and Susan Russell, p. 101. Denton: University of North Texas Press, 1992.

Clem, J. R. *He Bragged On Their Cotton*. Dallas: Banks Upshaw and Company, 1952.

Coltharp, J. B. "Reminiscences of Cotton Pickin' Days." *Southwestern Historical Quarterly* 73 (1970): 539–542.

Conrad, James H. "History Rich With Cotton Stories." *Greenville Herald Banner*, June 29, 1994.

Cox, Joe Fred. "Bale O' Cotton." *The Backroads of East Texas* 1 (1980): 21–22.

Crenshaw, Troy C. *Texas Blackland Heritage*. Waco: Texian Press, 1983.

Crews, Harry. *A Childhood: The Biography of a Place*. New York: Harper and Row, 1978.

Curlee, Abigail. "The History of a Texas Slave Plantation 1831–1863." *Southwestern Historical Quarterly* 26 (1922): 79–127.

———. "A Study of Texas Slave Plantations, 1822–1865." Ph.D. dissertation, University of Texas at Austin, 1932.

Daniel, Pete. *Breaking the Land: The Transformation of Cotton, Tobacco, and Rice Cultures Since 1880*. Urbana: University of Illinois Press, 1986.

———. *The Shadow of Slavery: Peonage in the South, 1902–1969*. Urbana: University of Illinois Press, 1972.

———. "The Transformation of the Rural South, 1930 to Present." *Agricultural History* 55 (1981): 231–248.

Dietrich, Wilfred O. "German American Pioneers in Washington County and Their Influence." *German-Texan Heritage Society Journal* 13 (1991): 123–125.

Dillow, Louise B., and Deenie B. Carver. *Mrs. Blackwell's Heart-of-Texas Cookbook*. San Antonio: Corona Publishing Company, 1980.

Dollard, John. *Caste and Class in a Southern Town*. New Haven: Yale University Press, 1937.

Domasch, Lydia. "Lydia Domasch." In *Cummins Creek Chronicle*, pp. 5–6. Round Top–Carmine High School, 1979.

Doughty, Robin W. *At Home In Texas: Early Views of the Land*. College Station:

Texas A&M University Press, 1987.

———. *Wildlife and Man in Texas: Environmental Change and Conservation.* College Station: Texas A&M University Press, 1983.

Dugas, Vera Lee. "A Social and Economic History of Texas in the Civil War and Reconstruction Periods." Ph.D. dissertation, University of Texas at Austin, 1963.

Edwards, Margaret. "Grandmother's Apron." *German-Texan Heritage Society Journal* 7 (1985): 237.

Eichler, Elmo. "Reflections." In *Cummins Creek Chronicle,* p. 14. Round Top–Carmine High School, 1979.

Evans, Samuel Lee. "Texas Agriculture, 1880–1930." Dissertation, University of Texas at Austin, 1960.

Ferris, William, ed. *You Live and Learn, Then You Die and Forget It All: Ray Lum's Tales of Horses, Mules, and Men.* New York: Anchor, 1992.

Ferris, William, and Charles Reagan Wilson, eds. *Encyclopedia of Southern Culture.* Chapel Hill: University of North Carolina Press, 1989.

Fischer, Florence. "Florence Fischer Talks About Old Time Burton." In *Hidden Memories,* edited by Pamela McGlaun, pp. 1–3. Burton: Burton High School, 1979.

Fite, Gilbert C. "The Agricultural Trap in the South." *Agricultural History* 69 (1986): 38–50.

———. *Cotton Fields No More: Southern Agriculture, 1865–1980.* Lexington: University of Kentucky Press, 1984.

Flynn, Robert, and Susan Russell, eds. *When I Was Just Your Age.* Denton: University of North Texas Press, 1992.

Foley, Neil. "The New South in the Southwest: Anglos, Blacks, and Mexicans in Central Texas, 1880–1930." Dissertation, the University of Michigan, 1990.

Foote, Horton. "Horton Foote." In *When I Was Just Your Age,* edited by Robert Flynn and Susan Russell, p. 18. Denton: University of North Texas Press, 1992.

Fox, Kermit W. *The Otto F. Fuchs Story.* Austin: Privately published, 1994.

———. *A Son of La Bahia Remembers.* Austin: Privately published, 1991.

———. "Thoughts on Which I Wrote." Unpublished manuscript, on file with the author. Austin: n.d.

Goode, Claude E. *Passing This Way But Once: Life of a Hunt County Farm Boy During the Roaring Twenties and the Great Depression Thirties.* Privately published, 1992.

Granade, James A. "The Twilight of Cotton Culture: Life on a Wilkes County Plantation, 1924–1929." *Georgia Historical Quarterly* 76 (Summer 1993): 264–285.

Grider, Sylvia. *The Wendish Texans.* San Antonio: Institute of Texan Cultures, 1982.

Gruver, Eric L. "Surviving the Agricultural Holocaust: A Texas Tenant Stays On the Land." Master's thesis, East Texas State University, Commerce, 1995.

Guelker, Freida Mae. "Born Not for Ourselves, but for the Whole World." In *Hidden Memories*, edited by Pamela McGlaun, pp. 21–26. Burton: Burton High School, 1979.

Hahn, Steven. "Hunting, Fishing, and Foraging: Common Rights and Class Relations in the Postbellum South." *Radical History Review* 26 (1982): 37–64.

Hartzke, Leila. "Mrs. Leila Hartzke." In *Cummins Creek Chronicle*, pp. 12–13. Round Top–Carmine High School, 1979.

Hinueber, Caroline [Ernst] Von. "The Life of German Pioneers in Texas." *Quarterly of the Texas State Historical Association* 2 (1898–1899): 227–232.

Hobson, W. O. *Early Days in Texas and Rains County*. Emory, Texas: 1917.

Hogan, William Ransom. *The Texas Republic: A Social and Economic History*. Norman: University of Oklahoma Press, 1946.

Howard, Dorothy. *Dorothy's World: Childhood in Sabine Bottom, 1902–1910*. New York: Prentice-Hall, 1977.

Hunter, W. D. "Present Status of the Cotton Boll Weevil in the United States." *Yearbook of the Department of Agriculture* 1904:191–204. Washington, D.C.: U.S. Government Printing Office, 1904.

———. "Some Recent Studies of the Mexican Cotton Boll Weevil." *Yearbook of the Department of Agriculture* 1907: 313–323. Washington, D.C.: U.S. Government Printing Office, 1907.

Institute of Texan Cultures. *The Czech Texans*. San Antonio: Institute of Texan Cultures, 1972.

Johnson, Charles S., Edwin R. Embree, and W. W. Alexander. *The Collapse of Cotton Tenancy: Summary of Field Studies & Statistical Surveys, 1933–35*. Chapel Hill: University of North Carolina Press, 1935.

Jordan, Terry G. *German Seed in Texas Soil: Immigrant Farmers in Nineteenth-Century Texas*. Austin: University of Texas Press, 1966.

———. *Texas: A Geography*. Boulder: Westview Press, 1984.

———. *Trails to Texas: Southern Roots of Western Cattle Ranching*. Lincoln: University of Nebraska Press, 1981.

Jordan, Terry G., and Matti Kaups. *The American Backwoods Frontier: An Ethnic and Ecological Interpretation*. Baltimore: Johns Hopkins University Press, 1989.

Kirby, Jack Temple. *Rural Worlds Lost: The American South, 1920–1960*. Baton Rouge: Louisiana State University Press, 1990.

———. "The Southern Exodus, 1910–1960: A Primer for Historians." *Journal of Southern History* 49 (November 1983): 588–600.

———. "The Transformation of Southern Plantations ca. 1920–1960." *Agricultural History* 57 (July 1983): 257–276.

Kleberg, Rosa. "Some of My Early Experiences in Texas." *Quarterly of the Texas State Historical Association* 1 (1898): 297–302.

Knutzen, Joe. "Blacksmithing." In *Cummins Creek Chronicle*, pp. 15–16. Round Top–Carmine High School, 1979.

Kotter, Stephen M., Patience E. Patterson, Dan K. Utley, and Henry B. Moncure. *Final Report of Cultural Resource Investigations at the Cummins Creek Mine, Fayette County, Texas.* Texas Archeological Research Laboratory, Studies in Archeology 11. University of Texas at Austin, 1991.

Krause, Lois. "Round Top Rifle Association Hall." In *Fayette County: Past and Present,* edited by Marjorie L. Williams. La Grange: Privately published, 1976.

Lawson, Marjorie. "The Schiege Cigar Factory Still Standing After 110 Years." *La Grange Journal,* October 3, 1985.

"Legacies and Legends." *German-Texan Heritage Society Journal* 14 (1992): 144.

Lich, Glen E. *The German Texans.* San Antonio: Institute of Texan Cultures, 1981.

Lipscomb, Mance, and Glen Alyn. *I Say Me For a Parable.* New York: Norton, 1993.

Lotto, F. *Fayette County: Her History and People.* Schulenburg: 1902.

Lowe, Richard G., and Randolph B. Campbell. *Planters and Plain Folk: Agriculture in Antebellum Texas.* Dallas: Southern Methodist University Press, 1987.

Mann, Susan A. "Sharecropping in the Cotton South: A Case of Uneven Development in Agriculture." *Rural Sociology* 49 (Fall 1984): 412–427.

Massey, Ellen G., ed. *Bittersweet Country.* Anchor: Garden City, 1978.

Matthies, Almuth. "Pop." In *Hidden Memories,* edited by Pamela McGlaun, pp. 15–20. Burton: Burton High School, 1979.

Matthies, Howard. "I'm Going To Do My Talking Standing Up." In *Hidden Memories,* edited by Pamela McGlaun, pp. 32–39. Burton: Burton High School, 1979.

Matustik, David. "Our Store." Austin *American-Statesman,* October 25, 1993, 12.

Meyer, A. H. *Soil Survey of Washington County, Texas.* Washington, D.C.: U.S. Government Printing Office, 1913.

Moore, Mary Ann. *Rekindled Embers: The Story of the Robertson Family of Washington County.* Houston: 1987.

Moulton, Elma S. *Cotton Production and Distribution in the Gulf Southwest.* U.S. Dept. of Commerce, Domestic Commerce Series No. 49. Washington, D.C.: U.S. Government Printing Office, 1931.

Mueller, John. "Memories." In *Cummins Creek Chronicle,* pp. 14–15. Round Top–Carmine High School, 1979.

Nation, Mrs. Cass. Letter to James H. Conrad, September 13, 1991. Archives, East Texas State University, Commerce, Texas.

National Youth Administration of Texas. *Cotton Growing in Texas.* Austin: 1938.

Natural Fibers Economic Research. "150 Years of Cotton in Texas." Typescript. University of Texas at Austin, July 1973.

Natural Fibers Information Center. *The History of Cotton in Texas*. Bureau of Business Research, University of Texas at Austin, n.d.

Neese, W. J. "W. J. Neese." In *Cummins Creek Chronicle*, p. 7. Round Top–Carmine High School, 1979.

Neville, A. W. "Backward Glances." *The Paris News* (various columns, 1930s through 1950s).

Otto, John S. "Slaveholding General Farmers in a Cotton County." *Agricultural History* 55 (1981): 167–178.

Owens, William A. *A Season of Weathering*. New York: Charles Scribner's Sons, 1973.

———. *This Stubborn Soil: A Frontier Boyhood*. New York: Nick Lyons Books, 1966.

Padilla, Juan Antonio. "Texas in 1820." *Southwestern Historical Quarterly* 23 (1919–1920): 47–68.

Peteet, Walton. *Farming Credit in Texas*. Texas Agricultural Extension Service Bulletin No. B-34. College Station: 1917.

Polk, R. L. *Texas State Gazetteer and Business Directory*. Detroit: R. L. Polk & Co., 1884, 1890, 1892, 1896, 1914.

Quesenberry, Paul. "Witching for Water and Oil." In *The Loblolly Book: Omnibus Edition*, edited by Thad Sitton and Lincoln King, pp. 193–202. Austin: Texas Monthly Press, 1986.

Raugh, Heinrich, and Joanna Christina Siebert. *Raugh Family Tree, 1819–1991*. 1991.

Reich, Steven A. "Soldiers of Democracy: Black Texans and the Fight for Citizenship, 1917–1921." *Journal of American History* 82 (March 1996): 1478–1504.

Robinson, David G., and Dan K. Utley. "The Case of the Misplaced Brick Slag: The Historical Mystery of the Guyler Plantation." *Heritage* 10 (1992): 18–21.

Rosengarten, Theodore, and Ned Cobb. *All God's Dangers: The Life of Nate Shaw*. New York: Alfred A. Knopf, 1974.

Russman, E. J. "The Cotton Gin." In *Diamond Bessie and the Sheperds*, edited by William M. Hudson, pp. 45–50. Austin: Encino Press, 1972.

Schultz, Mrs. Eddie. "Mrs. Eddie Schultz." In *Cummins Creek Chronicle*, pp. 7–9. Round Top–Carmine High School, 1979.

Sharpless, Mary Rebecca. "Fertile Ground, Narrow Choices: Women on Cotton Farms of the Texas Blackland Prairie, 1900–1940." Ph.D. dissertation, Emory University, 1993.

Silverthorne, Elizabeth. *Plantation Life In Texas*. College Station: Texas A&M University Press, 1986.

Simmons, Lee. *Assignment Huntsville: Memoirs of a Texas Prison Official*. Austin: University of Texas Press, 1957.

Sinks, Julia. *Chronicles of Fayette County.* Fayette County Historical Commission, n.d.

Sitton, Thad. *Backwoodsmen: Stockmen and Hunters along a Big Thicket River Valley.* Norman: University of Oklahoma Press, 1995.

———. *Ringing the Children In: Texas Country Schools.* College Station: Texas A&M University Press, 1987.

———. *Texas High Sheriffs.* Austin: Texas Monthly Press, 1988.

Sitton, Thad, and Lincoln King, eds. *The Loblolly Book: Omnibus Edition.* Austin: Texas Monthly Press, 1986.

Skrabanek, Robert. *We're Czechs.* College Station: Texas A&M University Press, 1988.

Smithwick, Noah. *The Evolution of a State: Recollections of Old Texas Days.* Reprint. Austin: University of Texas Press, 1983.

Stimpson, Eddie, Jr. *My Remembers: A Black Sharecropper's Recollections of the Depression.* Denton: University of North Texas Press, 1995.

Strong, Julie W. "Cotton Production in Rural Washington County, 1820–1941." Research report prepared for the Texas Historical Commission, Austin, n.d.

Taplin, Dave. "Picking and Pulling." In *Hidden Memories,* edited by Pamela McGlaun, pp. 27–31. Burton: Burton High School, 1979.

Tarlton, Dewitt Talmage. "The History of the Cotton Industry in Texas, 1820–1850." Masters thesis, University of Texas, Austin, 1923.

Texas State Board of Education. *A Report on the Adequacy of Texas Schools.* Austin: 1936.

Tiedt, Leola K. "Letter to Tyler." *German-Texan Heritage Society Journal* 7 (1985): 124–125.

———. "My Grandmother's Garden." *German-Texan Heritage Society Journal* 7 (1985): 124–125.

U.S. Agricultural Census (various years). Washington, D.C.: U.S. Government Printing Office.

Vance, Rupert B. *Human Factors in Cotton Culture: A Study in the Social Geography of the American South.* Chapel Hill: University of North Carolina Press, 1929.

Vaughn, George Lester. *The Cotton Renter's Son.* Wolfe City, Texas: Henington Publishing Company, 1967.

Von Hinueber, Caroline, "Life of German Pioneers in Early Texas," *Quarterly of the Texas Historical Association* 2 (1899): 227–232.

Wallis, Mrs. Jonnie Lockhart. *Sixty Years on the Brazos: The Life and Letters of Dr. John Washington Lockhart, 1824–1900.* New York: Argonaut Press, 1966.

Wassermann, Lillie. *The Common School Districts of Washington County, Texas, 1909–1967.* Brenham: Brenham Louise Giddings Retired Teachers Association, 1988.

Webb, Walter Prescott, ed. *The Handbook of Texas, Vols.* 1-3. Austin: Texas State Historical Association, 1952.

West, Tommy, "Ingenhuett Store Spans 125 Years and Still Humming." San Antonio *Express-News Magazine*, August 16, 1992, 28–31.

Weyand, Leonie R., and Houston Wade. *An Early History of Fayette County.* La Grange: La Grange *Journal*, 1936.

Whitener, Oliver. "Memoir," 1982. Unpublished manuscript, Baylor Institute for Oral History, Baylor University, Waco, Texas.

Wiener, Jonathan M. "Class Structure and Economic Development in the American South, 1865–1955." *American Historical Review* 84 (1979): 970–1006.

Wilkison, Kyle. "The End of Independence: Social and Political Consequences of Economic Growth in Texas, 1870–1914." Ph.D. dissertation, Vanderbilt University, Nashville, Tennessee, 1995.

———. "Plain Folk Critics of Capitalism: Cultural Persistence and Economic Change in Texas, 1870–1912." Paper presented to the annual meeting of the Texas State Historical Association, Austin, Texas, March 4, 1994.

Williams, R. W. "Backward Glances." Wolfe City *Sun*, Wolfe City, Texas (various columns, 1940s, 1950s).

Wills, Geoffrey. "Geoffrey Wills." In *Earth Has No Sorrow*, edited by Dee Azadian, p. 37. Austin: Voluntary Action Center of Caldwell County, Texas, 1977.

Windicott, W. "Annual Drive Had Gobblers on the Go," Austin *American-Statesman*, November 24, 1994, 1, 20.

Winfield, Nate, and Mrs. Nate Winfield. *All Our Yesterdays: A Brief History of Chappel Hill.* Waco: Texian Press, 1969.

ORAL SOURCES

Bauer, Jonnie. Taped interview with Jean E. Spraker, 1974. Winedale Historical Center, Winedale, Texas (hereafter, WHC).

Blume, Kermit. Taped interview with Thad Sitton, 1994. Baylor Institute for Oral History tapes, Baylor University, Waco, Texas (hereafter, BU).

Bowman, J. D. Taped interview with James H. Conrad, 1995. East Texas State University Oral History Program tapes, East Texas State University, Commerce, Texas (hereafter, ETSU).

Bowser, Bubba. Taped interview with Glen Alyn, 1977. Lipscomb-Myers Collection tapes, Center for American History, University of Texas at Austin (hereafter, LMC).

Buck, Gilbert. Taped interviews (2) with Dan K. Utley, 1993. BU.

Burton, James. Taped interview with Thad Sitton, 1994. Lower Colorado River Authority archive, Austin, Texas (hereafter, LCRA).

Collier, Bea Ruth Tatum. Taped interview with Thad Sitton, 1995. LCRA.

Cox, Joe Fred. Taped interview with James H. Conrad, 1995. ETSU.

Cox, Layton B. Taped interview with Thad Sitton, 1994. LCRA.

Crumley, D. E. Taped interview with Thad Sitton, 1995. LCRA.

Crumley, Prudie B. Taped interview with Thad Sitton, 1995. LCRA.

Davis, Howard H. Taped interviews (2) with Thad Sitton, 1994. BU.

Davis, Lily Lipscomb. Taped interview with Glen Alyn, 1977. LMC.

Dean, Mrs. Otis. Taped interviews (2) with James H. Conrad, 1994. ETSU.

Dean, Otis. Taped interviews (2) with James H. Conrad, 1994. ETSU.

Dement, J. M. Taped interview with Dan K. Utley, 1992. BU.

Dement, Robert. Taped interview with Dan K. Utley, 1993. BU.

Draeger, Gus. Taped interview with Thad Sitton, 1995. BU.

Ebner, Edna. Taped interview With Thad Sitton, 1994. BU.

Ebner, Edwin. Taped interview with Thad Sitton, 1994. BU.

Ehrigson, Lydia. Taped interview with Dan K. Utley, 1995. BU.

Ewing, Olivia ("Chang"). Taped interview with Glen Alyn, 1976. LMC.

Fox, Kermit W. Taped interviews (2) with Thad Sitton, 1994–1995. BU.

Fuchs, Henry Lee. Taped interview with Thad Sitton, 1994. BU.

Fuchs, Ora Nell Jacobs. Taped interview with Thad Sitton, 1994. BU.

Gilley, Nona Mae Tatum. Taped interviews (2) with Thad Sitton, 1994. LCRA.

Gipson, Susie Davidson. Taped interviews (2) with Sarah Sitton, 1981, 1986. Private collection of Sarah Sitton.

Gipson, Wanda DuBose. Taped interview with Thad Sitton, July 30, 1994. Private collection of Sarah Sitton.

Gutierrez, Cune. Taped interview with Thad Sitton, 1994. LCRA.

Hancock, Earnest. Taped interview with Thad Sitton, 1994. BU.

Henninger, H. C. Taped interview with Lonn Taylor, n.d. (1974?). WHC.

Henry, Ola B. Crumley. Taped interview with Thad Sitton, 1995. LCRA.

Hermann, Violet. Taped interview with Thad Sitton, 1994. BU.

Jacoby, Charles. Taped interview with Glen Alyn, 1977. LMC.

Jaeger, Henry C. Taped interviews (2) with Dan K. Utley, 1994. BU.

Janish, Frank J. Taped interview with Jean E. Spraker, 1974. WHC.

Keiler, Gus. Taped interview with Jean E. Spraker, 1974. WHC.

Keiler, Mrs. Gus. Taped interview with Jean E. Spraker, 1974. WHC.

Keiler, Teddy R. Taped interview with Jean E. Spraker, 1974. WHC.

Krause, Gladys J. Taped interview with Thad Sitton, 1994. BU.

Krinke, Gertrude Wegner. Taped interview with Thad Sitton, 1995. BU.

Lathan, Ed. Taped interviews (2) with Glen Alyn and Thad Sitton, 1975, 1995. LMC, BU.

Lincecum, Charlie. Taped interview with Dan K. Utley, 1992. BU.

Lipscomb, Elnora. Taped interviews (3) with Glen Alyn, 1973–1975. Transcripts: Files 2K197 and 2K198, LMC.

Lipscomb, Mance. Taped interviews (11) with Glen Alyn, 1973–1975. Transcripts: Files 2K197 and 2K198, LMC.

Lipscomb, Willie. Taped interview with Glen Alyn, 1977. LMC.

Loud, Johnnie. Taped interview with Thad Sitton, 1994. BU.

Manske, Mrs. Elenora. Taped interview with Jean E. Spraker, 1974. WHC.

Marburger, Leona. Taped interview with Jean E. Spraker, 1974. WHC.

Matthies, Howard. Taped interviews (7) with Thomas L. Charlton and Dan K. Utley, 1991–1992; Deb Hoskins, 1992; and Thad Sitton, 1994. BU.

Matthies, Olefa. Taped interviews (3) with Thomas L. Charlton, 1991–1992. BU.

McClure, C. R. Taped interview with Corrine Crow, 1973. ETSU.

McWilliams, Charles E. Taped interview with Thad Sitton, 1995. BU.

Meinen, Fritz. Taped interview with Jean E. Spraker, 1974. WHC.

Meinen, Mrs. Fritz. Taped interview with Jean E. Spraker, 1974. WHC.

Moseley, Ora Nell Wehring. Taped interview with Lois E. Myers, 1992. BU.

Peschke, Edith Gilley. Taped telephone interview with Thad Sitton, 1995. LCRA.

Reed, Edna Ruth Gilley. Taped telephone interview with Thad Sitton, 1995. LCRA.

Reed, Richard Rufus. Taped interview with John Henry Faulk, 1941. University of Texas Folklore Center Archives, Center for American History, Austin, Texas (hereafter, CAH).

Schmidt, Annie. Taped interview with Jean E. Spraker, 1974. WHC.

Schmidt, Elvera. Taped interview with Thad Sitton, 1995. BU.

Schmidt, Lawrence. Taped interview with Thad Sitton, 1995. BU.

Schmidt, Roy. Taped interview with Thad Sitton, 1995. BU.

Schmidt, Wallie. Taped interview with Jean E. Spraker, 1974. WHC.

Schoenemann, Herman, Sr. Taped interview with Thad Sitton, 1994. BU.

Sitton, Evarilla Harrell. Taped interview with Sarah Sitton, 1977. Private collection.

Smalley, Laura. Taped interview with John Henry Faulk, 1941. CAH.

Smith, Harriet. Taped interview with John Henry Faulk, 1941. CAH.

Sorrells, Willis. Taped interview with John Henry Faulk, 1941. CAH.

Stolz, Skeeter. Taped interview with Glen Alyn, 1980. LMC.

Tatum, Booth. Taped interviews (2) with Thad Sitton, 1994–1995. LCRA.

Tatum, Zelmo. Taped interview with Thad Sitton, 1994. LCRA.

Terrell, William J. Taped interview with Thad Sitton, 1995. BU.

Tiedt, Leola K. Taped interviews (2) with Thad Sitton, 1994–1995. BU.

Treybig, Otto. Taped interview with Jean E. Spraker, 1974. WHC.

Tunnell, Curtis D. Taped interview with Dan K. Utley, 1995. BU.

Ullrich, Ilo. Taped interview with Thad Sitton, 1994. BU.

Wade, Georgie Lee. Taped interview with Glen Alyn, 1977. LMC.

Wade, James ("Beck"). Taped interview with Glen Alyn, 1977. LMC.

Washington, Davis. Taped interview with Glen Alyn, 1977. LMC.

Wegner, Edward F. Taped interviews (7) with Dan K. Utley, 1992–1995. BU.

Wegner, Herbert. Taped interview with Thad Sitton, 1995. BU.

Wegner, Verlie. Taped interviews (2) with Lonn Taylor and Dan K. Utley, 1974, 1994. WHC, BU.

Whitener, Oliver. Taped interviews (3) with Thomas L. Charlton and Dan K. Utley, 1992. BU.

Wilhelmsen, Albert F. Taped interviews (2) with Thad Sitton, 1995. BU.

Wilhelmsen, Robert H. Taped interviews (2) with Thad Sitton, 1995. BU.

Williams, Grover, Sr. Taped interviews (5) with Dan K. Utley, 1991–1992. BU.

Index